CAMDEN COUNTY, NEW JERSEY

CAMDEN COUNTY NEW JERSEY

THE MAKING OF A METROPOLITAN COMMUNITY, 1626–2000

Jeffery M. Dorwart

RUTGERS UNIVERSITY PRESS
New Brunswick, New Jersey

Library of Congress Cataloging-in-Publication Data
Dorwart, Jeffery M., 1944–
    Camden County, New Jersey : the making of a metropolitan community, 1626–2000 /
Jeffery M. Dorwart.
        p.   cm.
    Includes bibliographical references and index.
    ISBN 0-8135-2957-3 (cloth : alk. paper) — ISBN 0-8135-2958-1 (pbk. : alk. paper)
    1. Camden County (N.J.)—History.   I. Title.
    F142.C16 D675 2001
    974.9'87—dc21

                                                                    00-045899

British Cataloging-in-Publication data for this book is available from the British Library.

Publication of this book was made possible, in part, by funding from the Camden County Board of
Freeholders, as a Millennium Project.

Making It Better, Together.

CONTENTS

ACKNOWLEDGMENTS

The decision to update and completely rewrite the 1976 history of Camden County, New Jersey, for the year 2000 was largely the vision of the Camden County Board of Chosen Freeholders, including Freeholder Director Jeffrey L. Nash, Deputy Director Frank Spencer, and Freeholders Riletta L. Cream, Annette Castiglione-Degan, Laurelle Cummings, Patricia E. Jones, and Edward T. McDonnell. Additional impetus for having the new history document the increasingly diverse, multicultural Camden County metropolitan community came from Ruth Bogutz, director of the Camden County Cultural and Heritage Commission, Ken Shuttleworth, director of the Camden County Division of Public Affairs, and Paul W. Schopp, former director of the Camden County Historical Society.

Special thanks go to Schopp, who in some ways is the coauthor of this history. He is the preeminent authority on the county's history, and he shared his unparalleled knowledge with me as he read and commented on every draft. Thanks must go as well to David Munn, president of the Camden County Historical Society, for reading the early chapters, and to the staff of the historical society, most notably Jean Crescenzi and Joanne Diogo-Seitter, for research assistance. Gary Golden, Julie Still, Elaine Navarra, Judy Odom, Mary Ann Nesbit, and Deborah Goldberg of the Paul Robeson Library, Rutgers University, Camden, aided my research in immeasurable ways.

At Rutgers University, Camden, Howard Gillette, my colleague and a specialist in urban history who is writing a study of Camden City neighborhoods, gave me timely advice and counsel. Several generations of my New Jersey history students, too numerous to list, also helped to make this history possible. Some deserve individual mention for their particular contributions. Vince Sarubbi and Robert DePersia discussed Camden County's Italian American history with me. Erin Basile wrote a history of the R. M. Hollingshead Company. Lori Fleming prepared a history of Collingswood. Eric Zeplin researched the Ellisburg Circle. Jon Anthony Korn presented the study of Laurel Springs. Jason DeCharleroy assembled a detailed report on the history of the Camden and Amboy Rail Road. Anthony Tinelli analyzed the creation of Audubon Park. Fatimah Hayes presented a sensitive study of the Fairview section of Camden City. Bart Everts wrote papers on the history of Admiral Wilson Boulevard. Michelle Smith studied the building of the Ben Franklin Bridge and its impact on the county. To these and the many other students who enthusiastically researched and wrote seminar papers about Camden County's history (now on deposit in the Camden County Historical Society), my warmest thanks.

CAMDEN COUNTY, NEW JERSEY

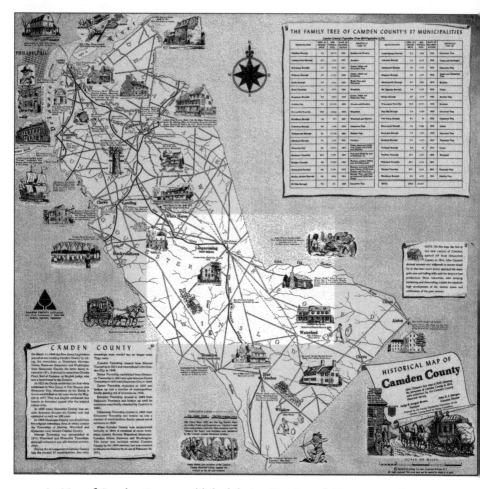

1. Map of Camden County published during New Jersey's Tercentenary in 1964. *(Camden County Historical Society Collection)*

INTRODUCTION

WHY STUDY CAMDEN COUNTY HISTORY?

Camden County, New Jersey, provides an ideal subject for the study of the development of American metropolitan communities. It contains one large central city that for most of the county's history was the center of economic and political life and culture. Nearby, urbanized suburbs developed along old turnpikes and railroad lines. Later, the railroads and the automobile created an outer ring of sprawling suburban neighborhoods expanding into the countryside. Throughout much of the county's history, the suburbs and countryside were integrated closely into a Philadelphia–Camden City metropolitan region. All roads and rails led to the Delaware riverfront, where county residents could take a ferryboat (or, after 1926, the bridge) across the river to Philadelphia for business, government, and entertainment.

Over time, changes in America's industrial economy and society brought about a decline of the central city. Simultaneously, urban middle-class residents and businesses moved to the surrounding suburbs. Gradually, the center of county life shifted from city to suburbs, and in the process the traditional metropolitan community began to break down. The evolving community had decidedly new ethnic, racial, and cultural characteristics. Once composed almost entirely of European Americans, Camden City became home primarily to residents of African, Hispanic, and Asian descent by the end of the twentieth century. As the former residents moved to the suburbs, where they settled among older rural European American neighborhoods, walls of mistrust arose between an increasingly impoverished and crime-ridden urban center and the prospering middle-class suburban regions.

At first view, it would seem that racial, economic, and cultural polarization caused the breakdown of the Camden County metropolitan community. Yet the process was far more complicated. In fact, as the county developed, the urban riverfront and suburban countryside became inseparable, and it is this intimate connection between city and suburb that explains the sometime turbulent evolution of a multicultural society.

MULTICULTURAL SOCIETY

During its long history, first as part of old Gloucester County and then as a separate governmental entity, Camden County has been home to every ethnic and cultural group in American history: European, African, Latino, Caribbean, Asian, and Native American; Protestant, Catholic, and Jew. All took part in shaping the county's history. At the same time, the county experienced every type of residential neighborhood, workplace, and way of life known to the American historical experience. From the nation's beginning, the tiny seventeenth-century community on the eastern shore of the Delaware River was part of the first pluralistic society that formed in the Middle Atlantic colonies of West New Jersey and Pennsylvania. Throughout the centuries, the county continued in this tradition, becoming by the close of the twentieth century one of the most ethnically diverse and culturally pluralistic communities in the United States.

For most of the county's history, Anglo-American Protestant culture dominated its society, politics, and economy. The original Native American (Indian) way of life soon disappeared, leaving only traces. African Americans, brought to the county as slaves, preserved remnants of their culture in remote rural black enclaves. Later, German, Irish, Italian, Polish, and Russian American Catholics and Jews conformed to the dominant Anglo-American Protestant institutions in order to obtain economic and political advantage. Likewise, Hispanic, Central and East Asian, Pacific, and Caribbean Americans, who came to the county toward the close of the twentieth century, also adopted them.

While acknowledging the imprint of Anglo-American Protestant values and institutions on Camden County, a multicultural approach to its history recognizes the county's rich diversity. The concept of a metropolitan county composed of different cultural and ethnic groups can be a valuable method with which to analyze the American historical experience in local community building. More important, it enables the people of Camden County to begin the new millennium with a better understanding of how their individual cultures contributed to the formation of the place where they make their lives today.

A BIRTHPLACE OF U.S. HISTORY

Another compelling reason to study Camden County's history is its role in the creation of the United States. Located on the eastern side of the Delaware River, opposite the historic Pennsylvania port city of Philadelphia, Camden County has a recorded history that extends back more than three centuries, making it one of the oldest colonial settlements in America. First as part of Gloucester County (1686) and then as a separate political entity (1844), Camden County stood near the center of every major historical development in Philadelphia that shaped the formation of an independent United States.

Camden County's origins can be traced to the period in the seventeenth century when Western European trading nations aggressively sought the resources of the North American seacoast. This competition brought Dutch fur traders, Swedish and Finnish farmers, Scottish-Irish Presbyterians, and English Anglican and Quaker colonists to the Delaware Valley. These first European Americans encountered and destroyed the local Native American culture and introduced black slavery (and, indirectly, African American cultures) to the southeastern bank of the Delaware River. At the same time, struggles in Western Europe for more religious and political freedom extended to the Delaware River as the first British settlers brought a charter assuring fundamental rights and liberties for the colonists.

The future Camden County became more closely connected to the wider American historical experience at the end of the eighteenth century, when its location directly across the river from the temporary national capital in Philadelphia placed it at the crossroads of the American Revolution and near the birthplace of the United States. British and Hessian troops and American volunteers foraged, camped, and at times fought in the area. Whig and Tory factions struggled to preserve the identity of their local communities.

After the war, between 1781 and 1800, the county reflected the nation-building process going on in Philadelphia. If local leaders on the Philadelphia side of the Delaware River followed Federalist principles of centralized government and developed an urban commercial town, those on the east side advanced the idea of the yeoman farmer embodied in Jeffersonian Republican ideals of an agrarian, democratic society and a decentralized government of independent freeholders.

CAMDEN COUNTY AS A REFLECTION OF U.S. HISTORY

In old Gloucester County during the first decades of the nineteenth century, the debate between Federalists and Jeffersonian Republicans over the nature of U.S. government and institutions became a bitter political contest that contributed eventually to the creation of Camden County. Incorporation of the City of Camden along the Delaware riverfront in 1828 had given rise to conflicts between urban manufacturing interests and an older agrarian commercial section. Construction of the first steam railroad in the county a few years later exacerbated the growing separation of rural agricultural and urban industrial sections. All along, Irish and German Catholic immigrants arrived to build the railroads and work in the factories, presenting the first challenge to the traditional Protestant agricultural leadership. Differences between the political leaders of the riverfront city and its immediate suburbs, versus the old elites of the more rural countryside, strongly influenced the partition of Gloucester County in 1844 and the establishment in 1851 of Camden City as the seat of the new county.

Yet turnpike and railroad construction in the years before the Civil War made the rural countryside and the riverfront city increasingly interdependent. In many ways already, Camden County had become a metropolitan community.

The Civil War put Camden County at the nexus of the American historical experience once more. The older agrarian section held traditional social and economic ties to the slave-owning agricultural South; and, despite a strong Quaker antislavery tradition, many county residents sympathized with the states' rights position of the rebellious Confederacy. Nevertheless, the industrial and manufacturing areas of Camden County's urban riverfront, and particularly the Irish and German immigrants, showed strong Unionist tendencies as they helped to build the Northern war machine. Now tied to the city financially, economically, and socially, the nearby rural suburbs and more distant farming hamlets supported the Union cause as well. The Civil War also provided a catalyst to organize countywide business and financial interests. During the war and immediate postwar era, local businessmen from all sections of the county consolidated small banks to provide capital for the increasingly complex and large-scale operations of textile, chemical, oilcloth, iron forging, shipbuilding, and, most important, food canning and agricultural industries.

Late-nineteenth-century industrialization brought waves of southern, southeastern, and eastern European immigrants to the Delaware Valley, predominantly Catholic or Jewish Poles, Russians, and Italians. Most settled on the Philadelphia side of the river, but thousands entered Camden County to work in riverfront factories or on commercial farms and orchards in the countryside. New immigration changed the county's ethnic and religious character and threatened its cultural homogeneity. Camden County's dominant Anglo-American Protestant leadership responded with the first Greater Camden Movement, a program to integrate the newcomers more fully by promoting urban jobs and ownership of houses in the railroad or trolley commuter suburbs. The process worked. On the eve of America's entry into World War I, Camden County appeared to be an orderly community of working middle-class neighborhoods, businesses, and cultural institutions. The new immigrants participated enthusiastically in this Greater Camden society.

After World War I, the wartime industrial expansion and building boom continued. The leaders of the Greater Camden Movement embraced the Coolidge administration's New Era of business and government co-operation during the 1920s. Development of paved automobile roads and the opening of the Camden-Philadelphia Bridge in 1926 rushed people to the suburbs. Camden City continued to prosper as well, and its population grew from 9,000 in 1851, when it became the county seat, to 125,000 by 1950. The city remained the center of county life. Everyone came to shop, do business and banking, and attend the motion picture theaters or social and cultural events held in the riverfront city at the Camden Convention Center, the Haddon Avenue Armory, and the magnificent new Walt Whitman Hotel. Many suburban commuters to Philadelphia continued to take the ferry from Camden rather than bypass the city on the automobile bridge. During the 1920s Camden County reached its peak as a truly metropolitan community, blending central city and suburban neighborhood in a dynamic county environment. Then, the stock market crashed in 1929 and ushered in the worst economic depression in modern U.S. history.

DECLINE OF THE METROPOLITAN COMMUNITY

The Great Depression of the 1930s revealed the underlying flaws in Camden County's urban fabric. Years of poor management, unrestrained development, and political corruption left scars on the city. Moreover, pressed against the river to the west and deep tidal creeks north and south, the city had no place to grow. Smoky factories and railroad lines cut through gritty, overcrowded ethnic working-class neighborhoods. Meanwhile, the approach to the Camden-Philadelphia Bridge had split the city in half and gutted one of its most historic and affluent neighborhoods. There was little parking space for the flood of suburban automobiles that came to the city daily. Already, neighborhoods started to separate along racial and ethnic lines. City and county governments seemed unresponsive, unaware or unable to improve the urban environment. Instead, the county paid increasing attention to its suburban areas in developing a park system, schools, a hospital—and better roads and bridges to rush people out of the city. Increasingly during the Depression and the New Deal, metropolitan Greater Camden became suburban Camden.

World War II pulled urban Camden County out of economic depression and diverted attention for a while from lingering social and economic problems. Once again, riverfront factories and shipyards boomed. Once more, suburban county residents flocked to the city to work, shop, bank, and attend the movies. So many jobs needed to be filled that local industries recruited nontraditional workers, including females, blacks, and the area's first Hispanics. The federal government built subsidized low-income rental housing projects for this influx of new war workers, altering in the process the traditional concept of neighborhood. The war increased prosperity, but also added to the industrial pollution, overcrowding, traffic congestion, crime, and municipal neglect that had become apparent during the Depression. The female and minority workers who found opportunities in the defense industries and in housing during the war were laid off as soon as the men returned from overseas. Big industries cut back on production, and some even closed their doors. Prewar difficulties returned. Housing shortages, inadequate schools and public services, and an outdated transportation system confronted an increasingly diverse urban community. Decay, crime, unemployment, and social unrest intensified.

For the white urban middle class and for businesses, the suburbs looked more and more inviting in the postwar years. It would take several decades for them to abandon Camden City altogether, but the final trek to the suburban county had started. Postwar consumer spending and the onset of the cold war boosted the county's economy during the 1950s and early 1960s through the expansion of local defense industries. Camden City showed signs of returning to its prewar glory days as a shipbuilding, electronics manufacturing, retail shopping, theater, business, and government center for the entire southern New Jersey region. However, the recovery also revealed outdated factory systems, overcrowded housing, decayed and restless neighborhoods, and steadily rising city taxes without an apparent improvement in the urban landscape or municipal services. Skilled workers for the newer, more technologically sophisticated industries and businesses moved to the surrounding suburbs. Soon the businesses themselves left the overcrowded, inefficient city, establishing office centers, shopping malls, and industrial parks in the suburbs.

Suburban transformation intensified during the last decades of the twentieth century. The remaining open land filled with sprawling industrial and business parks, housing developments, townhouses, and the low-income apartment complexes mandated by federal and state governments. Gas stations, fast-food restaurants, and strip malls lined once rural farm roads. These narrow two-lane highways became so overburdened that even the most remote areas experienced traffic jams. Sprawl placed a tremendous strain on natural resources and upon the rural landscape. Municipal and industrial waste filtered into drinking water supplies, polluted once pristine millponds, and choked sluggish, silt-filled tidal creeks.

Suburban Camden County began to suffer from the same malaise that had plagued urban Camden, particularly the older communities on the immediate fringes of the inner city. Poverty, unemployment, crime, abandoned businesses, vacant houses, crumbling neighborhoods, pollution, traffic jams, and higher taxes were not just Camden City problems. Decline of the inner suburbs removed the buffer zone between the city and the outer ring of prosperous middle-class suburbs of more recent origin, threatening to make these distant suburbs part of an urban fringe. This process revealed once more at the close of the twentieth century the historic nature of Camden County as a metropolitan community. The intimate connection between urban riverfront and suburban countryside had always shaped the political and economic landscape; and in the year 2000 Camden County recognized its historic origins and turned to reinvent the riverfront community where it all began nearly four hundred years before.

I

"We Hope West Jersey Will Be Soon Planted"

Native American Culture

The recorded history of the area that would become Camden County began when the first European visitors contacted the Native Americans along the eastern banks of the Delaware River early in the seventeenth century. At that time, the area between Timber and Pennsauken Creeks was covered with great oak and pine forests, tidal streams, and fertile wetland meadows. The place abounded with waterfowl, fish, small fur-bearing creatures, and large game animals. It was an ideal natural environment for the late-woodland-era, seminomadic Native American culture known as the Lenape.

The Lenape were organized into autonomous tribal units headed by sachems, or chiefs, and were governed by council meetings. When the first Europeans arrived, several Lenape communities existed along the tidal creeks. They lived in villages near the water during planting season, where they fished in the streams and slashed and burned trees to open ground sufficient to plant maize, beans, and peas. In the winter, the Lenape scattered to smaller woodland camps to gather firewood and hunt game. The Delaware Indians, as the Europeans called them, developed an elaborate system of narrow trails through thick forests and along high ground that led to fording places over tidal creeks and tributaries. Some paths wandered along the shore of the river; the most heavily used ones headed from the riverfront east toward the Atlantic seashore, where the Lenape collected dark purple and white shells to manufacture wampum belts of polished beads. The Native Americans used wampum for ceremonial purpose and as a form of money to conduct business with Europeans. Dutch fur traders, who established the first extended contact between Native American and European cultures in the Delaware River Valley, bought pelts and skins from the Lenape with wampum.

THE DUTCH WEST INDIA COMPANY

Agents for Amsterdam merchant burghers had explored the Delaware Bay since the beginning of the seventeenth century, searching for a northwest water passage to their East Asian trading posts. English navigator Henry Hudson, working for the Dutch East India Company, entered the bay in 1609, and during the following decade Dutch navigators sailed up the Delaware River at least as far as the Falls at present-day Trenton, New Jersey. They established an outpost in 1624 on a Delaware River island near present-day Burlington City. The Dutch organized the West India Company, claimed the uncharted territory between Long Island (New York) and the Delaware Bay, and founded New Netherland, with a large trading post at New Amsterdam (New York City). From this base, on what they called the North River (Hudson River), the Dutch moved down to the Delaware River (which they named the South River) and in 1626 built Fort Nassau, a fortified fur-trading post, on land probably probably gained from local natives in exchange for trinkets.

Located near the confluence of the Delaware River and Big Timber Creek, Fort Nassau was the first European community in what today is Camden County. Although garrisoned only part of the time, the post took on characteristics of a permanent settlement. There was a large house for the Dutch commissary and his three African slaves, a storehouse for furs and pelts, and probably some small log cabins for West India Company agents and at least eight Walloon (Belgian) couples who planned to settle there. This first European community on the east bank of the river kept garden plots and several dozen goats for milk and cheese. A high wooden palisade and small iron cannon provided security against feared Native American attacks, such as the one that wiped out a similar Dutch trading post downriver on the west side of the bay at Swanendael (near present-day Lewes, Delaware).

Fort Nassau served as the Dutch government center on the South River. West India Company officials sent all correspondence and instructions there, and the commissary bargained with the Lenape for furs and negotiated with European interlopers who interfered with the company's trade monopoly in the Delaware Valley.

New Sweden on the Delaware

The tiny fortification at the mouth of Big Timber Creek was poorly situated to defend the Dutch West India Company's interests on the South River. Captain Andries Hudde's guns could barely reach midstream, never mind guard the mouth of the Schuylkill River nearly opposite on the western side, which led to the rich fur-trading region of the future British colony of Pennsylvania. Bold Swedes and Finns (Finland was a province of Sweden), who founded New Sweden in 1638, simply slipped past Fort Nassau, seized control of the local fur trade, and established tiny settlements along both sides of the river (including Puchack on Pennsauken Creek in present-day Camden County). Sweden had neither the resources nor the manpower to sustain New Sweden, and the Dutch restored authority over the Delaware River in 1655. Nevertheless, the Swedish/Finnish cultural influence, transmitted to the incoming British, far outweighed that of the more powerful New Netherlands colony, whose cultural heritage remained dominant on the North River.

During their brief hegemony over the Delaware Valley, the colonists of New Sweden designed log cabins, farm buildings, and waterwheels that were adopted by British settlers, who began arriving on the east side of the Delaware in the 1670s. During their first winter in the Delaware Valley wilderness, the English Quakers who founded the community that became Camden County received shelter among the Swedes at New Stockholm (near present-day Swedesboro in Gloucester County). The Swedish settlement across the river at Wicaco (the Southwark section of present-day Philadelphia) provided boats for the pioneering British Quakers to travel upriver and locate land that could be cleared for houses and planting.

Swedish guides and interpreters helped the English find the best spots along the tidal creeks and conclude treaties of purchase with Native American residents. In 1677 New Stockholm landowners Israel Helmes, Peter Rambo, Lacy Cock, and Wolley Dalbo assisted the English to procure the Arwamus territory below Newton Creek in exchange for duffel cloth, blankets, iron tools, flintlock guns, trinkets, beads, tobacco, and seven "Ankers of Brandy." The Swanson family of Wicaco, who had kin in New Stockholm, witnessed deed signings, establishing the close connection between the future Philadelphia and Camden that helped shape the county's history.

The Swedes cooperated with the first British settlers on the Delaware River in part because they wanted to hold on to their property, acquired earlier from the Native Americans, when the British assumed control over the Delaware Valley. That the British arrived after the Dutch and Swedish settlers may seem surprising. Britain was the most powerful and aggressive Western European trading nation in the seventeenth century, drawing upon the combined resources of England, Ireland, Scotland, and Wales, and upon the entrepreneurial skill of an expanding bourgeois capitalist class. Moreover, after the defeat of the Spanish Armada in 1588, Britain gained mastery over the Atlantic sea lanes and trade routes. With such advantages, Britain surged ahead of other European trading states to colonize North America, establishing settlements on the Chesapeake Bay and in New England. But the English Civil War, which led to the beheading of King Charles I in 1649 and the rise of the Puritan Commonwealth under Oliver Cromwell, interrupted British colonization efforts in the Middle Atlantic region. Consequently, Dutch and Swedish traders and settlers took advantage of Britain's domestic crisis to stake early claims to the Delaware Valley.

BRITAIN SEIZES THE DELAWARE VALLEY

With the restoration of the British monarchy in 1660 came renewed interest in colonizing the Delaware Valley region. Nearly bankrupt from the recent civil war, the English crown saw the exploitation of New World lands as a way to generate revenue and reward allies. King Charles II gave his brother James, duke of York, patent to all lands between the Connecticut River and the Delaware Bay. The duke dispatched a royal commission to America in 1664, ostensibly to inspect the existing New England and Chesapeake colonies, but in fact to remove pesky Dutch officials from his new acquisitions. Loyal man-at-arms Colonel Richard Nicolls, who led the commission, seized New Amsterdam and renamed it New York in honor of his master.

Nicolls's fellow commissioner Sir Robert Carr sailed to the mouth of the Delaware River in a forty-gun warship and captured the Dutch outpost at Fort Casimir (present-day New Castle, Delaware), thus eliminating Dutch rule in the Delaware Valley. The duke's men allowed the Dutch and Swedish settlers to keep their land so long as they obeyed the duke's laws. The British commissioners distributed land patents to New England, Long Island, and other tracts, unaware that the duke of York had already granted this property to powerful allies, including John, Lord Berkeley, and Sir George Carteret, governor of Jersey, the island in the English Channel where the Royalists had sought refuge during the civil war. Not surprisingly, the duke of York christened his gift New Jersey.

Founding West New Jersey

The manner in which the two noble proprietors of New Jersey managed the duke of York's grant explains why English Quakers founded the community that one day became Camden County. In the north, Carteret survived much controversy over proprietary and taxing rights to develop a thriving colony in the eastern half of the duke's patent (East New Jersey). Lord Berkeley, on the other hand, failed to exploit his real estate to the south and went bankrupt. After Dutch warships returned momentarily to the Delaware River in 1673, Berkeley decided to sell his share of New Jersey to the wealthy London brewer Edward Byllynge for £1,000.

A former officer in Cromwell's army and a recent convert to the teachings of George Fox, founder of the Religious Society of Friends (Quakers), Byllynge belonged to a group of Quaker entrepreneurs who dreamed of establishing a religious and economic refuge in the New World to escape growing persecution and confiscation of their property by Anglican Church and British government officials. After a missionary trip through Maryland, New Jersey, and New York in 1672, Fox reported that the

Delaware Valley offered a fruitful land for establishing a Quaker common-wealth. He found only a few native villages standing in the way of European settlement. Fox's observations influenced prominent London Quaker William Penn to plan a colony on the west bank of the river, on land given to him by the king to pay off debts owed Penn's father.

Fox aroused Byllynge's interest as well. The London brewer could not take advantage of the situation, however, because he went bankrupt from excessive fines and property confiscation levied as punishment for his membership in a Quaker meeting. A fellow army officer and Quaker convert, John Fenwick, agreed to hold the thousand-pound note for Byllynge. But the duke of York refused to recognize the entire transaction, because Fenwick most likely had been at the head of Cromwell's cavalry at the execution of the duke's father. Fenwick exacerbated the situation by claiming that he had bought proprietary rights and intended to go to the Delaware Valley as governor of a new province. He bolted without consulting Byllynge or the Quaker meeting and founded his own colony on the Delaware River in 1675 along Salem Creek. An angry Byllynge submitted the dispute to meeting, and fellow London brewer Nicholas Lucas, merchant Gawen Lawrie, and William Penn agreed to serve as trustees for the Byllynge/Fenwick purchase. Penn was particularly anxious to have a secure Quaker community across the river from his planned City of Brotherly Love (Philadelphia).

The trustees settled affairs so that "things may go on easy without hurt or jar; which is the desire of all Friends; and we hope West Jersey will be soon planted." They smoothed relations with the crown and defined the boundaries between Berkeley's former holdings and those of the Carteret family, signing the Quintipartite Deed in 1676, which divided the duke's grant into East and West New Jersey. The Quaker trustees of West New Jersey organized a joint stock company, dividing the territory into one hundred proprietary shares and granting the contentious Fenwick ten full shares. The remainder went to prominent Friends who sought to escape intolerance and persecution by going to the New World. Surprisingly, the sale of proprietary shares went slowly. To further the project, the trustees issued "The Concessions and Agreements of the Proprietors, Freeholders and Inhabitants of the Province of West New Jersey in America."

This document guaranteed religious toleration for most, the right to hold property free from feudal restrictions, trial by jury, and representative government by elected officials. It also organized the property into ten equal parts (Tenths), outlined procedures to form constable wicks (townships), divided up farmland, and established local courts of justice. A board of land commissioners, appointed by the trustees, served in America as community managers until sufficient numbers of settlers allowed for the organization of provincial, county, and local governments. The West Jersey trustees instructed the commissioners to take soundings on the Delaware River and surrounding creeks and to find healthy ground upon which to build a town and plant a community. The commissioners were also directed to parley with the Native Americans to purchase land and obtain signed deeds, although the Lenape held no concept of land ownership.

ENGLISH QUAKERS ARRIVE

English Quakers from London, Yorkshire, and Dublin were the first to take advantage of the West Jersey purchase, sailing to the Delaware Valley in 1677. They refused to land at the only English community on the river at Salem Creek because Fenwick was in charge there. Fortunately, the Swedish community upriver at New Stockholm, on Raccoon Creek, provided shelter for the winter of 1677–78. When the spring thaw arrived, the Quaker pioneers pushed further upriver and built Burlington Town on the eastern bank. The Yorkshire people held patent to the First Tenth and claimed the best town lots on the high ground fronting the river and the prime spots for laying out plantations along the tidal creeks. Although unhappy with their inferior town plots, the London Quakers stayed long enough in Burlington to help construct a meetinghouse, central market square, courthouse, and public buildings. By 1679, however, several London Quakers who had signed the Concessions as original shareholders started looking for better properties downriver, where a group of Dublin Quakers had arrived recently in the Third Tenth.

COOPER CREEK COLONY

Located between Pennsauken and Timber Creeks, the Third (or Irish) Tenth offered an attractive area with four fast-flowing tidal creeks to provide access to the meadows and woodlands of the interior. London and Dublin Quakers staked out claims there in the late seventeenth century, obtained surveys, registered deeds in Burlington, and started to build houses.

They settled along Cooper's, Newton, and Timber Creeks, forming the original communities that would define the entire history of the county.

Master bricklayer Francis Collins, an original signatory of the Concessions and holder of four-sevenths of one proprietary share, made the first survey of land in the Third Tenth, although Richard Arnold from Burlington already held land on Newton Creek. A London Quaker, Collins had spent several years on a less desirable town plot in Burlington, where he helped to build brick meeting and counting houses. The fiercely independent and entrepreneurial English Quaker pioneer wanted his own plantation. As one of the early road commissioners in West Jersey, Collins traveled the winding Indian path that went from Burlington to Salem, and he took up more than a thousand acres of prime real estate where the road crossed Deer Creek (later Cooper's Creek), near present-day Haddonfield. Collins's property extended south to the next creek (Newton) and included a town plot on the riverfront between Newton and Big Timber Creeks (present-day Gloucester City). He developed a landing on Cooper's Creek and built a plantation house. Mostly, Collins speculated in real estate, selling prime tracts between 1684 and 1695 to John Kay, Simeon Ellis, and John Hugg—future leaders of the community destined to become Camden County.

Another Burlington Quaker, William Cooper, a former London ironmonger, joined Collins in the Third Tenth in 1681, purchasing rights to a three-hundred-acre tract from the proprietors. Cooper settled on the southern bank at the mouth of Deer Creek. It was the best spot in the area, a magnificent pine-covered point of high ground jutting out at a bend in the Delaware River. The Lenape occupied this fertile land during the planting season, and Cooper bargained for the property, paying for it with tools, jewelry, cloth, wampum, and liquor. According to tradition, Cooper shared the land and coexisted peacefully with the Lenape. Meanwhile, he erected a large house, blacksmith shop, and stable on his Pyne Poynt plantation. His house served for a time as a Friends meetinghouse and possibly an inn (although the Coopers received no tavern license until 1727).

Most important, as early as 1682 the West Jersey Friends took a wherry (an oar- and sail-powered longboat used as a ferry) from Cooper's riverfront landing to attend meeting across the river in Shackamaxon (later the Kensington section of Philadelphia). Thus Cooper established the riverfront area (now Camden City) as a ferry landing that linked the Quaker communities of West Jersey to those of Philadelphia. These historic social, economic, and cultural ties between Philadelphia and Camden would remain a constant characteristic of the county's development. After Cooper bought out the original ferry license holder, William Roydon, in 1688, the Cooper family held a near monopoly on all ferry traffic crossing the river between Cooper's and Newton Creeks. Proprietary restrictions against owning both sides of a tidal creek were rarely enforced, so the Cooper family accumulated land all along Cooper's Creek, purchased part of the island in the river at the mouth of their creek from proprietary shareholder John Petty, and established, through kinship ties with other leading Quaker families on both sides of the river, a dynasty that controlled local politics and the economy for nearly a century.

NEWTON COLONY

Another group of English Quaker shareholders of the West Jersey proprietorship claimed property along the meandering Newton Creek. They included wealthy London linen draper and merchant Robert Turner, serge maker Robert Zane, stuff weaver Thomas Thackara, and master carpenter William Bate (sometimes Bates). Having resided most recently in Dublin, the Newton Creek colonists were dubbed Irish Quakers, and the Third Tenth, where they settled, was called the Irish Tenth. Zane served as the group's advance agent, arriving in the Delaware Valley before 1679, when he was listed as a "New Salem merchant."

In this capacity, Zane located unclaimed lands along the river for his shareholding partners and another group of Quakers, among them merchant Anthony Sharp, whose nephew Thomas Sharp joined the first Newton Creek settlement in 1681. Zane purchased a boat from the Swedes at Wicaco, directly across the river from the mouth of Newton Creek, and sailed up the tidal creek. He employed a Swedish guide and interpreter to bargain with the Lenape. According to tradition, the Dublin Quaker met and married supposed Native American Alice Alday during negotiations, but this story of Native American ancestry for the Newton Creek community is most likely part of the region's rich folklore. Zane's will named his wife, Elizabeth, the daughter of Philadelphia Quaker Henry Willis, as guardian of his children and five indentured servants.

Zane's partners arrived in 1682 to occupy their individual plantations,

and they staked out claims to a common meadow at the mouth of New-
ton Creek to provide winter hay for their livestock. Zane selected the best
spot for his farm on a cleared meadow that fronted both Cooper's and
Newton Creeks and probably on the site of his Lenape "wife's" village.
Thackara settled immediately to the south, across the creek from William
Bate's property. Master carpenter Bate soon built a meetinghouse for the
Dublin Friends on Newton Creek. Sharp and his "Negro man" took a
smaller plot of land below the others, closer to the riverfront and at a fork
in the creek, where he served for years as the local land surveyor, county
clerk, and Newton colony historian.

Turner, who held half of the Irish Quaker proprietary share and most
likely never settled in West Jersey, sold nearby tracts of land to London
tallow chandler Mark Newby. Reportedly, Newby operated West Jersey's
first banking house from his one-room log cabin along Newton Creek, using a hoard of Irish copper half-pence that he had brought with him from
Ireland to finance land purchases. After Newby's death, his widow Hannah managed the 250 acres of meadowland and 300 acres of timber that
constituted the plantation. Meanwhile, Turner sold a tract below Newby's
to cooper Archibald Mickle, founder of one of the most prominent families in Camden County history. A few years after the Mickle purchase,
Turner sold yet another large tract along the riverfront, east of Mickle's,
to Philadelphia master carpenter John Kaighn. The Kaighn family developed the 455-acre farm and tiny waterfront village of Kaighnton, an area
remembered today by Kaighns Avenue in Camden City.

GLOUCESTERTOWN

By 1685 the Burlington Court, which served as the government for the
West Jersey province, resolved that the justices and freeholders of the Third
and Fourth Tenths (who grumbled constantly about the long trek to the
provincial capital in Burlington) could form a county government. In May
1686 Cooper, Collins, Sharp, Bate, and Newby, the leaders of the Third
Tenth (designated by the provincial court as the upper precinct of the new
county named Gloucester) traveled to a house below Newton Creek to
meet with representatives of the Quaker Fourth Tenth, which extended
from the Gloucester River south toward Fenwick's Salem colony and was
designated as the lower precinct. To appease the Swedish farmers, Presby-

terian planters, and influential Quaker families who resided in the Fourth Tenth (including Constantine Wood, Thomas Gardiner, and John Ladd), the freeholders from the Third Tenth agreed to hold alternate court sessions in each precinct. The first would be held at Red Bank on Woodbury Creek, which adjoined the lands of the Wood, Ladd, and Gardiner families; the next would meet in a riverfront collection of houses on the north bank of the Gloucester River, laid out as Gloucestertown.

The earliest Gloucester County Court sessions of 1686 convened first at Henry Tredway's tavern in Red Bank and then at the large riverfront house of Gloucestertown brewer and ferry owner John Reading, who also served as the first county clerk to record business. The first court provided for election of justices and freeholders, passed ordinances to register earmarks for cattle and hogs, and appointed tax assessors and collectors. Also, the first Gloucester County government instructed road commissioners to make a "passable" highway (the Irish Road) and construct a "good and usable" bridge over the Gloucester River (now referred to as Timber Creek) to connect settlers in the lower precinct with the more influential freeholders of the upper precinct.

Accommodation with the freeholders below Timber Creek was deceptive. The powerful clique of Quaker families who resided along Cooper's and Newton Creeks and on the north side of Timber Creek had no intention of sharing the county seat with the few Friends, Presbyterians, and Swedes from the lower precinct. A bitter court case between Woodbury Creek tavern owner Tredway and Newton Creek founder Zane, who accused Tredway of stealing his hog earmark (a serious offense in the eyes of these pioneering plantation owners), ended Tredway's privilege of holding county court sessions at his inn. After Zane's suit, no further Gloucester County government business was conducted in the Fourth Tenth (although the area gained revenge a hundred years later when Gloucester County relocated the seat of government to Woodbury).

The removal of Tredway led to the creation of a county government seat in the little riverfront collection of houses that lay between Newton and Timber Creeks. Gloucestertown residents John Reading, Dorothy and Matthew Medcalfe, and Sarah Bull, wife of proprietary shareholder Thomas Bull, entertained the first gatherings of freeholders and justices in their houses to organize a town appropriate for the county seat. They agreed in 1689 to build "two public and commodious landings in the most convenient places on the banks of the Gloucester River and the branch of the Newton Creek" and authorized the surveying of roads from the Delaware riverfront to the "high or great road through the midst of the Town bounds." They hired Newton Creek surveyor Thomas Sharp to survey town plats, lay out streets, and design a central market square.

Gloucester County government, now meeting exclusively in Gloucestertown, ordered construction of a courthouse, jail, whipping post, and stocks. A shortage of tax money or perhaps public disinterest delayed final construction of county buildings until the mid-1690s, however. Most likely, county court sessions were held during this interval at clerk Reading's house, until it burned down in 1698 (and with it all early county records). Furthermore, the creation of separate "constable wicks," or townships, in 1694–95 allowed the individualistic upper precinct Quaker farmers to tend to their own local affairs rather than travel to Gloucestertown, which was nearly cut off from the rest of the county at high tide on the creeks and river. In addition to Gloucestertown Township, the original townships in the Third Tenth included Waterford (between Pennsauken and Cooper's Creeks), Newton (between Cooper's and Newton Creeks), and Gloucester (between Newton and Timber Creeks). In the Fourth Tenth were Deptford and Egg Harbor Townships.

Seventeenth-Century Society

Proprietors and freeholders in these original townships—perhaps two hundred people in the late seventeenth century—shared common English bourgeois cultural values and middle-class economic backgrounds. Most of the original landowners had been merchants, shopkeepers, artisans, skilled craftsmen, or mechanics in the old country. They ranged from modestly wealthy Quaker families to those inhabitants called "low in the world" by William Penn. Most likely, constant fines and imprisonment for attending meeting or failing to support the established church impoverished some, and others came from the growing class of individuals dislocated by social and economic changes in seventeenth-century Britain. These poorer inhabitants of the Third Tenth signed contracts of indenture with more prosperous proprietors, who paid their passage to West Jersey in return for a term of servitude. Robert Zane and Mark Newby each sponsored five indentured servants, who owed five years of service in return for passage to the New World.

Among Gloucester County's first leaders in the upper precinct were educated gentlemen who owned books and small libraries. Several, including Zane and Thomas Sharp, had studied law. A few shared William Penn's ideas about town planning and government, and had a concept of bourgeois community organization. The largest landowners ran their plantations as would English country gentlemen, suggesting prior farming experience in the British countryside. Attachment to the teachings of George Fox created a sense of community as well. Quaker freeholders in the Third Tenth (perhaps 50 percent of the late-seventeenth-century population) attended the Friends meeting and conducted their personal and community lives with guidance from the meeting. With choices for marriage limited, the first Quaker settlers tended to intermarry with Friends along the tidal creeks, in Burlington County, and across the river in Philadelphia.

Development of kinship ties became the single most important factor in shaping Camden County's original community. Estates were consolidated and community leadership was perpetuated in the hands of the families, kin, and ancestors of the first English Quaker families. The Bate and Thackara families preserved their lines through intermarriage with the Cooper, Clement, Ellis, Spicer, and other prominent pioneering families. Marriage forged powerful political alliances among rival tidal creek townships. Margaret and Priscilla Collins, daughters of Cooper Creek pioneer Francis Collins, married, respectively, Elias Hugg and John Hugg Jr., sons of the most prominent Gloucestertown and Timber Creek family, establishing a hundred-year alliance. Newton Creek constable William Bate's son Jeremiah married the daughter of county judge Samuel Spicer, owner of the first ferry across Cooper's Creek, thus assuring his position as a township constable.

SEVENTEENTH-CENTURY POLITICS AND LAW

The fragmented records of the original Gloucester County Court (1686–1703) reveal life in the future Camden County during the last years of the West Jersey proprietary government. The county's recording clerk, Thomas Sharp, spent a great amount of time and energy elaborately drawing cattle

and hog identifications in a county earmark book, attesting to the importance of livestock and agriculture in this tidewater community. The county
government authorized bounties of up to 10 shillings for the ears of wolves,
panthers, and bears, which reportedly attacked local farm animals in the
still wilderness county. The Gloucester Court directed a three-member
road commission to improve Indian trails for the passage of horseback
riders and possibly two-wheeled carts (there would be no four-wheeled
coaches on county roads until after the 1730s). The first roads connected
Cooper's ferry landing to the Salem Road, near present-day Haddonfield,
and Gloucestertown to the Salem Road where it crossed the headwaters
of Timber Creek. Unfortunately, the county neglected bridges over the
creeks. Complaints from two Long Island travelers who fell off the rick-
ety Little Timber Creek bridge and would have drowned "but for the
Almighty" revealed the road commissioners' failure to repair the structure.
The county fined the commissioners for their oversight. Highway maintenance seemed indifferent as well. The county struggled to collect taxes in
scarce silver coin or barleycorn, wheat, rye, and Indian peas to support
road improvement through the undeveloped countryside, where travelers
often went twenty miles before seeing another farmhouse along the narrow horse paths.

Gloucester County government was far more successful in its enforce-
ment of moral order, replicating the conduct of the dominant Burlington Court and the monthly Friends meeting. Like its models upriver, the
Gloucester County Court fined residents for having children born illegally
out of Quaker meeting. In one case, the local justices sentenced a county female to be stripped naked to the waist and whipped in front of the Gloucester Court. In another case, two villagers convicted of theft were sentenced
to have the letter "T" burned into their hands to the bone unless they agreed
to five years of indentured servitude in the West Indies. They chose the
latter. Despite the severity of seventeenth-century justice, the Gloucester
County Court avoided the more violent punishments that could be found
in East Jersey, New England, and other New World communities. Gloucester County burned no one at the stake and never tortured prisoners to
death. Even a convicted child murderer was simply fined by the Gloucester Court in the late seventeenth century for this most heinous crime.

The creation of county government and laws had more to do with Burlington Quaker politics than with punishment for sins that were already

subject to scrutiny by the monthly meeting. Deputy Governor Samuel Jennings, who held kinship and business ties to Quakers in the Third Tenth, expected Gloucester County to support the proprietary government against assaults from non-Quaker newcomers and from a contentious faction of rebellious Quakers, and he was not disappointed. Knowing that Jennings controlled the distribution of unclaimed proprietary lands, Gloucester County representatives William Cooper and Thomas Thackara sided consistently with Jennings against the followers of Quaker George Keith, who refused to accept the basic tenets of George Fox, founder of the Religious Society of Friends.

At the same time, Gloucester County justices and freeholders defended the original proprietors against Anglican and Anabaptist religious factions in Burlington. Justice Andrew Robeson, a Scottish-Irish Presbyterian, was arrested and fined for threatening to throw the anti-Quaker Governor Jeremiah Basse into the Delaware River and for showing "contempt of the present Government." Newton Township constable Jeremiah Bate was fined for opposing Basse. In the end, such unrest in West Jersey (and more violent activity in East Jersey) convinced the British government to unify the two proprietary provinces into the royal colony of New Jersey. The pioneering period came to a close with the last court session of June 1703, and a new historical process began along the tidal creeks on the east side of the Delaware River, which would eventually lead Gloucester County to revolt against British rule.

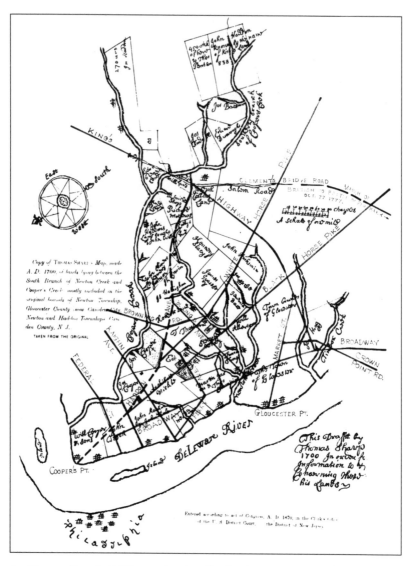

2. Thomas Sharp's 1700 map showing first landowners, as published in George R. Prowell's *History of Camden County* (1886) and annotated with some current roads superimposed over the old settlements. *(Camden County Historical Society Collection)*

2

"A County Where Business Is Exceeding Plenty"

Tidewater Plantation Society

A select group of prosperous landowning families descended from and holding extensive kinship ties to the original settlers dominated life in Gloucester County during the eighteenth century. Although surrendering their right to govern when West Jersey became part of the royal province of New Jersey in 1703, the proprietors and their kin continued to control affairs by maintaining proprietary rights to undeveloped land. This landed gentry held the largest tracts along the tidal creeks and tributary streams that defined the region's distinctive cultural geography. Here they operated plantations of more than three hundred acres, partly cleared for planting and with meadows fenced for pasturage and wooded tracts and cedar swamps. Their estates were each valued at nearly £1,000.

The original proprietary families and their kin controlled the landing places on the creeks that linked the county to markets on the Delaware River and in Philadelphia. Near these creek landings they built their two-story brick and frame houses with bricks produced locally by a kiln established in 1712 by the Huggs near Gloucestertown. The plantation houses had full cellars and detached stone kitchens, barns, milk houses, cider mills, and stables. Large landowners dammed streams to make millponds for their sawmills and their grist and bolting mills, which ground grain and sifted flour into meal. Several owned fulling mills for cleaning, stretching, dying, and pressing cloth. They secured legislation to bank the creeks, keep out tidal waters, and expand their wetland hay meadows and high arable land. Over the course of the eighteenth century, these families made the region bounded by the Delaware River to the west, Oldman's Creek on the south, Pennsauken Creek to the north, and extending eastward toward the Great Egg Harbor River and Atlantic Ocean into a northern tidewater plantation society.

The most prominent plantation and mill-owning families that dominated life between Timber and Pennsauken Creeks in the upper part of old Gloucester County (forming the boundaries of modern-day Camden County) were even more tightly linked through kinship and business ties than those in the county below Timber Creek. The Spicer, Morgan, Coles, Burrough, Lippincott, and Inskeep families led affairs in Waterford Township between Pennsauken and Cooper's Creeks and to the east as far as Egg Harbor River. Newton Township's elite, residing between Cooper's and Newton Creeks, included the Cooper, Mickle, Kaighn, Clement, Gill, Haddon-Estaugh, Hopkins, Stokes, Ellis, Matlack, and Kay families. The Hillman, Hinchman, Tomlinson, Cheesman, and Blackwood families defined the sprawling Timber Creek region. The Hugg and Harrison families dominated life at the county seat of Gloucestertown at the mouth of Big Timber Creek.

These founding families and their kin in Burlington and Salem Counties and across the river in Philadelphia influenced county politics through domination of the boards of justices and freeholders and the offices of sheriff, tax assessor, collector, and overseer of roads. They directed where county roads and bridges should be built to improve access to and enhance the value of their holdings. They established township and county laws and determined how to distribute tax money. Most important, the Cooper, Kay, Kaighn, and Hinchman families represented the county proprietary interests at the provincial assembly that met alternately in Burlington and Perth Amboy after the 1703 surrender of West Jersey government to the crown. Here they voted with their peers from other counties to create land banks, back the issuance of paper currency, and provide credit to property owners and business interests. And they determined how the county would respond to provincial and imperial tax policies, to economic coercion, and eventually to the growing demand for autonomy and independence from Britain.

INDENTURED SERVANTS

The gentry class shaped social and religious life in the upper part of Gloucester County. They built Quaker meetinghouses in Newton Township and Haddonfield, and Presbyterian churches in Longacoming (modern-day Berlin Township, settled at least by 1718) and Blackwoodtown (1690s). The leading Gloucester County families took care of the infirm and indigent through the Quaker meeting or the poor house and sponsored indentured servants. Indentured servitude became an elaborate social, economic, and moral institution in eighteenth-century Gloucester County, providing care for and educating poorer children and orphans. Young female apprentices would learn "the Trade or Mystery of Housewifery, as Sewing Knitting & Spinning." Masters forbade their apprentices to "commit fornication, nor contract Matrimony within the Said Term, play at Cards, Dice or any other unlawful Game" or "haunt Ale-houses, Taverns, or Play-houses." Every leading Gloucester County family held indentured servants, as revealed by the many announcements in the Philadelphia newspapers of runaway servant boys and girls (mostly of Irish heritage) from Gloucester County plantation and mill owners. John Gill, Timothy Matlack, Richard Chew, John Blackwood, Benjamin Cooper, Abraham Mickle, William Hugg, and Peter Cheesman all offered rewards between 1742 and 1750 for the return of runaway indentured servants with time still to serve.

SLAVERY

Of the mid-eighteenth-century county population of about 3,500 people, nearly 150 were African slaves. The Cooper, Matlack, Hugg, Coles, Hillman, and Hinchman families were among the largest slaveowners. Most families held one or two black slaves as female household help or male farmhands. But sawmill owner and planter Abraham Porter owned "four young Negro men, three boys, one woman, and one girl" to work his five-hundred-acre Timber Creek plantation in the 1740s. Gabriel Davis, proprietor of an inn on Timber Creek, kept three black men, one woman, a

boy, and a girl. "Black girl, Nina, mulatto girl Fan, Negro girl named Ve-
nus, [and] Negro boy, Piro" worked Jacob Stokes's large Newton Township
plantation. The Blackwood family used blacks in their saw and fulling mills
on Timber Creek, and Joseph Ellis had three black slaves in his Gloucestertown tan yard. Even quiet Quaker preacher John Estaugh and his wife
Elizabeth Haddon of Haddon Field owned the slave Primus. Reputedly, the
West Jersey Quakers treated their blacks as part of the family and better
than larger slaveowners in East Jersey to the north or the Chesapeake
region to the south. But Gloucester County tidewater plantation society
could be equally harsh. Daniel Cooper's freedom-minded "Negro Man
Quaco had an iron Collar with two Hooks to it, round his Neck, a pair of
Hand-cuffs with a Chain to them, six Feet long."

Daniel Cooper sponsored slave auctions at his ferry landing and at
Benjamin Cooper's ferry upriver. The Coopers sold African slaves during the mid-eighteenth century even as Quakers across the river in Philadelphia banned the slave trade there. Consequently, the Philadelphia
merchant houses of Willing, Morris and Company and Stocker and Fuller
disposed of their slaves at Daniel Cooper's Ferry. Occasionally, the Cooper's
Ferry slave market auctioned a large cargo of Africans from a slave ship
anchored in the Delaware River. The August 1762 sale featured morning
and afternoon sessions to display a new shipment: "just imported, a parcel
of fine young Negroe Slaves, Men, Women, Boys and Girls, and to be sold
at Daniel Cooper's Ferry, in the Jerseys, opposite the City of Philadelphia."
This cargo, shipped directly from West Africa, attracted local tidewater
planters. "It is generally allowed," noted a Philadelphia newspaper adver-
tisement, "that the Gambia Slaves are much more robust and tractable, than
any other Slaves from the Coast of Guinea, and more capable of under-
going the Severity of the Winter Seasons in the North-American Colonies, which occasions their being vastly more esteemed and coveted in this
Province, and those to the Northward than any other Slaves whatsoever."

"A County Where Business Is Exceeding Plenty"

The Cooper's Ferry slave auction, dealing mostly in smaller "parcels of
likely Negroe Wenches and boys," was only one part of the general market of Barbados spirits, Teneriffe wines, and imported merchandise. In-

deed, Cooper's Ferry served as an occasional marketplace for all of Gloucester County, and Philadelphia buyers crossed the river from Arch Street to browse among the "horned cattle" brought in by area farmers. Marmaduke Cooper offered his fine stud horses and mares for sale or breeding, while Job Whitall sold pork and bacon. Isaac Hinchman displayed his imported Pomeranian and Irish linens and his London and Bristol glassware for sale at Benjamin Cooper's fifteen-room tavern. Gloucester County gardener Richard Collings sold imported seed for turnip, broccoli, kale, celery, lettuce, asparagus, cucumbers, carrots, onion, mustard greens, melons, and flowers to the likes of Elizabeth Haddon-Estaugh, who built Haddon Field estate at the head of Cooper's Creek, about seven miles from the Delaware riverfront ferry landings.

Arguably, Elizabeth Haddon became the single most important female real estate developer in Camden County history, establishing a plantation in 1713 and a town at the other end of Cooper's Creek from the slave auction settlement at the mouth of the creek. In the process, Haddon accumulated the largest personal estate in the area, valued at her death in 1762 at £8,000. Haddon arrived in Gloucester County in 1701 to lay claim to Richard Matthews's one-eighth of one share of the West Jersey proprietorship, which had been purchased by her father, John Haddon, a London Quaker ironmonger. Unable to make the trip to America himself, Haddon dispatched his highly educated daughter as his legal representative. Aided by kin and fellow Friends Francis Collins, John Gill, John Kay, and Samuel Clement, Elizabeth Haddon located and surveyed the four hundred acres of prime tidewater land at the head of Cooper's Creek in present-day Haddonfield. Along the way, she met and married Quaker preacher John Estaugh, who became an able partner in the development of Haddon Field plantation, the sale of town lots, and the establishment of the Haddonfield Friends Meeting in 1721 on a lot donated by John Haddon.

After Estaugh's death on a missionary trip in the West Indies, Elizabeth developed her estate and sold town lots along the King's Highway, where it crossed the head of Cooper's Creek, to skilled craftsmen and merchants like brewer Timothy Matlack and blacksmith John Kaighn. At the same time, she managed the Pennsylvania Land Company and became a stockholder in the London [Land] Company. Estaugh-Haddon served as recording clerk of the Women's Friends Meeting in Newton Township, developing a female support group for Quaker widows, single females, and working-class women—those most vulnerable to exploitation under English law. She supported Sarah Dimsdale, Rachel Lippincott, Elizabeth Kaighn, and the "widow Cooper." Before her death in 1762, Haddon-Estaugh turned over interests in the land companies to her kinswoman Sarah Hopkins.

The favorable entrepreneurial environment on the east side of the Delaware River contributed to Haddon-Estaugh's success as a business-woman. The Gloucester County plantation, mill, and tavern owners in the upper precinct built a prosperous business community based on the tidal streams between Timber and Pennsauken Creeks. One Cooper's Creek mill owner boasted that his property was "situated on a never failing stream, and in a County where business is exceeding plenty." John Blackwood described his Timber Creek property as "half a mile from a very good Landing, convenient for Trades Men." Samuel Blackwood announced that his landing, situated eight miles from Gloucestertown, had become "an old accustomed Place for Business." Blackwood's Timber Creek fulling mill offered "as cheap rates as at any mill in New Jersey or Pennsylvania, with Press-Shop, Dye-house, Tenter-bars, and all other Tools and Utensils necessary for carrying on the Fulling Business." Planters and mill owners floated their cedar shingles, cordwood, and agricultural products in flat-boats from Roe's Landing (later Chew's Landing) and other places along the branches of the fast-flowing Timber Creek tidal system for shipment to Philadelphia.

A Suburb of Philadelphia

The region between Timber and Cooper's Creeks attracted Philadelphia investors and real estate entrepreneurs who sought to make the area a suburb of the big port town across the river. Wealthy Quaker entrepreneur William Wharton described the benefits of the excellent water and rich meadowlands along the tidal creeks and the availability of valuable woodlands. Their location but a few miles from Philadelphia's markets, Wharton announced, made such plots "very convenient for the farmer, in that he may, several times a week, dispose of his produce on the most advantageous terms." Local proprietors agreed, advertising for sale one-hundred-acre tracts of land complete with apple and peach orchards, fenced pastures, two-story houses with full cellars, detached kitchens with stone fireplaces and draw wells at the door. Most included frame barns for hay, stables, sheds, cider mills, and milk houses. Isaac Cooper offered his Cooper's Creek property with eighty acres of "grubb'd" (freshly tilled) land, twenty acres of drained meadow "fit for the Scythe," and thirty acres of valuable woodland.

Property sold most quickly near good landings on Timber, Newton, and Cooper's Creeks and close to a Friends meetinghouse. Gentry proprietors developed building lots along the "great country road" between Gloucestertown and the head of Cooper's Creek (present-day Haddonfield). The best lots bordered the road between Cooper's Ferry and Haddonfield (Haddon Avenue) "now open'd and clear'd" from Cooper's Ferry to the Salem Road. By the 1750s land sales also increased along the recently finished King's Highway between Burlington and Salem, a "good Road fit for all Wheel Carriages."

The colonial tidewater community on the New Jersey side of the Delaware River became a popular place to invest, do business, or find respite. Local proprietors promoted land sales among the more prosperous Philadelphians anxious to escape from a busy city perceived already as overcrowded, dirty, and plagued with yellow fever. Thus West Jersey Quaker proprietor Jacob Spicer described Gloucester County as "very pleasant and healthy." William Hugg promised that the fresh air, clean water, and bountiful gardens of Gloucestertown's riverfront lots would "suit a genteel family, who have an inclination to retire from the noise and bustle of the city." The Huggs established a regular ferry service between their Delaware riverfront town and Gloucester Point below Philadelphia to encourage development of Gloucestertown properties.

Philadelphia merchant Jacob Cooper inherited one hundred acres below Cooper's Creek from his family in 1764. The first of many Philadelphia suburban developers to exploit real estate opportunities across the river, Cooper cleared a lane (Market Street) to his brother Daniel Cooper's ferry landing and widened the horse trail to the river, making Cooper Street. Probably copying the plan of the riverfront town of Philadelphia, Cooper surveyed streets perpendicular to the river and cross streets for a town in an orthogonal grid. In 1771 he advertised lots in his planned town in the Pennsylvania press and at the London Coffee House on Front and High Streets, Philadelphia. Cooper promoted the riverfront properties as offering rich soil for gardens and fruit trees and boasting pure water for brewing beer, fishing, and sailing. Cooper named his project Camden Town. The name derives either from the Cooper family's ancestral home of Campden, in Gloucestershire, England, or, more likely, from the title of the Lord Chief Justice of England, Charles Pratt, the earl of Camden, who showed much sympathy for the American grievances against British tax policies.

The buyers of the original Camden Town lots revealed that the entrepreneurial Cooper most likely named his real estate development in honor of that British friend of American maritime interests in order to attract Philadelphia's leading merchants and opponents of the discriminatory British navigation laws. Philadelphia merchants Thomas Mifflin, Samuel Miles, and Robert Morris, who used Cooper's ferries to sell slaves and other goods, bought the first lots. Southwark boat builder Henry Casdorp, ship's carpenter William Rush, Northern Liberties shipbuilder Isaac Coates, and ship chandler Nathaniel Falconer purchased waterfront lots across the river in Camden Town as well. George Bartram, son of colonial America's leading horticulturalist, John Bartram (who owned an estate along the Schuylkill River), also purchased Camden Town lots, perhaps to replicate his father's agricultural and horticultural experiments in the rich soil of the Gloucester County riverfront.

Trouble with Britain, however, leading to the Revolutionary War, killed the first attempt to make Camden a suburb of Philadelphia. The project failed as the original lot owners became deeply involved in the resistance movement and, eventually, revolution. Morris became the organizer of finances for the Continental Congress, Miles a militia leader, and Mifflin a quartermaster general in the Continental Army and later governor of Pennsylvania. None ever returned to his investments on the other side of the river. Development of Camden would not occur until the early decades of the nineteenth century, when the town emerged as the leading urban center in the county. Meanwhile, the tiny fishing village of Gloucestertown (modern-day Gloucester City) achieved its moment of glory in county history as the center of local political and military organization in the decade before the Revolutionary War.

GLOUCESTERTOWN ORGANIZES THE COUNTY FOR WAR

Gloucestertown was not much of a place in the late eighteenth century. Unlike Cooper's Ferry or Haddonfield, the riverfront village of no more than a dozen houses and two taverns, located between the mouths of Newton and Big Timber Creeks, grew little during the century. For a time, the town served as a vital ferry landing for travelers to Southwark or as a depot for goods that came down Timber Creek from the interior. Located well off the main roads through the county and surrounded by creeks, Gloucestertown gradually lost business to Cooper's Ferry to the north, Haddonfield to the east, and Woodbury to the south. Nevertheless, Gloucestertown was a center of political life throughout most of the eighteenth century, and citizens there organized the local movement to gain independence from Great Britain.

The Gloucester County Board of Justices and Freeholders, created by the provincial assembly in 1713 to raise tax money for the maintenance of county buildings and composed of two elected freeholders from each township, convened at Gloucestertown to conduct government business. The overseers of the poor assessed obligations to the indigent and managed the workhouse. The overseers of roads tried to improve the nearly impassable dirt traces by requiring county residents to fill low, wet spots in roadbeds or by raising public subscriptions to erect causeways and bridges over fast-flowing tidal creeks. Meanwhile, county tax assessors and collectors raised revenues. Legal affairs were settled on court day at the county courthouse on High (later Market) Street, located one block from the river. The nearby county "gaol" imprisoned "insolvent debtors," runaway servants, and common criminals. The whipping post erected in the courthouse yard about 1734 was employed frequently to punish minor crimes. In at least a half dozen cases, the county executed capital felons by hanging. High Sheriff Joseph Hugg's hangman executed two in 1721, and in 1750 County Sheriff Samuel Harrison's executioner hanged three.

When county residents first organized their government at the end of the seventeenth century, Gloucestertown seemed the best place for a county seat. It was located on the Delaware River halfway between the lower county townships of the Fourth Tenth (Greenwich, Deptford, and

Woolwich) and the upper county townships of the Third Tenth (Waterford, Newton, and Gloucester). Moreover, Gloucestertown developed as a strictly secular community, differing from the neighboring Quaker-dominated county seats of Salem and Burlington. Unlike Cooper's Ferry, Haddonfield, or Woodbury, it had no Friends meetinghouse. The Blackwoods and other fiercely anti-English Scottish-Irish families from the Timber Creek region congregated in Gloucestertown, and aggressive Presbyterian preachers like George Whitefield and Benjamin Chestnut selected the Timber Creek community as the location for revival sermons. Whitefield claimed that he stirred fifteen hundred "Hearers" in a county that totaled barely three thousand residents (although many crossed from Philadelphia and Chester to hear the Presbyterian revivalist). One of Gloucestertown's few permanent Quaker residents, Robert Friend Price, the county's first true politician, sought favor with all rival sects. Price regularly opened his house, Windmill Place at the mouth of Great Timber Creek (modern-day Westville), to preachers like the Presbyterian John Brainerd and the Methodists Joseph Pilmoor and Francis Asbury.

The riverfront town also attracted the more militant county residents, including Timber Creek sawyer-planter Abraham Porter, tanner Joseph Ellis, innkeepers John Hider and William Hugg, and County Sheriff Samuel Harrison—all Gloucester County militia officers and veterans of the colonial wars. During the French and Indian War of 1756–63, Gloucestertown became the center for recruiting West Jersey militia, and in 1761 "Rioting Soldiers" seeking back pay damaged the "County House." After the war, in 1763, William Hugg stored in his tavern 159 muskets, "the Quota of Arms and Ammunition which belongs to the County of Gloucester." Also, the town hosted the Gloucester [Fox] Hunting Club, organized at Hugg's Tavern in 1766. The hunting club became the gathering place for future Revolutionary War militia officers, such as young Franklin Davenport of Woodbury, and the organizers of the Philadelphia Light Horse Troop. Indeed, many of Philadelphia's wartime and postwar leaders gathered at the club in Gloucestertown, including Samuel and Robert Morris, Robert Wharton, John Cadwalader, Charles Willing, Thomas Mifflin, and John Dickinson.

Thus the Delaware riverfront county seat provided the natural base for the first local stirrings of protest that led to armed resistance against

Britain. Between 1764 and 1776, Hugg's Tavern served as the meeting place (and proprietor John Hugg functioned as the recording clerk) for the Gloucester County association to endorse the American nonimportation movement to boycott British goods, promote domestic manufacturing, and organize committees of observation and correspondence. In the end, the meetings at Hugg's Tavern in Gloucestertown brought the long isolated (and often antiwar) communities between Pennsauken and Oldman's Creeks into the movement to resist British economic and tax regulations and to participate actively in armed revolt.

The Gloucester County planter elite's involvement in the larger colonial protest movement began in 1764, when the British government imposed a stamp tax on legal documents and newspapers to defray the extraordinary expense accrued in defending the American colonies during the recent French and Indian War. This interference with local business provoked the Quaker landed gentry and business community to resistance. Gloucester County's Quaker proprietary representatives to the provincial assembly, John Hinchman and Robert Friend Price, eagerly joined the call for a Stamp Act congress to protest the tax. Though a Friend and married into the Quaker gentry elite Mickle family, the politically active Price promoted all religions and interests in the area. The local tidewater planter elite encouraged the protest with fifty-two signatures on the petition in 1769 that urged Hinchman and Price to oppose British economic regulations and taxes at the provincial assembly in Burlington. The same Gloucester County proprietary families supported formation of committees of observation and nonimportation associations when the British closed Boston's port and imposed the Intolerable Acts to crush Massachusetts's opposition to more taxes and the quartering of troops. Such interference with local affairs agitated Gloucester County, leading to early support for the local committee of correspondence's humanitarian relief fund for the people of Boston. The West Jersey protestors also endorsed the action of protestors in nearby Cumberland County, New Jersey, who burned a cargo of tea in a Greenwich warehouse to protest a new tax that raised the price of tea in America.

Tidewater plantation leadership continued on the Committee of 77, organized at "a general meeting of the inhabitants of the county of Gloucester in New Jersey held at the Court-house on the 12th of December, 1774," to correspond with other county committees and elect representatives to a provincial congress. Delegates from the townships above Timber Creek came from the leading families. The Spicer, Morgan, Stokes, Coles, and Inskeep families headed the Waterford Township delegation. Mickle, Clements, Gill, and five Cooper family leaders sat for Newton Township, and Tomlinson, Cheesman, Hider, and Hillman for Gloucester Township. Gloucestertown Township representatives Price, Hinchman, William Hugg Jr., Joseph Hugg, and Joseph Ellis coordinated the movement, with Ellis and the Huggs urging a more militant approach. Participation caused a crisis among local Quaker members. The Haddonfield Monthly Meeting disowned John Cooper for membership on the Committee of 77 and separated Hinchman from the Unity of Friends for promoting military preparations.

The Gloucester Committee of 77 guided the county toward further resistance and full cooperation with other patriots throughout Pennsylvania and New Jersey. A radical Gloucestertown faction, led by French and Indian War veterans Ellis and the Huggs, pushed the county toward war. Ellis organized the first countywide nonimportation association during the 1760s and served as treasurer of the relief fund to send money to the people of Boston blockaded by the British. He attended every local meeting of the committees of observation and correspondence and recruited county militia in 1775 after the Battle of Lexington and Concord initiated armed resistance to British rule. The militant Hugg family coordinated Gloucester County's unfolding resistance movement. William Hugg Jr. provided rooms in his tavern for illegal protest meetings, while his brother Joseph served as clerk for the county committees of observation and correspondence, calling the county to the meetings and recording the minutes. Hugg, Ellis, Hinchman, Price, and John Cooper met with representatives from other New Jersey counties to choose delegates to serve in the Continental Congress. Hugg, Ellis, and activist John Sparks of Woodbury, a delegate to the Committee of 77 from Deptford Township, located spots in the Delaware River to sink *cheveaux-de-frise,* huge iron-tipped logs intended to obstruct passage by British warships and troop transports upriver to Philadelphia. The Gloucester County Committee of Observation appointed Samuel Harrison and Joseph Hugg to cut logs and erect the *cheveaux-de-frise.*

WAR COMES TO THE COUNTY

The Revolutionary War was fought in Gloucester County between late 1777 and early 1778. British General Sir William Howe drove overland from Head of Elk on Chesapeake Bay to capture Philadelphia in September 1777, bringing the county near the center of military operations. The Continental Army's commander-in-chief, George Washington, hoped to isolate Howe in the city by preventing supplies and reinforcements from coming up the Delaware River. He ordered the delivery of more logs for the *chevaux-de-frise* and the construction of fortifications on the Gloucester County shore at Billingsport below Mantua Creek and at Red Bank on Woodbury Creek (Fort Mercer). Meanwhile, militia artillery captain Samuel Hugg, Franklin Davenport, and other Gloucester Hunting Club gentlemen erected a battery at the mouth of Mantua Creek, between the two forts.

The raising of a New Jersey riverfront defense brought Salem, Cumberland, and Gloucester County militias trudging through the communities below Timber Creek. As they went to build and man the forts at Billingsport and Red Bank, they broke into the meetinghouse in Woodbury and into private farmhouses seeking food and shelter. The local militia fed their horses on neighborhood hay piles, seized cattle, sheep, and pigs, and rarely paid for the supplies. Captain Hugg secured the permission of local farmers to borrow wagons to carry ammunition to his Mantua Creek battery, but Quaker planter Job Whitall reported that "Ye militia took our light covered wagon in ye Night without leave & hasn't returned it." Worse, "Capt Jos. Blewer [of the Pennsylvania Committee of Safety in charge of building the fort at Billingsport] took my little Brown mare without leave to ride up to Washington's Camp, as he said."

The American militia proved more of a nuisance than a threat. Not so the three battalions of elite Hessian grenadiers and infantry chasseurs sent across the river from Philadelphia by General Howe in October 1777 to reduce the fort at Red Bank. On 21 October more than two thousand men under Count Emil Ulrich von Donop crossed to Cooper's Ferry, marched to Haddonfield and down the King's Road, turned to cross Big Timber Creek at Clement's Bridge, and advanced toward the river along Woodbury

Creek (Red Bank Avenue). Gloucester County farmers working in the fields reported that "our women blowed ye horn & we went home, got our horses & wagon & loaded it with goods & ye reason was because Ye English troops was close by."

Units of the Continental Army repulsed the Hessian force in a bloody fight at Fort Mercer. The invaders retreated over Timber Creek, burying some of their dead at the Ashbrook Burial Ground near Clement's Bridge, then marched back through Haddonfield and crossed from Cooper's Ferry to Philadelphia.

The Battle of Gloucester

The county had seemingly escaped depredation, but shortly it would experience considerable violence. In November the British reduced Fort Mifflin, on the Pennsylvania side nearly opposite Fort Mercer, and then returned to Gloucester County with a much larger force than earlier to seize the fort at Red Bank. The Americans abandoned the fort before the attack, and Lord Charles Cornwallis dismantled the abandoned earthworks overlooking the river, moved upriver, and established headquarters in Hugg's Tavern.

Cornwallis set out pickets at Little Timber Creek Bridge (near present-day Brooklawn) and dispatched troops to forage for food. On 24 November 1777 the marquis de LaFayette, Morgan's Rifles, and Henry Lee's light horse attacked the British and Hessian forces. Militia Colonel Joseph Ellis of Gloucestertown and Captain Jacob Browning of Waterford Township commanded Gloucester County militiamen at the battle near Gloucester Bridge over Little Timber Creek. More than forty British and Hessians and twenty Americans were killed. As the Americans drove the invaders from Gloucester County, the British ransacked local houses, kitchens, and barns, taking horses, bread, pies, milk, clothing, and cooking utensils. British troops (and, possibly, local Loyalists) burned farm buildings and the Hugg plantation, and hacked up pigs and cattle. Nevertheless, Gloucester County escaped more bloody incidents, such as the one that occurred in March 1778 at Hancock's Bridge on Lower Alloways Creek in Salem County, where a British patrol bayoneted to death American militiamen and an elderly county judge while they slept.

The upper part of the county (present-day Camden County) along Cooper's Creek and through Haddonfield, Ellisburg, and over the border into Burlington County became the seat of war briefly in early 1778, as Sir George Clinton prepared to evacuate the British occupation army from Philadelphia. Clinton sent an advance guard across the Delaware River to secure Cooper's Ferry and other landings for his army to cross and march north through New Jersey to New York. Reportedly, the British forces (probably aided by local Loyalists familiar with the countryside) seized several patriots from Dr. Benjamin Vanliers's Newton Township house and ransacked Continental treasurer John Gill's place in Haddonfield. They also killed or captured several Gloucester County militiamen along the way; Major William Ellis and Aaron Chew ended up in a prison ship in New York harbor. In March 1778 Continental Army General Anthony Wayne and Polish volunteer Count Casimir Pulaski led troops against a unit of the Queen's Rangers (Loyalists) near Cooper's Creek in the vicinity of present-day Sixth and Market Streets in Camden City. The British occupation army evacuated Philadelphia in June, crossed into Gloucester County, and camped in Haddonfield, where they destroyed several houses. Clinton marched through Mount Holly, eventually fighting a battle against Washington's army in Monmouth County before withdrawing to New York.

Aftermath of War

There was a momentary erosion of law and order in Gloucester County after the British evacuation. Armed men posing as militia searched private homes for deserters or Loyalists and stole money and clothes instead. Lawless men shot sheep and cattle grazing in pastures. Local militia intimidated Quaker farmers with threats of arrest. Travelers were robbed on the highway, and horses were stolen, even from prominent county leaders such as Elijah Clark in Haddonfield. In response, New Jersey Governor William Livingston placed Colonel Ellis in command of the Gloucester County militia, with headquarters in Haddonfield. Ellis restored order. Anyone venturing through the county or crossing the river to Philadelphia had to secure a pass. Deserters were rounded up and brought to Trenton for court-martial and possible execution. Meanwhile, the marshals of the local Court of Admiralty, Isaac Kay of Newton Township and John Stokes of Haddonfield, convened auctions to settle disputes over the disposal of cargoes seized by local privateers. "On Tuesday the fifteenth instant, will be sold by Public Vendue at Samuel Cooper's Ferry, the Prize Schooner GOOD INTENT," Stokes announced in December 1778.

The Inferior Court of Common Pleas held an inquisition against fifty-eight Gloucester County residents in November 1778 "for joining the army of the King of Great Britain, and other offences against the form of their allegiance." The court instructed the Gloucester County Commissioners of Confiscated Estates, Joseph Hugg and John Sparks, to seize the personal estates of Loyalists for use by the nearly bankrupt State of New Jersey. Those indicted included Gloucester Township mill owner Jeremiah Prosser, former Gloucester County justice Isaac Lord, and former county sheriff John Hinchman, a Timber Creek tidewater planter and longtime county representative to the provincial assembly. Two weeks later, the Gloucester County Court of Oyer and Terminer sentenced seventeen men to death for high treason, including Lord. Most received pardons. It is likely that the county court executed only William Hammet for treason (in January 1779), although earlier two local residents had been hanged for guiding Hessian forces to Fort Mercer. Hinchman escaped to join the British in New York, and he resided for a time in a Loyalist colony in Nova Scotia. He returned to Timber Creek after the war, living on his wife's property and dying in 1787 in complete obscurity.

The war hurt patriot landowners as well as those Loyalists who had their property confiscated by the state. Patriotic Gloucester County farmers, particularly Timber Creek plantation owners Major George Payne and John and Thomas Hampton, whose military service had prevented them from tending their farms to bring in revenue-producing crops, saw their properties auctioned off to pay debts or back taxes. Under a state act of October 1780, township constables were authorized to recover back taxes in inflated Continental currency. Gloucester County's representatives, John Cooper, John Sparks, Thomas Rennard, and Isaac Kay, endorsed such measures, which benefited their fellow prosperous plantation owners who held the Continental money. The Coopers, Huggs, Blackwoods, Clements, and other prewar gentry elite families, who controlled county business before the war, quickly bought up postwar properties at public auction. William Hugg operated the Gloucester County Loan Office in his tavern between 1786 and 1799, where he gave low-interest loans to Joseph Ellis,

James Cooper, Franklin Davenport, and other patriots who emerged from the war in a sound financial state, having sponsored wartime privateers or purchased confiscated Tory estates and bankrupt plantation properties.

Wartime prosperity propelled these families to the forefront of Gloucester County's postwar political economy. Ellis served as the county's representative to the state assembly (1781–85), along with Joseph Cooper, and from 1787 to 1794 he was a member of the New Jersey Legislative Council. John Blackwood joined Cooper in the assembly from 1791 to 1794, and Abel Clement was there from 1789 to 1797. Also, Blackwood served as clerk of the Gloucester County Board of Justices and Freeholders, 1792–98 (reorganized in 1798 as the Board of Chosen Freeholders), and as county sheriff, 1787–98. Joseph Hugg replaced Blackwood as sheriff, serving until 1803, while Samuel Hugg became Gloucester County's representative to the New Jersey Legislative Assembly in 1781–83 and 1790–91. Samuel's most important task, however, was to head the committee to build a new courthouse after a suspicious fire burned down the old one in late March 1786. Hugg hoped to reconstruct the Gloucester County courthouse and jail in Gloucestertown, but a powerful faction from the lower precinct wanted the county seat and courthouse moved to Woodbury—a momentous decision that would lead to a movement in the upper precinct to separate and form a new county.

3

"Most Interesting Election Ever Held in This County"

Courthouse Fire

Fire destroyed the county courthouse and jail in Gloucestertown in March 1786. Reportedly, a horse thief incarcerated in the jail and facing a death sentence set the fire. But there were larger questions. Prior to the fire, residents of the eastern townships of Galloway, Old Egg Harbor, and Tuckahoe had petitioned for a new county, claiming that it was too difficult for them to travel from the seashore to Gloucestertown to conduct legal business or pay taxes. After the fire, Sarah Steelman and most male freeholders from the distant townships again petitioned the state legislature for their own county.* At this moment, the Gloucester County Board of Justices and Freeholders voted to move the county seat to Woodbury, a town below Big Timber Creek that was far more accessible to the shore townships and had closer kinship ties to them (particularly among the Steelmans and lower county families of Swedish ancestry). When they learned

---

* Steelman's signature suggests female participation in late-eighteenth-century local politics under the state constitution of 1776; only in 1844, with adoption of a revised constitution, would women, blacks, and the "insane" be barred from voting in New Jersey.

about the removal of the county seat from Gloucestertown, the eastern coastal townships withdrew their petition to create a new county.

WOODBURY AS THE COUNTY SEAT

Woodbury's development as the county seat coincided with the shaping of a new federal constitution and government across the river in Philadelphia between 1787 and 1799. Concurrently, Gloucester County undertook a major reorganization of its government by removing justices from the representative board and creating a Board of Chosen Freeholders in 1798. The once quiet West Jersey Quaker town pulsed with the spirit of militant nationalism. "An unusual noisy time about Woodbury this P.M.," complained Woodbury Quaker merchant Samuel Mickle, "a very general Parade of the Militia with Cannon, small arms, drum and fife, etc., and flag hoisted on top of the courthouse." Every birthday celebration for President George Washington evoked more patriotic military displays and parades by the "Free Masons in their Masonic Dress," led by Grand Master Franklin Davenport, a Woodbury attorney, war hero, and militia leader. The military spirit undermined the local Friends peace testimony. Threats of disownment failed to discourage Gloucester County tidewater planters from raising and training horses for the newly created War Department's light cavalry or local craftsmen from making weapons for the federal government. A Woodbury Quaker blacksmith told the Friends meeting that "if he made none, others would."

Clearly, the once-dominant Quakers no longer controlled Woodbury or Gloucester County. In an effort to preserve the traditional Quaker way of life, the monthly meeting in Haddonfield disowned members for military activity, refusal to free slaves, and other "horrid atheistical expressions." The attrition increased, and Friends neglected their obligations. Mickle lamented to fellow Quaker James Whitall of Red Bank that the Deptford Friends School had lost support: "I observed to him the languor and indifference now, contrasted with lively animation in the school 20 years ago [1779], when the Trustees very generally attended and when the house was crowded with spectators."

Presbyterians, Methodists, and Episcopalians made great strides in the county by linking the Revolutionary War and national spirit to their

religious outlooks. Revolutionary War leaders Michael Fisher, Peter Cheesman, and John Blackwood expanded the Presbyterian church in Blackwoodtown (established 1751). War veterans Davenport and Reverend
Andrew Hunter organized the Presbyterian church at the county seat in
Woodbury (founded on Woodbury Creek before the war by lower county
Revolutionary War leaders and tidewater planter gentry Archibald Mof-
fett, Randall Sparks, and Elisha Clark). The militant "spirit of Methodism"
permeated Gloucester County as well. Kendal Coles, Dr. Benjamin Vanlier,
William Rudderow, and the Inskeep family enlarged the Episcopal congregation in Waterford Township, while county wartime leaders George
Vanlier and the Chew, Clark, Tonkin, and Paul families established Methodist meetings in Gloucester, Greenwich, and Deptford Townships. After
the war, Francis Asbury, superintendent of the Methodist Episcopal Church
in America, established a meetinghouse in Woolwich Township. By then,
the Methodists had become so aggressive in Woodbury that preacher Jesse
Chew disrupted the Woodbury Friends Meeting and, according to Samuel
Mickle, had to be "silenced by one of our elders."

Yellow Fever Strikes

Gloucester County Quakers suggested that the decline in their faith contributed to divine retribution in the form of the yellow fever plague. After
all, yellow fever made it "very mortal up Timber Creek" in August 1792
after John Hider, Richard Cheesman, and John Thorne organized the Protestant Episcopal church at Chew's Landing. When Joseph Thorne allowed
the Methodists to hold a service in his Haddonfield tavern, yellow fever
struck that predominantly Quaker town. Of course, yellow fever had
plagued Philadelphia throughout the eighteenth century, but the severe
epidemics during the 1790s that coincided with fading Quaker influence
seemed to hit the Delaware Valley harder than at any previous time. Several thousands died in the Pennsylvania port city during the worst epidemics of 1793 and 1798, while thousands more of the poorer residents
huddled in tent shelters along the Schuylkill River.

Those Philadelphia Quakers with kin in southern New Jersey fled to
Gloucester County, Woodbury merchant Mickle grumbled, bringing "pes-
tilence in our neighborhood." Soon yellow fever appeared in Haddonfield,

Woodbury, Mantua, and along Oldman's Creek at the extreme southern boundary of the county. It hit Cooper's Ferry, killing the wealthy Italian American merchant Vincent M. Pelosi, who had moved there from Philadelphia for the supposedly healthy atmosphere. Gloucester County residents convened town meetings to consider ways to stop communication between Philadelphia and the Jersey side of the Delaware River. Instead of banning travel, they decided to raise money to feed the suffering poor along the Schuylkill, provide nurses, and undertake funerals for victims of the "putrid" disease who came to the county to die. For a moment, Gloucester County leaders considered using local blacks to carry bodies to graves and bury the dead from Philadelphia, "it being generally allowed that the black people are less liable than whites to take the infection." (Yellow fever victims may have been buried within the boundaries of present-day Camden City). Yellow fever deaths among blacks soon ended the idea that somehow they were immune to the disease. In any case, Gloucester County's Quakers opposed such exploitation of black slaves, servants, and laborers, whom they were busily trying to free.

ABOLITION

The movement to abolish slavery in the Delaware Valley had its roots in Philadelphia and Burlington County, but Gloucester County assumed a more active role during the Revolutionary War. In 1777 James Cooper called upon members of the Haddonfield and Woodbury Friends meetings to free their slaves. Friends who refused faced disownment, and Marmaduke Cooper was read out of meeting for keeping his slaves. Such agitation contributed to the state's decision to stop further importation of African slaves. By 1792 the Quaker tidewater planters of the Haddonfield Meeting held no slaves and announced that they would employ free black labor instead.

Tidewater planters below Timber Creek seemed reluctant to free their slaves, however. To revive the local abolition movement, Joseph Clement, Franklin Davenport, Jacob Wood, Joseph Sloan, and Samuel Mickle organized the Abolition Society for Gloucester County at the courthouse in Woodbury in 1792. The following year, Mickle became society treasurer and raised funds for the work of abolishing slavery in Gloucester County.

Response was poor, and by 1798 only nine of the fifty dues-paying members of the society bothered to attend its annual meeting. Gradually, individual tidewater planters along Timber Creek manumitted slaves on their own. Joseph Hugg freed one slave each year in 1788, 1789, 1793, and 1800, but William Hugg kept his slaves until 1812.

Many freed blacks fled to remote woodland spots, forming enclaves such as Guineatown above Timber Creek on the former Hugg plantation (near present-day Bellmawr). Also, runaway slaves formed hidden communities to escape the slave hunters who scoured the county. Local Quakers supported runaways, hiding them in the barns and cellars that made up the stations of the "underground railroad" that hurried escaped slaves northward through Gloucester County. According to tradition, Haddonfield Quakers provided a "free haven" in the 1790s for runaway black slaves on land owned by Philadelphia Friend Ralph Smith, who later established the black enclave of Snow Hill that became the African American–governed borough of Lawnside in 1926. It is believed that Reverend Richard Allen of Philadelphia, founder of the African Methodist Episcopal Church, dedicated Mount Pisgah mission in Free Haven about 1815. Meanwhile, blacks guarded their freedom in these sanctuaries and, in at least one case at Guineatown, probably killed a slave catcher who ventured into their enclave. Elsewhere in the county, the major effort to prevent slave catchers from seizing runaways and to form entire African American neighborhoods occurred upriver in Camden Town, which by the first decades of the nineteenth century had started to rival Woodbury as a center of business and society.

The Village of Camden

Camden Town recovered slowly from the failure of Jacob Cooper's pre–Revolutionary War real estate project. Efforts by Jacob's ardently pro-Federalist cousin Joshua Cooper to develop a neighborhood around a lane that he named Federal Street in 1803 faltered as well. Finally, a group of investors from Philadelphia and neighboring New Jersey counties, and a new breed of aggressive Gloucester County entrepreneur (encouraged by the speculative spirit unleashed by the Jeffersonian Republicans, who controlled national and state politics), created the first true city on the eastern side of the Delaware River. One of these investors, Edward Sharp, purchased a forty-acre tract west of Market Street in 1812 from the estate of Joshua Cooper, and he bought additional lands and seven-tenths of Windmill Island (in the river between Philadelphia and Camden) in 1818. Between 1818 and 1820, Sharp laid out "Camden Village" along a wide avenue leading to a proposed bridge to Windmill Island. Sharp hired master bridge builder Amos Campbell of Woodbury, master carpenter Gideon V. Stivers of Essex County, and Philadelphia house builder Samuel Lanning to construct the Windmill Island Bridge, houses in Camden Village, and St. Paul's Methodist Espiscopal Church. (Lanning and Stivers later became Camden City's first mayors, 1828–36.)

Sharp recruited a number of investors who later helped build Camden County, including George Genge, Hugh and Joseph J. Hatch, and Dr. Samuel Harris. Harris set up a practice on the Jersey side of the river in 1811 after investments in Philadelphia real estate proved unprofitable. Sharp also interested kin of upper precinct tidewater planter families, among them Richard Matlack Cooper, president of the State Bank of Camden (founded in 1812), and Newton Creek planter Isaac Mickle Sr. Sharp found no investors among the Woodbury people below Timber Creek, however. Without the support of the county seat, Sharp stood little chance of securing legislation for a bridge. Consequently, the Camden Village entrepreneur petitioned for a public vote in 1819 that would decide whether to move the Gloucester County government out of Woodbury and to Camden. Sharp claimed that the courthouse and jail in Woodbury had decayed beyond repair and offered no fireproof clerk's office to maintain county records. Though politically motivated, his attack on county facilities had substance. "Males and females and persons confined for debt, as well as for crimes," a county grand jury discovered, "are suffered to be together in one apartment in said Prison."

BATTLE OF THE TOWNSHIPS

Sharp's petition exposed local sectional political party lines, economic issues, and cultural differences between the upper and lower precincts. The original townships above Timber Creek—Newton, Gloucester, and Waterford—focused on the bustling riverfront town of Camden as the center of life. The townships below Timber Creek—Deptford, Greenwich, Wool-wich, and Franklin (created 1820)—looked for political and economic direction to the courthouse village of Woodbury. Meanwhile, the remote Atlantic seacoast townships of Galloway, Egg Harbor, Weymouth, and Hamilton sided with whichever group promised to ease their tax burdens. The process would lead in 1837 to the amicable creation of Atlantic County and to a "good deal of hard feeling between opposition parties" in the formation later of Camden County.

Gloucester County's Federal Republicans (later the Whig party), led by Woodbury attorney, county judge, and Worshipful Master of the Free Masons Franklin Davenport and by Deptford Township farmer Michael C. Fisher, bitterly opposed Sharp. The Democrat Republicans (later the Jacksonian Democratic party) of the upper precincts just as warmly endorsed the Camden entrepreneur's plans. For a while, the Woodbury forces organized and campaigned more effectively to keep the county buildings in Woodbury. During the 1820s the first countywide newspaper, the *Columbian Herald* of Woodbury (later the *Woodbury Constitution*), spread pro-Woodbury opinions through the politically sensitive Timber Creek border region between the upper and lower precincts. The newspaper created images of urban crime, riotous mobs, wild drinking, profanity, and awful disease in Camden Village for its rural subscribers in Chew's Landing, White Horse, Clementon, Blackwoodtown, Limber Bridge, and Thomas Bee's Store (near present-day Williamstown).

After Woodbury merchants and farmers and the Haddonfield planter gentry elite defeated Camden's effort to swing the Gloucester County vote for Andrew Jackson in the presidential election of 1824, Camden leaders renewed their campaign to remove the county seat from Woodbury. This time, led by steamboat entrepreneur John W. Mickle, their forces appeared to be better organized than in 1819. Jacob Glover, a Deptford Township mill owner, tidewater planter, and director of the Gloucester County Board of Chosen Freeholders, called an emergency meeting at the courthouse in Woodbury "to prevent so ruinous a project." Glover also convened anti-Camden rallies at Paul Sears's tavern near Cross Keys, William Turner's tavern (present-day Turnersville), and Jebediah Elwell's inn near Woodbury Dam. Greenwich Township mobilized a "County Seat Committee of Vigilance." The Woolwich Township representative on the Gloucester County

Board of Chosen Freeholders, Charles Creighton Stratton (a Swedesboro farmer who served as a Whig in Trenton and governor of New Jersey, 1845–48), circulated a remonstrance against the Camden movement, purportedly signed by sixteen hundred Gloucester County voters.

The upper precinct townships rallied behind Camden, gathering in support at Isaac Ellis's inn in Waterford Township. The friends of Camden assured voters that if the county government were relocated upriver, they would construct a new courthouse, like the one recently erected in the Burlington County seat of Mount Holly, for less money than it would cost to repair the old courthouse in Woodbury. At the same time, the opportunistic Gloucester County seashore townships of Galloway and Egg Harbor played both sides, resolving to support whichever exempted them from county taxes. "If the friends of Woodbury will not comply with the above resolution . . . ," the coastal townships warned, "the said lower townships will unanimously give their suffrage to Camden."

This time, the lower precinct townships gave Woodbury a majority of the 4,156 votes cast in February 1825 at "a very general election to which the sick, lame and blind were brought forward." Surprisingly, Gloucestertown Township supported Woodbury, probably because Jacob Glover, who was the county bridge keeper as well as director of the Board of Chosen Freeholders, promised to fund a covered truss bridge over Little Timber Creek at the southern end of town, which might revive Woodbury's lagging business. Woodbury celebrated the election victory with a banquet and torchlight parade, like those held on the national level during the recent hotly contested presidential election. Torchlights illuminated the Gloucester County Courthouse while cannon fire and cheering crowds announced victory. "Thus has ended, in the total defeat of the Camden Party," the *Woodbury Constitution* observed, "the most interesting Election ever held in this County."

INCORPORATING CAMDEN CITY

Even though Edward Sharp's problems in securing support for his Windmill Island bridge led to his bankruptcy during the Panic of 1819, Camden Village boomed during the first decades of the nineteenth century.

Dozens of manufacturing shops opened along the waterfront. Benjamin Allen operated a forty-vat tannery, Isaac Van Sciver a carriage manufactory, Samuel Bates an iron forge and workshop, and Elias Kaighn a foundry to manufacture iron edge tools and carriage springs. Jacob Lehr ran a candle factory, while William Carman, who married into the Cooper family, opened a large sawmill and lumberyard at the foot of Cooper Street in 1822. Rural farmers apprenticed their sons to these city craftsmen, revealing an early expression of an emerging metropolitan society. The town contained livery stables, a hay market, wheelwrights to repair carriages, and a dozen inns, taverns, and pleasure gardens at the ferry landings.

The flood of pleasure seekers who arrived from Philadelphia to frequent Camden Village's taverns and the Vauxhall, Columbia, and other beer gardens contributed to the incorporation of a city government with the power to enforce law and order. "The woods and orchards lured multitudes of Philadelphians to these shores in search of shade, air and recreation," the Camden County chronicler George Prowell observed, "and the police force of [Newton] township afforded little restraint upon those inclined to turbulence, and there were many such." Reinforced by the locally famous hard apple cider and apple brandy, Philadelphians caroused in the narrow dirt streets of Camden Town and generally disrupted the peace. Rumors that Philadelphia gamblers planned to open a racecourse somewhere in the vicinity of the town made incorporation more urgent. Consequently, the Camden Town land developers, merchants, and builders John K. Cowperthwaite, John Lawrence, Richard Fetters, and John W. Mickle, along with attorney Jeremiah H. Sloan (already angry at Haddonfield's refusal to hold the Newton township meeting in Camden), petitioned the state government for articles of incorporation.

Incorporated on 14 February 1828, Camden City turned its back on Gloucester County affairs, dominated by the Woodbury Whigs. Mickle and Sloan strengthened Camden City's Democratic party organization to support Andrew Jackson for president in 1828. They also led South Jersey's efforts between 1828 and 1830 to persuade the Whig-dominated state assembly to charter a steam railroad (surveyed originally to travel east through Burlington County's seat, Mount Holly, but now planned to connect South Amboy through Bordentown to Camden). In the process, Mickle, Sloan, and Gloucester County Democrats united Camden with the single most important political and economic organization in New Jersey during the antebellum era: the Camden and Amboy Rail Road and Transportation Company, which combined with the Delaware and Raritan Canal Company in 1831 to form a monopoly over rail and steamboat travel between Philadelphia and New York.

The Camden and Philadelphia Steamboat Ferry Company

The politics surrounding the development of the Camden and Amboy and its subsidiary, the Camden and Philadelphia Steamboat Ferry Company, contributed to Camden City's rise to economic and political importance (and, eventually, to the creation of Camden County). Incorporated in 1830, the Camden and Amboy Rail Road and Transportation Company had laid tracks from Bordentown to Camden by the end of 1834, and the first passenger train entered the city on 5 January 1835. One of the original stockholders, J. W. Mickle, sold to the Camden and Amboy his former Windmill Island Bridge Company property, which included a wide avenue to the riverfront surveyed by Edward Sharp in 1818. The Camden and Amboy extended tracks for its steam carriages down Bridge Avenue in 1835 and constructed the Railroad Hotel at the foot of Federal Street (known as Elwell's Hotel after its proprietor, James Elwell).

The railroad needed a ferry terminal and apparently bargained unsuccessfully with local Whig party leader Abraham Browning for his Market Street landing. Consequently, Mickle, now a director of the railroad company, incorporated the Camden and Philadelphia Steamboat Ferry Company in 1836 with the Camden and Amboy as majority stockholder. He purchased the Federal Street ferry landing and Windmill Island from real estate and shipping tycoon Jacob Ridgway and obtained the Pennsylvania legislature's approval for digging a Windmill Island Canal for passage by his steamboat ferries. Although Mickle's political opponents in the New Jersey legislature delayed the required state approval for the Delaware River passage, Mickle completed the canal and started ferryboat service through it before obtaining final approval. "At sunset this evening," his nephew Isaac Mickle observed on 22 August 1840, "the Steam-boat

William Wray passed through Windmill Island Canal, to signify that the long-pending and celebrated bargain between Jacob Ridgway and the 'Odious Monopoly' [the Joint Company] has been consummated."

Enthusiasm for Camden's railroad and steamboat ferry spread throughout the upper townships of Gloucester County, bringing together city and countryside to develop the riverfront city. Camden's leading manufacturing interests met with upper county tidewater planters at the Railroad Hotel to discuss common interests in developing the riverfront region between Cooper's and Newton Creeks. The ubiquitous Captain J. W. Mickle often chaired the meetings, attended by his steamboat ferry board of directors, which included Lanning, Stivers, and Dr. Samuel Harris, who had been Edward Sharp's associates on the Windmill Island bridge project. Carriage makers Isaac Cole and Isaac Van Sciver represented Camden City's growing manufacturing section. Lumber merchant Carman, who married Daniel Cooper's daughter Mary Ann and built up the Carmanville neighborhood, promoted the interests of the powerful Cooper family, without whose support no Camden project could be entirely successful. Newton Creek tidewater farmer Joseph Kaighn, who in 1820 had fought against removal of the county seat to Camden, broke with his conservative Quaker kin Joseph Glover and Joseph Sloan to advance Kaighn family connections to the new steam and iron business. As a result, Charles Kaighn developed a ferry terminal, hotel, and industries at Kaighn's Point.

CREATING CAMDEN COUNTY

The steamboat ferry company gave the Gloucester County Democratic party an organizational base in Camden and a connection to a powerful statewide ally, the railroad, in the movement to create Camden County. However, it took the successful effort of the seashore townships to separate from Gloucester County and form the Whig-dominated Atlantic County for the final process to begin. On 10 February 1837 a pro-Camden organization of "Many Citizens" published a notice in the Camden and Woodbury newspapers for a meeting to consider the formation of a new county that would comprise the original townships of Waterford, Newton, and Gloucester and the newly incorporated townships of Camden (1831),

Union (1831), and Washington (1831).* John K. Cowperthwaite, a Waterford Township landowner and the current mayor of Camden City, led a rally two days later at the Vauxhall Garden Hotel on Cooper Street in Camden. Opportunely, in his dual role as Gloucester County's collector of accounts, Cowperthwaite confiscated the *Woodbury Village Herald* when its owner, County Clerk Joseph Sailor, was charged with printing counterfeit bills. Cowperthwaite brought the weekly newspaper to Camden and made it the voice for advocates of a new county.

Anti-Camden Whig factions still controlled local and state politics, however. These rural farmers revived earlier attacks on Camden's corrupt urban society. In December 1843, on the eve of the final campaign to divide the county, the *Woodbury Constitution* reported that intruders had burglarized the houses of Camden City's leading citizens—merchant William B. Hatch and lawyers William N. Jeffers and Richard W. Howell. "Look out citizens for thieves," the newspaper warned. "They are all about, and may pounce upon you before you are ready." At the same time, an anti-Camden citizens' organization held a rally at the Woodbury courthouse to oppose the scheme of "dividing the county."

The Camden partisans bided their time until the election of Jacksonian Democrat James Knox Polk as president in 1844 gave the Democratic party control over the New Jersey legislature. Then Camden's Jacksonian Democrats, led by steamboat ferry company directors Fetters, Cole, J. W. Mickle, and Dr. Isaac S. Mulford (Mickle's brother-in-law), petitioned for county status. Camden City drugstore owner Joseph Charles Delacour, sausage maker William A. Hammell, and city councilman John Sands also signed the petition. "Nothing is thought or heard of now but the new county proposed to be called Delaware," Camden City journalist Isaac Mickle Jr. reported in February 1844. "Camden goes for it strongly and Woodbury and Haddonfield against it."

When farmers in the upper part of Waterford Township formed Delaware Township in 1844, leaders of the new county movement changed the name of their proposed government from Delaware to Camden. The bill to create Camden County barely passed the Democratic-controlled

---

*Washington Township would return to Gloucester County in 1871 as part of a deal to place the county hospital in Camden County.

state assembly, as Gloucester County state representatives Nathan T. Stratton, Samuel W. Cooper, and Benjamin Harding bitterly opposed the division. The only Gloucester County vote for Camden came from Gloucestertown shopkeeper Thomas B. Wood, a state representative from recently formed Union Township. Wood's vote enabled passage of the new county bill, and Camden County leaders rewarded him by making him the county's first clerk. The boundaries of the new county extended from the south branch of Pennsauken Creek on the northeast to Big Timber Creek and Great Egg Harbor River to the southwest. The legislative act creating the new county authorized the formation of committees to divide county property, draw up a frame of government, and select a county seat. Seemingly, the political battle among townships that had convulsed Gloucester County for nearly twenty-five years was over.

DISPUTE OVER THE COUNTY SEAT

From the outset, controversy accompanied the organization of Camden County's new government. The joint Gloucester and Camden committee to divide public property fought over the boundaries that placed the county almshouse and farm (which Gloucester and Camden would share until 1860) within Camden County. These institutions were located below Timber Creek, which meant that "the inhabitants of a portion of this new county of Camden, will pass through the county of Gloucester on their way to the new seat of justice." The *Woodbury Constitution* published a large map that revealed the "Gerrymandered County of Gloucester," suggesting that the new county sought to take control of the older one. Meanwhile, town meetings held at the Gloucester County Courthouse in Woodbury and at a schoolhouse in Haddonfield demanded repeal of the "arbitrary, oppressive and anti-democratic" act that had divided Gloucester County against the will of the majority of its residents.

Failing to stop the formation of Camden County, the Haddonfield Quaker gentry, tied closely to the Woodbury faction, decided to take control of the new county government for the tidewater Whig planters. The Haddonfield clique included Judge John C. Clement, his sons-in-law Joshua Browning and Jacob L. Rowand, drugstore owner Thomas Redman Jr., and Haddonfield storekeeper David Roe, leader of the Gloucester

County prohibition movement opposed to Camden City's liberal liquor-licensing policy, which promoted dozens of wild saloons and pleasure gardens. These religious and temperate Haddonfield gentry would not allow such a sinful city to become the county seat or dominate local business and government. In one last effort, the anti-Camden party pressed Gloucester County Whig leader John C. Smallwood, president of the New Jersey State Senate, to reverse the state legislation. Unsuccessful, they turned next to Woolwich Township farmer Charles C. Stratton, the governor of New Jersey and a bitter opponent of the Camden and Amboy Rail Road, to overturn the law creating Camden County. After these Whig leaders failed to block creation of the new county, the Haddonfield group campaigned to locate the county seat of government anywhere but in Camden City, a place that Abraham Browning's wife, Elizabeth Matlack, derided as "Sausageberg."

The anti-Camden forces tied up the selection of a county seat for seven years. In a series of bitterly contested elections between 1844 and 1848, the rural hamlets of Mount Ephraim, White Horse, Chew's Landing, Haddonfield, and remote Longacoming (present-day Berlin Township and Borough) obtained enough votes to block Camden City from obtaining the necessary majority. The vote for Longacoming in 1848 was so large that the Camden County Board of Chosen Freeholders purchased property and let out contracts to construct county buildings there. But Camden City partisans cried fraud and demanded a new election. It had become a "public scandal," declared an editorial signed by "Farmer" in the anti-Jackson and anti-Camden *Woodbury Constitution.* "Modern history furnishes no example that will admit of any comparison."

CAMDEN CITY BECOMES THE COUNTY SEAT

Tired of the incessant squabbles, the New Jersey Supreme Court mandated in May 1851 that Camden City, winner of the latest election for county seat, be made the permanent center of government. Predictably, the decision failed to end the controversy. Now, rival ferry factions—led by J. W. Mickle of the Camden and Philadelphia Steamboat Ferry Company, located at the foot of Federal Street, and by Abraham Browning of the West Jersey Ferry Company, at the Market Street riverfront—competed for the placement of county buildings near their landings. In the end, the Cooper family, holding interests in both companies, decided the issue. Abigail Cooper offered the county a plot of land between Federal and Market Streets, an equal distance from both ferries and on the "Road to Woodbury" (present-day Broadway). The Board of Chosen Freeholders accepted the offer and a plan for a courthouse drawn by Samuel Sloan. In 1852 the freeholders contracted with Daniel A. Hall for construction of the facility on Abigail Cooper's lot opposite the William Carman mansion on Federal Street. More than a decade after its creation, Camden County dedicated its first courthouse in March 1855, a two-story brick building complete with an iron cage to hold convicted murderers.

EARLY MANUFACTURING

Location of the county government in Camden accelerated the riverfront city's development as an antebellum manufacturing, business, and entertainment center, established already with introduction of the steam ferry and railroad. During the 1830s, Joab Scull had opened a general store and spice grinding and packaging company at Second and Federal Streets, which became William S. Scull Coffee and Tea Company in 1858. Elias Kaighn erected a foundry to manufacture iron plows at Front Street and Kaighn Avenue. Charles Freeman established an oilcloth factory above Market Street in 1833, and Robert and George H. Smith began a pottery for production of glazed earthenware. During the following decade John and James G. Capewell built their flint glass manufacturing works on Kaighn's Point below Locust Street, William Waldo Fleming founded his Nickel Works on Cooper's Creek, and the heirs of Marmaduke Cope constructed a paper mill at Cooper's Point. John F. Starr (son of Philadelphia iron tank and boiler manufacturer Moses Starr) built the West Jersey Iron Foundry on Bridge Avenue in Camden to produce steam engines and sugar mill and pumping machinery, and to repair Camden and Amboy locomotives. Around the same time, Jesse W. Starr opened the first hardware store in the city in 1845.

The industrial boom along the riverfront continued throughout the 1850s. John H. Dialogue opened the Kaighn's Point Foundry to repair Camden and Amboy steam ferryboats. In 1852 Amasa B. Mathis built wooden and sail ships on the Pyne Poynt waterfront, and two years later David Taylor and Chalkley Mathis established a shipyard nearby at Point and Erie Streets. John W. Mickle incorporated the Camden Gas Works, which provided the first gas lighting for the city's streets in 1852, and the Camden Waterworks (1854). William S. Doughten and Henry B. Wilson (father of Admiral Henry B. Wilson, namesake of the boulevard) founded a large riverfront lumber mill and timber yard on Front Street below Chestnut and incorporated the Stockton and Newton Turnpike Company to facilitate travel to their Camden waterfront business. English inventor Richard Esterbrook set up the first steel pen manufacturing plant in the United States in 1858 at the foot of Cooper Street.

First Urban Neighborhoods

Industrial and commercial development stimulated urban neighborhood growth in Camden County along the Delaware riverfront before the Civil War. Camden City's population swelled from 3,298 in 1830 to 9,479 in 1850 and 14,358 by 1860. Nearby Gloucestertown Township (which became a manufacturing center during this era as well) grew from fewer than 400 people in 1830 to more than 2,000 by the eve of the Civil War. In Camden City, Robert Stevens of the Camden and Amboy Rail Road and Transportation Company built worker housing on Stevens Street below Bridge Avenue for the Irish and German immigrants who moved to the Camden riverfront. William Carman erected company housing along Linden and Pearl Streets for his lumberyard and sawmill employees. J. J. Benson, a Camden and Amboy official and owner of the Diamond Cottage pleasure garden, constructed additional worker housing for the ever-expanding railroad company on Benson Street below Stevens. In Gloucestertown, Philadelphia textile entrepreneur David S. Brown built company housing for his urban mill workers.

Philadelphia merchant Richard Fetters became the most successful urban housing and land developer of the antebellum period. Introduced to the opportunities of the Camden waterfront by his brother-in-law Ebenezer Toole (manager of the Kaighn's Point Ferry Company), Fetters purchased large tracts of land between Line and Cherry Streets and Third Street and the Delaware River from Charity and Grace Kaighn in 1833 and 1835. There he surveyed streets and laid out building lots. Fetters constructed inexpensive housing for Philadelphia and South Jersey laboring folk who moved to Camden in the 1840s and 1850s to work in the growing manufacturing section around Kaighn's Point (which included Capewell's glassworks, Kaighn's iron foundry, Wilson's lumberyard, and Dialogue's iron forge and later shipyard).

Fetters encouraged the settlement of blacks in his Fettersville development, selling lots along Cherry and Spruce Streets to laborers from Philadelphia. He established a common community garden and Methodist school for "the people of color," while other residents organized the Macedonia Church. Just below Fettersville, Benjamin Vandyke, Daniel Wilkins, and other middle-class black Philadelphians bought John Kaighn's old cornfield in the vicinity of Seventh Street south of Chestnut, founding another black neighborhood at Kaighnsville in 1838.

GLOUCESTERTOWN INDUSTRIALIZES

Philadelphia textile entrepreneur David Sands Brown wanted to exploit the resources of Kaighn's Point as well, particularly the supply of labor in Fettersville and Kaighnsville. He incorporated the Washington Manufacturing Company and in March 1844 tried to purchase from the Mickle family a large waterfront lot bounded by the Delaware River and Newton Creek. "Mr. David Brown, the head man of the concern has taken a great fancy to that property, and has insinuated that they would give us eighty thousand dollars for it," Isaac Mickle explained. "The land has been in the name so long and we want money so little that we concluded not to sell."

Brown next looked below Newton Creek to the sleepy waterfront village of Gloucestertown. Philadelphia entrepreneurs had long considered the area prime investment property. In 1816 Philadelphia Mayor Robert Wharton bought the ferry service running between Gloucester and Greenwich Point (Southwark section of Philadelphia) and tried unsuccessfully to interest Pennsylvania developers in Gloucestertown. Woodbury hotel owner Jesse Smith, James Matlack, John C. Smallwood, and other Gloucester County and Philadelphia entrepreneurs founded the Camden and Woodbury Railroad Transportation Company in 1836 and laid eight miles of track from the Camden and Amboy terminal in Camden City through Gloucestertown to Woodbury. Completed in 1839, the Camden and Woodbury Railroad ran as many as six steam trains daily at first, but then went bankrupt. Henry R. and John D. Campbell operated a horse railroad on the tracks from 1843 to 1846.

Brown, on the other hand, succeeded spectacularly, transforming the little village into an industrial town. In 1845 he opened the Washington Manufacturing Company textile mills and the Gloucester Manufacturing Company to bleach, dye, and print designs on cotton products for the Washington mills. Brown incorporated the Gloucester Land Company the following year to build housing, a store, and an assembly hall for his skilled textile workers; many Irish Catholics used the hall to hold mass before establishment of St. Mary's Roman Catholic parish and church. Brown developed the Gloucester Saving Fund and Building Association in 1849 to assist workers to buy their own houses, and he purchased a steamboat ferry company and wharf in 1857.

Brown's success stimulated other investors. William S. McCallister opened a lumberyard and house construction business in the 1850s. Hugh and Robert Lafferty established a sugar refinery in 1853, unloading imported cane from the Mercer Street wharf. Richard F. Loper operated a machine shop at the foot of Mercer Street to develop steam ferryboat engines, propellers, and machinery. Later, John Siter bought the shop to manufacture textile machinery.

Abraham Browning of Camden and a Philadelphia syndicate opened the short-lived Gloucester China Company, creating the Southwark Holloware product line. Browning also incorporated the Woodbury and Camden Turnpike Company in 1849 and the Gloucester Turnpike Company in 1850 to build a planked road to Gloucestertown. Caught up in the nationwide movement for transportation improvements during the 1840s, Browning and other Camden County leaders, in both the city and the countryside, united between 1839 and 1859 to incorporate nearly a dozen private turnpike companies. Chartered by the state legislature to take over public highways and operate them as private toll roads, these companies connected the rural county to the booming manufacturing, business, and government center along the waterfront. The turnpike-building frenzy opened the countryside to development and provided avenues to build Camden County's first metropolitan community.

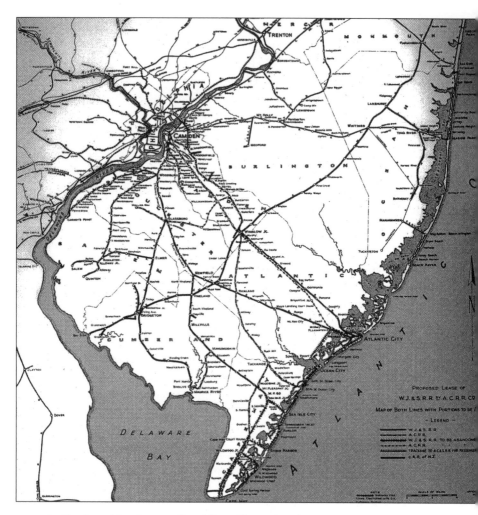

3. Southern New Jersey railroad lines, illustrating the various stations in Camden County. *(Paul W. Schopp Collection)*

4

"CLEAN, PURE LIFE ESSENTIAL TO SOCIAL ADVANCEMENT"

THE TURNPIKE COMPANIES

From the Camden area's earliest colonial history, even the most remote farms and rural hamlets looked to the Delaware riverfront for economic and political direction. The tidewater planters traveled to Gloucestertown for government and justice, and they floated timber and grain from their mills down the creeks to the waterfront markets on both sides of the river. It took the turnpike-building movement of the decades before the Civil War, however, to connect the eastern villages and countryside irrevocably to the riverfront urban market and begin the formation of a Camden County metropolitan region.

HADDONFIELD AND CAMDEN TURNPIKE COMPANY

The descendants of the original Cooper's Creek tidewater planter families incorporated the first turnpike in the nineteenth century to link Camden County to Camden City. Their eighteenth-century ancestors had established the most direct land route from the riverfront (Cooper's Ferry) to the rural county (Haddonfield) in the upper precinct. Now, in 1839, the Browning, Cooper, Nicholson, Redman, and Gill families chartered the Haddonfield and Camden Turnpike Company and sold stock to build a wide, graveled toll road between the city and the King's Highway in Haddonfield. Economic depression delayed the sale of shares until 1847, when the company incorporated and the state legislature granted title to the public highway (Haddon Avenue) between Haddonfield and Camden City.

The turnpike's first board of directors tied old Gloucester County pioneering families to the new Camden County entrepreneurial spirit. John Gill IV's great grandfather, for example, had helped Elizabeth Haddon found Haddonfield in the early part of the eighteenth century. Moreover, Gill was related through marriage to the Hopkins, Willits, Cooper, Browning, Nicholson, and other original Cooper's Creek families. He operated an old tidewater plantation and belonged to the Gloucester Fox Hunting Club and other historic organizations that had defined colonial Delaware Valley society. Gill was a modern nineteenth-century businessman and entrepreneur as well. He favored the adoption of steam power for farm machinery, sawmills, and transportation. He supported the entrepreneurial banking system, serving as president of the State Bank at Camden. Most important, Gill advanced internal improvement projects, such as the Haddonfield and Camden Turnpike and the White Horse Turnpike Company, which extended a toll road to Longacoming in 1854. Gill hoped to make Haddonfield an integral part of the political and economic boom created by the formation of the new county and the industrial development of the Camden City waterfront. Gill also brought his fellow gentry elite to the turnpike schemes, including Samuel Nicholson, Thomas Redman, and John Estaugh Hopkins (the county's leading dealer in marl fertilizer).

Haddonfield merchants and businessmen eagerly subscribed to the turnpike company to improve their access to the waterfront market. Mill owner Josiah B. Evans and earthenware pottery maker Richard W. Snowden (a state assemblyman and a Camden County freeholder) became company directors. Other directors included Joseph Porter (a Haddonfield storeowner and postmaster), Charles H. Shinn (a land developer, pleasure garden proprietor, and trustee of the Grove Street School), coal and lumber merchants Joshua P. Browning and Charles L. Willits, and house builder Jacob Stivers. Turnpike directors Jacob L. Rowand, Joseph W.

Cooper, and Daniel Conrad promoted closer rural ties to the urban center. Rowand moved to a country estate between Camden City and Haddonfield, where he established the hamlet of Rowandtown (modern-day Westmont). Rowand encouraged land sales and attracted businesses to his settlement by improving the turnpike past his property. Likewise, J. W. Cooper, director of the State Bank of Camden and one of the largest landowners along Cooper's Creek and principal stockholder in the Cooper's Point Ferry, speculated that the turnpike would increase the value of his urban and rural properties. At the same time, Conrad wanted the turnpike to connect his terra cotta works at Conradsville, in the lower county near Longacoming, to the Camden waterfront market.

Other turnpikes, though they made less immediate impact on developing a metropolitan community, also linked rural countryside to urban waterfront. Timber Creek shipbuilder Edmund Brewer, Tansboro glassworks and stagecoach owner Joel Bodine, and Camden waterfront entrepreneur John W. Mickle incorporated the Williamstown and Camden Turnpike Company in 1849 to improve communication between the city and the remote southeastern part of the county. Mickle, Gill, Samuel Nicholson, Samuel S. Willits, and Joseph B. Cooper incorporated the White Horse Turnpike Company, which in 1854 built the road that became today's White Horse Pike.

J. W. Mickle joined Camden waterfront developers John M. Kaighn and Abraham Browning, Centre Township mill owner John D. Glover, and Chew's Landing and Camden City druggist and physician John R. Sickler to form the Camden and Blackwoodtown Turnpike Company in 1855. This toll road (the present-day Black Horse Pike) provided the first gravel highway between Camden and the hamlets of Mount Ephraim and Chew's Landing and the growing factory villages in the vicinity of Blackwoodtown. Meanwhile, Jacob Troth, a sawmill owner and director of the Camden County Board of Chosen Freeholders, helped to incorporate the Camden, Ellisburg and Marlton Turnpike Company. Troth speculated in land along the route. "I sold my mother's wood to day for thirty six dollars an acre to Jacob Troth," Isaac Mickle reported. Troth outbid Joseph Stoy of Stoy's Landing near Haddonfield on Cooper's Creek (present-day Westmont) by "coming down [at once to Camden] and closing the bargain."

MOORESTOWN AND CAMDEN TURNPIKE

The Moorestown and Camden Turnpike Company had a direct impact on the development of Camden County's first suburbs. Chartered in 1849, the turnpike crossed Cooper's Creek at the truss bridge (Federal Street) and traveled northeasterly toward Pennsauken Creek and through Moorestown and Mount Holly in Burlington County. It traversed the Cooper, Browning, Coles, Burrough, Lippincott, Rudderow, and Stokes lands, which in their subdivision and development became the foundations for Stockton Township (1859), Merchantville Borough (1874), and Pennsauken Township (1892).

Director William Folwell, who inherited a large tract of land at Spicer's Ferry on the east side of Cooper's Creek through marriage to Rebecca Rudderow, expected the turnpike to help the sale and development of his property. Another founding director, Joseph A. Burrough, envisioned the roadway as a means to transport grain from his gristmills directly to the city waterfront and timber and board to and from his sawmills on the south branch of Pennsauken Creek. Benjamin Cooper and his son-in-law Samuel Lippincott, also members of the first board of directors, predicted that the wide, straight, and gravel-surfaced Moorestown toll road would greatly stimulate the sale of land along the route. Cooper was one of the largest real estate developers in mid-nineteenth-century Camden County. He had supported the creation of the county and the establishment of the county seat in Camden City, where he lived, in order to wrest control of taxation and land development policy in the upper precinct away from the Gloucester County landowners of the lower precinct.

The Camden to Moorestown road opened the lands on the northeastern bank of Cooper's Creek to developers. It was virgin farm and woodland, with a few black enclaves, including Sordentown and Jordantown, most likely planted during the 1840s by Quaker abolitionists Thomas Clement and Benjamin Cooper. Initial sales were slow. The Pavonia Land Association, incorporated in 1852, sold only a few houses, the most notable built in 1854 for the engineer of the Camden City Water Works located on the Pavonia riverfront two miles above Camden City. The Stockton Land Company had more success in promoting Abraham Browning's former plantation nearby; and company directors Cooper, Joseph Kay, and Charles Knight went to Trenton in 1857 to petition for a separate township to further development. Stockton Township was incorporated in 1859, but the economic depression of the late 1850s and the onset of the Civil War delayed large-scale suburban development on the east side of Cooper's Creek.

THE HORSE RAILROAD

For some investors, the turnpike movement was too slow to transform the rural countryside into a metropolitan region. The companies maintained their roadways poorly, tollgates interrupted travel, and the high rates charged for a horse and wagon or a horse and carriage discouraged commuter and commercial traffic to the city. William Folwell, Josiah B. Evans, and Samuel S. Willits, all directors of the Moorestown and Camden Turnpike Company, thought that a horse railway might improve transportation between Camden and Haddonfield. Camden City developer Richard Fetters, Cooper's River industrialist William Coffin, and suburban developers Joseph B. Tatem and Edward Bettle joined them in March 1859 to incorporate the Camden and Haddonfield Passenger Rail Road Company. The company raised subscriptions and negotiated a right-of-way to run tracks down Haddon Avenue over the rutted, often muddy turnpike. Opposition from rival turnpike speculators and probably from the Camden and Amboy Rail Road board of directors, not to mention problems with the city government and a variety of local interests, proved insurmountable. The line was never built.

A few days after the formation of this first horse railroad company, the Camden, Moorestown, Hainesport, and Mount Holly Horse Railroad Company chartered to lay tracks from the foot of Federal Street out the turnpike to Moorestown and Hainesport. The company had grandiose plans to run branch lines along Market Street to State Street and down Newton and along Kaighns Avenues in Camden City and to connect the city to Burlington County. Once again, rival political and business interests stopped construction of the Hainesport enterprise, although the Camden and Amboy Rail Road opportunely acquired the defunct horse railroad company's track surveys, right-of-way, and plans and used them later to build the Camden and Burlington County Railroad. Several other efforts to build a horse railroad in Camden County before the Civil War also failed. Not until the Camden Horse Railroad Company was incorporated in 1866 and laid tracks in 1870 would a horse railroad begin running in Camden County, in 1871.

CAMDEN AND ATLANTIC RAILROAD

The years before the Civil War saw the development of Camden County's second major steam railroad main line: the Camden and Atlantic Railroad.* Camden City's leading antebellum transportation entrepreneurs, John W. Mickle and Abraham Browning, who held stock in and served as directors of local railroad, turnpike, and steam ferryboat companies, recognized that the railroad offered a better chance to develop land and business in the suburbs. In March 1852 they joined forces with Philadelphia and Atlantic County merchants and land developers to incorporate the Camden and Atlantic Railroad.

The idea for a railroad extending from the Camden City waterfront to the Atlantic seacoast came originally from Atlantic County industrialist Jesse Richards, who organized the Camden and Egg Harbor Railroad Company in 1836. Richards planned to construct a line from Camden City through Burlington County to Tuckerton near the coast. Although this original scheme failed, it was revived by Richards's son Samuel, a Waterford Township glass baron and land developer, and by Dr. Jonathan Pitney and Enoch Doughty, Atlantic County real estate developers who wanted to build an Atlantic seashore resort city on Absecon Beach. They sold ten thousand shares of stock to thirty-eight stockholders. Major stockholders and directors of the company came from the iron manufacturing area in the pine barrens of southeastern Camden County and neighboring Atlantic County. These included: William Coffin, former owner of the Winslow Glass Works; Stephen Colwell, operator of the Weymouth Forge and a leading landowner; William W. Fleming, Atsion land developer and operator of the first nickel and cobalt refinery in Camden City; and, most

---

*The Camden and Amboy was the first, while the short-lived Camden and Woodbury Railroad was little more than a local short line.

significantly, Atlantic County's largest landowner, store owner and lumber merchant Doughty.

Camden County's glass barons had most to gain from a railroad connection to Camden City. Located in the remote southeastern corner of the county in Winslow and Waterford Townships, the glassworks had to transport their products by mule train over the often muddy and rutted turnpikes, which proved costly and inefficient. Thomas and Samuel Richards of the Jackson Glass Works in Waterford Township, Andrew K. Hay of the Waterford Glass Works, and Joseph Porter, manager of the Winslow Glass Works, sat on the first board of directors of the Camden and Atlantic Railroad Company.

The railroad steamed through Haddonfield in 1853, continued to Longacoming (renamed Berlin, possibly to attract German laborers, craftsmen, and settlers), and extended over the Egg Harbor River and marshlands to Absecon Island by 1854, where Pitney and Doughty established the resort of Atlantic City. Arrival of the railroad stimulated expansion at the Jackson Glass Works (present-day Atco) and Waterford Glass Works (Winslow). Andrew Hay also planned the development of new timber, potato, fruit, and grain businesses (to replace the nearly defunct charcoal and iron industries) and proposed to ship these products to Philadelphia from the Winslow station. However, the Camden and Atlantic was built primarily to carry middle-class Philadelphia and Camden City excursionists to the Jersey shore and to promote Atlantic City business. At first, there were few suburban commuter stations or railroad stops for commerce along the route. But the resort business thrived for only three months, and the shipment of agricultural products and glassware from Hammonton and Winslow could not alone sustain the railroad for the rest of the year. To stimulate additional ridership and revenue, the board of directors organized land development companies, bought land along the railroad, laid out lots, and advertised the benefits of healthy rural living for those who worked in Camden City and Philadelphia.

Camden and Atlantic Railroad directors Coffin, Fleming, and Samuel Richards incorporated the Haddonfield Land and Improvement Company in 1854 to develop a suburban neighborhood on the outskirts of Haddonfield. They purchased a 130-acre tract from turnpike director Gill, surveyed building lots, and developed a pleasure garden (with a racetrack) near Cooper's Creek. The project proved unprofitable. Richards was more successful with the Camden and Atlantic Land Company, chartered in 1853 to settle Atlantic City and properties along the railroad. The land company purchased tracts around Longacoming and in 1856 built a railroad station (later named Berlin) that encouraged buyers of building lots and settlement of fruit and vegetable farmers in the Longacoming neighborhood. Meanwhile, Philadelphia paint manufacturer John Lucas purchased property in the old sawmill village of Gibbsboro and in 1852 built the White Lead, Zinc and Color Works near the White Horse station on the Camden and Atlantic Railroad line. After the Civil War, Lucas became president of the railroad and secured a one-mile-long spur from the main track to his Gibbsboro factories.

WEST JERSEY RAILROAD

The Camden and Atlantic Railroad largely bypassed Gloucester County glassworks, mill towns, and factory and farming villages. Consequently, a year after organization of the Camden and Atlantic Railroad Company, directors Mickle and Browning joined Gloucester County glassworks owner Thomas H. Whitney of Glassboro to incorporate the West Jersey Railroad and run tracks from Camden to Bridgeton (Cumberland County) through Glassboro (Gloucester County). Since the closure of the Camden and Woodbury Railroad in 1846, there had been no rail connections from Camden City into Gloucester County, and the Woodbury and Camden Turnpike Company that Whitney had helped to found in 1849 proved no substitute for a railroad. The West Jersey Company surveyed a line in 1853–54 from Camden City to Gloucester, Salem, Cumberland, and Cape May Counties, terminating at Cape Island at the southernmost tip of New Jersey. It would be a difficult and expensive engineering project, requiring extensive construction of culverts, trestles, and bridges to cross the many creeks, swamps, and lowlands of these remote rural counties.

During the Civil War, yet another company composed of Camden City and Philadelphia seashore resort developers chartered the Cape May and Millville Railroad line, completing the railroad to Cape May City in 1863. Eight years after the war, the Pennsylvania Railroad would absorb the West Jersey and associated lines as part of its lease on the Camden and Amboy.

ECONOMIC DEPRESSION AND CIVIL WAR

A slowdown in the northern industrial economy in the late 1850s after two decades of frantic growth delayed the expansion of Camden County's metropolitan community. Moreover, a terrible fire on the ferry *New Jersey*, which killed sixty people and led to the indictment for murder of steamboat company executives, discouraged Philadelphia merchants and workers from moving to the new suburban developments in Camden County. Sales of building lots and passenger traffic on the ferries fell dramatically. At the same time, the West Jersey Railroad stopped construction abruptly, and leading investor Abraham Browning dropped out. The Camden and Haddonfield Passenger Company (a horse-drawn street railway) and the Kaighn's Point and Philadelphia Ferry Company failed. Lumber merchant Henry B. Wilson and attorney Joseph M. Kaighn assumed receivership over the bankrupt ferry line.

Meanwhile, the Capewell Glass Company (absorbed in 1854 by the United States Glass Manufacturing Company) went bankrupt in 1857 and closed two years later. William Coffin's nickel works on Cooper's Creek struggled to survive, and Philadelphia entrepreneur Joseph Wharton took over operations and reorganized the company as the American Nickel and Cobalt Works in time to begin production for the Union war machine.

The Civil War helped to revive Camden County's economy, strengthening older businesses and creating new industries. During the war, the Reading Iron Works took over the struggling Camden Tube and Tool Company (formerly John Kaighn's Central Iron Foundry) and modernized it for war production. Merrill A. Furbush established a factory to manufacture textile machinery and tools on Cooper's Creek. Charles B. Coles and Willam S. Doughten opened a large lumber business and box manufactory at Front and Chestnut Streets. Henry Bottomley built the Camden Woolen Mills to produce uniforms for the military (although the plant did not start production until after the war).

The Camden and Amboy Rail Road added cars and locomotives to keep the troops and war matériel moving through New Jersey to the Camden waterfront, where the company increasingly controlled riverfront property. The rival Camden and Atlantic Company and the Raritan and Delaware Bay Rail Road opened a station at Jackson (present-day Atco) to carry troops from New York to Philadelphia on the Camden and Atlantic line. Opposition from the Camden and Amboy led to failure of the Raritan and Delaware Bay line, although it was later reorganized as the New Jersey Southern Railroad Company. The war also meant that Camden City became the commercial, financial, and banking center of southern New Jersey. The Farmers and Mechanics Bank reorganized as the First National Bank of Camden, and the State Bank of Camden as the National State Bank of Camden. Federally mandated consolidations made local banks into national institutions, established a stable currency, and provided the capital to expand the Philadelphia–Camden County metropolitan economy.

The Civil War unified urban and rural sections of Camden County. Secession of the Confederate states and the seizure of Fort Sumter removed sympathy for states' rights in rural Camden County. Moreover, the war momentarily stopped the Camden County Democratic party's bitter opposition to the Republican party's interest in allowing blacks to participate in county affairs. "The citizens of Camden, without distinction of party," met at the courthouse in Camden in April 1861 "for the purpose of expressing their sentiments in regard to our national differences." Urban Democrats and rural Republicans pledged allegiance to the Union and approved Camden attorney Samuel Hufty's resolution to form a home brigade, the First Regiment of Camden Reserves of the City of Camden. The meeting resolved that "the City Council of this City, and the Board of Chosen Freeholders of this county, be requested to provide a sufficient appropriation in money for the equipment of those persons who may volunteer in defense of our common country in this solemn crisis of our history."

The County Goes to War

Five hundred citizens responded to the courthouse rally by volunteering at once for military service. Abraham M. Browning quit college and enlisted. Camden attorneys George M. Robeson (later secretary of the Navy in the administration of Ulysses S. Grant), James M. Cassady, and Hufty enrolled in the home guard. So did Camden newspaper editor Philip J. Gray and iron industrialist and leading abolitionist Jesse Starr. Port collector Isaac W. Mickle, a Mexican War veteran, formed the Camden Light

Artillery Company. Camden merchant and realtor William B. Hatch, founder of the Camden volunteer Washington Grays, became a colonel in the Fourth Regiment, New Jersey Volunteers. Hettie Painter, "a doctress by profession," rushed off to become matron of the brigade hospital for the New Jersey Volunteers, while her husband, Joseph, a Camden store-keeper, served as the brigade commissary.

Rural villages opened recruiting stations in general stores and local taverns to enlist farm lads into the Union Army, while recruiters appeared on nearly every street corner in Camden City. The volunteer Stockton Cadets, Camden Light Artillery, Washington Grays, and Anderson Guards of Gloucester (City) mustered into service at Trenton with the Fourth Regiment, First Division, New Jersey Volunteers. The German (American) Rifle Company drilled at Maurer's Hotel. A cavalry troop organized at Cooper's Point, and the Jersey Blues formed in South Camden. Lads between the ages of ten and eighteen joined Stevens's Zouaves (sponsored by James Stevens, cashier of the Farmers and Mechanics Bank of Camden) and drilled three times a week at the corner of Second and Stevens Streets. "The boys conduct themselves in the most orderly manner, and we will soon ascertain whether our city cannot produce as fine a Cadet company as Philadelphia or any other city," the *Camden Democrat* promised.

The first rush of war excitement soon faded. Union forces stumbled badly at the battles of First Bull Run, the Peninsula, and Antietam. Many soldiers succumbed to disease and infected wounds. Camden County had lost more than a hundred men by late 1862, including popular city attorney Isaac W. Mickle and businessman William B. Hatch, killed in action at the Battle of Fredericksburg. The Lincoln administration's introduction of a draft under the Enrollment Act of 3 March 1863 (for "all able-bodied male citizens to constitute the national forces and liable to perform military duty") further diminished Camden County's enthusiasm for the Civil War. Antiwar Quakers and local gentry elite paid for substitutes to fill the draft quotas. "Drafted Men wishing to procure Substitutes with out any trouble, can do so by calling our Office," announced the Turner, English and Company Substitute and Volunteer Agency, located on Market Street in Camden. At least some of the bounty money for substitutes went toward building the Camden Dispensary, the county's first municipally supported hospital.

RACIAL TENSION

Opposition to the war developed in Camden County following Abraham Lincoln's Emancipation Proclamation. The anti-Lincoln and antiwar *Camden Democrat* claimed that the "war has been changed from its legitimate purpose of enforcing the Constitutional authority of the Government, to that of freeing the Negro." The Democratic Party Association of Camden, which "abhorred Abolitionism," became increasingly strident in its opposition to continued fighting as the number of blacks drafted in the county grew. To meet the county's quota of 802 men in early 1864, Camden City and the surrounding townships began to draft blacks. Ten of the seventeen draftees in Centre Township (incorporated out of Union Township in 1855) were black. Stockton, Newton, and Gloucester Townships also filled their quotas this way. Racial tension combined with opposition to the war to create violence in Camden County during the presidential election of 1864, which pitted Lincoln against the local favorite, Democratic party candidate General George B. McClellan of New Jersey, who had kin in Philadelphia and Camden City.

The *Camden Democrat* framed the entire election campaign around the question of race. It warned voters to elect McClellan and the countywide Democratic ticket in order to stop the onslaught of "black Republican" mercenaries who filled the Union Army, which was already "demoralized by the Negro element." Rallies held by "the Democratic and conservative citizens" of Camden County, led by Abraham Browning, warned voters against the impact of black Republicanism on their traditional way of life.

More virulent, the local leader of the antiforeign, antiblack American party, John H. Jones (who became Camden City mayor in 1874), bitterly attacked the "half-humanized Negro." A South Camden "White Woman" wrote an editorial urging city voters to save the county "by giving us a white Man for our next President—one who will keep the half-humanized Negro in his *proper* place." Such hate-filled rhetoric led to a race riot in November 1864 "between the whites and blacks" of Camden City's South Ward (location of an emerging African American middle-class community). "Sticks, stones, and pistols were used," an observer noted. Such racial tension would continue after the war, when Camden's African Americans tried to vote in 1870 for the first time under the Sixteenth

Amendment to the U.S. Constitution. County Republican leader Colonel James Matlack Scovel called out the Sixth Regiment of the New Jersey National Guard to protect black voters.

RECONSTRUCTION ERA

Scovel represented Camden County's postwar Republican party leadership during the era of Reconstruction, when Republicans in the U.S. Congress tried between 1865 and 1877 to reestablish the economy and society of the former Confederate states. At the local level, county Republicans expanded the Camden County metropolitan community, a process begun hesitatingly before the Civil War. These men included General William J. Sewell (a railroad entrepreneur and town builder), Edward Collings Knight (a merchant-industrialist and railroad and land developer), industrialist John F. Starr, banker and real estate developer Alexander G. Cattell, and many others. Between 1865 and 1877 these county leaders laid the foundations for a great urban industrial center along the waterfront, built new railroad lines through the county to connect rural and urban sections, and chartered street railways.

Equally significant, between 1865 and 1901 they firmly established Camden County's first suburban communities in Stockton Township on the northeast and in Haddon Township southeast of the city. These included the boroughs of Merchantville (1874), Haddonfield (1875), and Collingswood (1888), and Pennsauken Township (1892). The trend started when postwar Philadelphia and Camden City Republican and business leaders settled in Merchantville, located in the eastern part of Stockton Township.

MERCHANTVILLE

During the Civil War, a group of Philadelphia merchant brokers, bankers, and directors of the Pennsylvania Railroad Company, including Alexander G. and Elijah G. Cattell, decided to make their homes in Camden County. Perhaps the Cattells' close friend and business associate George M. Robeson, a former Camden County prosecutor and Republican party leader, encouraged their purchase of inexpensive but fertile farmland and virgin woodland convenient to the city in Stockton Township. The Cattells chose to buy near the cluster of houses called Merchantville, where prominent Philadelphia dry goods merchants had already built several country estates in the 1850s, from which they commuted down the Moorestown Turnpike to the city. As directors of the Pennsylvania Railroad Company, the Cattell brothers knew that the Camden and Amboy Rail Road (later absorbed by the Pennsylvania Railroad) planned to construct a line through Merchantville, and so they speculated in land along the proposed route. They laid out building lots and established Trinity Methodist Episcopal Church (1866) and the Oak Grove Academy. As expected, the railroad came to Merchantville in 1867, and building lots sold rapidly.

Selected by Republican party bosses to run for the U.S. Senate from New Jersey, Alexander Cattell established permanent residency in Merchantville. There he led (behind the scenes) the movement by Merchantville landowners to incorporate a borough in 1874. They wanted control over their own development because Stockton Township's leaders, who resided in the western section along Cooper's Creek, used Merchantville taxes to develop their own area. Cattell's influence can be seen in the unprecedented speed with which the state created the first borough form of government in Camden County. Introduced to the legislature in the morning, the Merchantville borough act passed both houses in the afternoon and was signed into law by Governor Joel Parker (once a bitter foe of the wartime Republican party) in the evening of the same day. In 1889 Cattell further shaped his new home by heading a syndicate that bought the Camden Horse Rail Road Company to run the county's first electric trolley to Merchantville in 1892.

Merchantville became the most popular suburb in Camden County for Philadelphia and Camden City business and industrial entrepreneurs of the Victorian era. Extension of the electric trolley greatly encouraged urban commuters to settle in the town. Also, Cattell attracted Christian E. Spangler, a fellow railroad syndicate director and Philadelphia dry goods merchant, and John J. Burleigh, chief of telegraph operations for the West Jersey Railroad. One of the few Irish Catholics to break into the Camden County Protestant business elite, Burleigh used his Economy Land

Improvement Association to finance relocation of urban middle-class Catholics to Merchantville, and he helped to establish a Roman Catholic parish and church there. Among the other urban industrialists who resided for a time in Merchantville were Isaac Ferris, a Camden City shoe manufacturer, Warren Webster, director of the Steam Water Heater Manufacturing Company, and Arthur Dorrance, president of the Joseph Campbell Preserving Company.

STOCKTON TOWNSHIP

Postwar development continued in the rest of Stockton Township as well. In 1866 Samuel H. and Emmor D. French opened the Stockton Rifle Range and Stockton Park. Camden Transfer Line stagecoaches shuttled visitors from the West Jersey Ferry to the rural amusement park at the junction of the Moorestown Pike (Federal Street) and the Burlington Pike (Westfield Avenue). Thousands of urban middle-class excursionists from Philadelphia and Camden City visited the park to play tennis and cricket, hear band music at the pavilion, and boat on the artificial lake. The park introduced potential buyers of building lots to rural Stockton Township, and Emmor French developed the Folwell Tract (Spicer's Ferry) on the east side of Cooper's Creek.

John Wright, a Camden coal and lumber merchant (and the nephew of one of Camden County's largest landowners, Richard M. Cooper), and his business partner Alfred Cramer purchased a large tract near Stockton Park for development. In 1874 Wright established the middle-class neighborhood of Wrightsville (formerly Spicerville) on the east side of Cooper's Creek. Wrightsville proved so popular that Cramer organized his own company. The former Blackwood farmer and Creesville store owner purchased tracts of land from the Thomas H. Dudley, Samuel H. French, and Benjamin W. Cooper estates and from the Lemuel Horner farm, surveying more than three thousand building lots. He purchased title to the Pavonia Land Association holdings, which included the shad fishing grounds along the Delaware River.

Cramer organized the Cramer Hill, Pavonia, North Cramer Hill, Rosedale, and Dudley housing developments, constructing tidy brick row houses, single-family dwellings, and stores. Cramer attracted the Philadelphia urban middle-class by extending easy credit terms through his building and loan associations. German, Irish, and later Polish American mechanics, tradesmen, and skilled workers from the city purchased houses in his carefully planned bourgeois suburban neighborhoods as fast as he built them. German Americans predominated, including the Bachmann, Buren, Hettel, Reninghaus, Stadtler, Stoeckle, Stier, and Tiedemann families. Saints Peter and Paul (German) Roman Catholic Church established its Pavonia Mission in 1892. The Pennsylvania Railroad's Pavonia Car Works, Shops and Freight Yard at Twenty-seventh and Howell opened in 1888, encouraging greater settlement of skilled workers. Cramer sold North Cramer Hill houses to hundreds of Pennsylvania Railroad engineers, telegraph operators, machinists, motormen, car cleaners, mechanics, car makers, and laborers. Finally, Stockton Town annexed the Pavonia, Cramer Hill, Dudley, Wrightsville, and Rosedale developments in 1894. In turn, the state joined Stockton to the city of Camden as the Eleventh and Twelfth Wards of East Camden in 1899.

All along, business and industry looked to the available land in Stockton Township for factory development on the east side of Cooper's Creek. The United States Chemical Company built a chemical and fertilizer plant near the Federal Street Bridge over Cooper's Creek in 1869. The Overbrook Mills opened in the western part of Stockton Township in the late 1870s to comb, draw, spin, and weave worsted textiles. Nearby, J. L. Cragin and Company of Philadelphia manufactured Dobbin's Electric Soap and Bradford's Fig Soap.

In the northeastern part of Stockton Township, Augustus Reeve acquired five kilns at the Pea Shore Brick and Terra Cotta Works, operating since the 1840s on the river above the mouth of Cooper's Creek, and began shipping products to the city from the Fish House station of the Pennsylvania Railroad, Amboy Division. Hugh and Joseph Hatch took over the Fairview Brick Works, already operating under a lease agreement on their land along the riverfront three miles above Camden. Soon, the Hatch brick factory turned out millions of paving and building bricks to develop metropolitan Camden County neighborhoods. The Hatch industries hired African, Irish, and German American laborers, many of whom resided around the tiny village of Pennsauken, first settled in 1878 east of Merchantville.

PENNSAUKEN TOWNSHIP

Even more isolated from Camden City affairs than Merchantville, Pennsauken, led by the Hatch brothers, started a movement to break away from Stockton Township. The region along Pea Shore on the Delaware River and the south branch of Pennsauken Creek, in the extreme north-eastern corner of Camden County, developed largely in isolation from the rest of the county. (River Road, the first highway through the area from Cooper's Creek to Pennsauken Creek, was not completed until 1868.) It was site of Puchak, the only colonial Swedish settlement in what became Camden County. It also sheltered more black enclaves than any part of the county, among them Jordantown, Sordentown, Morrisville, and Home-steadville. One of Camden County's earliest riverfront resort communities could also be found there; it included the Tammany Pea Shore Fishing Club (founded by Philadelphians as a pleasure resort in 1809), the Mozart Club (1869), and the Beidemann Club (1878).

The remote place also gave birth in the 1830s to the county's ill-fated silkworm industry. More important, the Pea Shore area boasted some of the best shad fishing banks on the Delaware River; the Wood, Cooper, Morgan, Fish, Browning, Rudderow, and other pioneering families all op-erated net fisheries in Fish House Cove. By the early 1890s the Hatch kilns and other businesses brought hundreds of new workers to settle the area and made Pennsauken village a busy town. In order to control their own taxes and development, the Hatches led the movement for separation from Stockton Township. Incorporated in 1892, Pennsauken Township extended from Pennsauken Creek to East Camden, from the Delaware River south to the boundary with Delaware Township, and southeast to Collingswood, which had just broken away from Haddon Township and incorporated as a borough in 1888.

COLLINGSWOOD AND WESTMONT

The development of farmland in what was then Newton Township, on the extreme southern extent of Haddon Avenue where it merged into the

White Horse Turnpike, began before the Civil War. Isaiah Stone bought property on Browning Road, set up a general store, and sold some Stonetown lots in the 1840s. Major development started when a wealthy Philadelphia merchant involved in the East India trade, John C. DaCosta, purchased a large farm at the turnpike entrance. In 1853 DaCosta became an incorporator, major stockholder, and director of the Camden and Atlantic Railroad. He secured a railroad stop on his farm (near the present-day Ferry Avenue station on the regional high-speed rail line) and subdivided his property into building lots.

After the Civil War, local developers brought the area into Haddon Township (incorporated in 1865), extinguishing the remnants of Newton Township. The Camden and Atlantic established a railroad stop and telegraph station near the Collings farm road in 1871, and the township voted in 1877 to name the place Collingswood. Edward Collings Knight, a wealthy Philadelphia import-export merchant and sugar refiner, purchased the old family homestead from his cousin Edward Zane Collings and organized the Collingswood Land Company, intent upon developing a suburban community. Joseph Stokes Collings opened a general store and post office there in 1882, and Richard T. Collings developed building lots along the railroad, including the old DaCosta property.

The Knight and Collings enterprise purchased farmland once owned by others of their ancestors, including the Zane, Stokes, Collins, Bates, Thackara, Champion, and more pioneering Newton Township families. They backed William Jones's Kalium Spring Water Company, which sold supposedly medicinal mineral water from a spring on the old Stokes farm near Newton Creek. They built Knight's Park to preserve the natural rural environment in the midst of suburban growth and then advertised the healthful benefits of this new suburb to urban residents. The Option Law of 1873 allowed them to forbid the issuance of liquor licenses in the community so as to promote sober middle-class development. "Excelling in natural beauty many of the suburbs contiguous to Camden, Collingswood presents, in addition to a diversity of building sites, a government that excludes the baneful saloon and a population united against vice in all forms," the developers promised. Collingswood was "a near approach to the Utopia, where seekers of homes who desire beautiful environment and the clean, pure life essential to social advancement, can find almost ideal conditions."

Glenwood, immediately below Collingswood, promoted the healthful benefits of its Crystal Lake, formed by damming Newton Creek, where Camden poet Walt Whitman reputedly took restful baths. Founded before the Civil War as Rowandtown, this stop on the Camden and Atlantic Railroad grew little until the immediate postwar era. By 1871, however, seven trains a day arrived at the station. James Flinn established a paint and varnish factory near an old Crystal Lake sawmill. The burgeoning Haddon Township village built a new schoolhouse in 1872 and changed its name to Glenwood—unfortunately claimed already by a town in North Jersey. Tired of having their mail delivered to the other Glenwood, residents voted in 1884 to change the name of their town once more, to Westmont (according to tradition, after a popular race horse of the same name). Some residents preferred the name of the nearby railroad stop, West Haddonfield, because of the implied proximity to Haddonfield, that "quaint and historical town where you breathe a delightful air of sweet comfort and congeniality."

Haddonfield Becomes a Borough

The historic colonial town of Haddonfield showed remarkable growth after the Civil War. Samuel Nicholson (a director of the Haddonfield and Camden Turnpike) and William Coffin and William Massey (director and president, respectively, of the Camden and Atlantic Railroad), along with the Haddonfield Improvement Company, sold building lots in Haddonfield during the early 1870s. "Many businessmen in the city have made it their permanent residence," the *West Jersey Press* announced in 1875, "in consequence of the convenience afforded by the railroad, and an excellent turnpike." Massey sought to improve the Haddonfield railroad station and the town's street lighting and other municipal services, supporting a postwar faction of new residents who wanted to incorporate the town.

Older residents bitterly opposed the movement to form a Haddonfield borough government, fearing tax increases and an intrusion of urban life. In the end, Haddonfield incorporated as a borough in 1875, although schools and roads remained under the control of Haddon Township. Massey's crusade to modernize the Camden and Atlantic also succeeded. The track bed between Camden and Haddonfield was widened, new rails were laid, and steam heat replaced wood-burning stoves to warm passenger cars. However, Massey found most Camden and Atlantic Railroad directors reluctant to extend improvements beyond Haddonfield or to promote suburban land development by opening new stops. Indeed, the Camden and Atlantic would not undertake a major suburban project until 1884, when, influenced by Pennsylvania Railroad Company stockholders, it helped develop the highlands between Waterford and Atco as the borough of Chesilhurst (incorporated 1887).

In 1876 the Camden and Atlantic's directors relied on the excursion trade to make a profit, and they raised ticket prices instead of expanding suburban business. That year the company purchased Kirkwood Lake and established Lakeside Park, running ten excursion trains a day during the summer to the rural resort. There would be no attempt at suburban development here until 1885, when the Penn Guarantee Trust Association developed Lindenwold a mile south of Lakeside Park. In the end, the board's conservative policies and the railroad's high ticket prices prompted Massey, Samuel Richards, and several other directors to break with the company in 1876 and build the rival Philadelphia and Atlantic City Railway.

5

"WHY DO YOU LIVE IN PHILADEPHIA OR CAMDEN, WHEN YOU CAN LIVE AT LAUREL SPRINGS?"

Camden County's first suburbs, immediately east and south of Camden City, arose from a combination of turnpike, street railway, and railroad development. The second phase of the county's suburban growth, west of the White Horse Pike and the Camden and Atlantic Railroad line, occurred through the efforts of the Philadelphia and Reading Railroad system, which included the Atlantic City Railroad main line and the Williamstown and Gloucester branches. Here turnpikes and street railways played a minor role, as suburban neighborhoods were first planted as railroad stops along the Philadelphia and Atlantic City Railway.

PHILADELPHIA AND ATLANTIC CITY RAILWAY

By 1876 the Camden and Atlantic Railroad Company had reached a turning point. The glass industry along the line had suffered numerous economic setbacks. The Jackson Glass Works became unprofitable with exhaustion of local timber and charcoal supplies to heat the furnaces, and it burned down in 1877. The Waterford Glass Works collapsed after the death of its innovative manager, Joseph Porter. Glass baron William Coffin Jr., one of the warmest proponents of Camden and Atlantic expansion, died in Philadelphia in 1874. Continued reliance on the troubled glass industry meant less profit for the railroad company, but the Camden and Atlantic's management made little effort to attract commuter traffic by developing more stations and stops along the line to assist in the development of permanent suburban neighborhoods. The Lakeside Park pleasure garden and picnic grounds were built in 1876 at Kirkwood station (formerly the White Horse and Marl City stations), near the property owned by railroad directors Ephraim Tomlinson and Joel P. Kirkbride. Unfortunately, the park brought in limited revenue, despite the railroad's "abundant transportation facilities which has secured a liberal patronage for the park from Philadelphia." To make up for the loss of commercial and suburban revenue, the railroad simply raised excursion rates to the resorts.

The more entrepreneurial railroad president Edward V. Massey, a Philadelphia brewer and South Jersey land speculator, and Samuel Richards, owner of the defunct Jackson Glass Works and primary stockholder in the Camden and Atlantic Land Company, which sought to develop suburban building lots, left the Camden and Atlantic Company board of directors and on 26 March 1876 chartered the Philadelphia and Atlantic City Railway Company. They determined to construct a 54.5-mile narrow gauge railroad west of the older line, connecting Camden City to the seashore and passing through the undeveloped rural communities that lay between the White Horse and Blackwoodtown Turnpikes. With limited capital, the new company chose to buy rights-of-way in the cheaper undeveloped lands west of the White Horse Turnpike, even though the rougher terrain and frequent stream crossings obstructed a straight line to the shore. The new line would have problems laying track and required more banked curves and construction of trestles. Moreover, the company bought inexpensive, used narrow gauge rail from the recently closed Centennial Exhibition in Philadelphia, making the hastily built Philadelphia and Atlantic City Railway a more dangerous system than the Camden and Atlantic. It also purchased exhibition buildings for use as the Bulson Street freight terminal in Camden City and as the passenger depot at the other end of the line in Atlantic City.

The Philadelphia and Atlantic City Railway Company started operating between Bulson Street in Camden and Atlantic City in July 1877. The cut-rate narrow gauge railroad faced problems from the outset. A construction train derailed near Williamstown, killing three, and a passenger train derailed at Tansboro, killing one. Trestles were unsafe and tracks banked improperly, forcing reduced speed and thus increased time to bring excursionists to the seashore. Nevertheless, the short-lived line (absorbed by the Philadelphia and Reading Railroad Company in 1883) built passenger platforms and flag and water stops along its path, many destined to become suburban municipalities. It opened the extreme lower county to suburban development, intruding on real estate developments promoted with little success by the Camden and Atlantic Railroad. The new line established stops at Tansboro, Cedar Brook, Braddock, and Blue Anchor, and at Williamstown Junction it connected to the Williamstown and Delaware River Railroad. At each place, the new line boosted business and settlement. "In the midst of the Jersey pines on the Atlantic City R. R.," Cedar Brook promoter John R. Duble announced, "this place is particularly recommended as a summer home for pulmonary sufferers." (Later, the Ancora Tuberculosis Hospital would be erected nearby.)

GLOUCESTER CITY

Construction of the Camden, Gloucester and Mount Ephraim Railroad in 1874 marked the culmination of the expansion of Gloucester City that industrialist David S. Brown had begun before the Civil War. Although Brown had created a vibrant manufacturing center on the Delaware riverfront at Gloucestertown, the town suffered layoffs and cutbacks in production during the economic depression of the late 1850s. The Civil War had not expanded industry in Gloucestertown, as it had in Camden City, and business fell off at the sugar refinery and textile mills. The only new wartime industry, the Gloucester Iron Works, which made shell casings for the government, found little work after the war. Part of the problem stemmed from the town's inability to attract investment capital or new industry. Gloucestertown's lack of good rail connections between its industries and the Camden City waterfront and its dearth of modern municipal services discouraged business expansion.

Incorporation of the town as Gloucester City in 1868 generated new investment and industries. Brown built the Gingham Mill in 1870 and bought the Gloucester Iron Works in 1871, expanding production. He opened the Ancona Printing Company Works (1871) and the Gloucester

Terra Cotta Works (1872), chartered the Gloucester City Savings Institution in 1872, and incorporated the Gas Lighting Company of Gloucester the following year. Brown's most important investment, however, was his organizing of the Camden, Gloucester and Mount Ephraim Railway. This narrow gauge "Peanut Line" connected Gloucester City's waterfront factories to the Kaighn's Point ferries in 1873 and extended to Mount Ephraim in 1875. When the Philadelphia and Reading Railroad acquired the Philadelphia and Atlantic City line in 1883, it also bought the Peanut Line to gain its Kaighn's Point terminal.

BATTLE OF THE RAILROADS

Competition from the narrow gauge Philadelphia and Atlantic City line forced the Pennsylvania Railroad Company to attempt to take it over in 1881. With its control of the Camden and Amboy and the West Jersey railroads through Camden County, the Delaware Valley's largest employer could be assured of a monopoly with acquisition of the narrow gauge line. However, the directors of the Philadelphia and Atlantic City Railway, who had broken with the Camden and Atlantic in 1876, had no desire to be reabsorbed by another railroad, and they rejected the Pennsylvania Railroad's offer. The Pennsylvania Railroad then took over the Camden and Atlantic and closed its connecting tracks at Winslow Junction (where all rail lines crossed) to competitors, accepting traffic only from its own system. This tactic forced the Central Railroad of New Jersey's Southern Railroad line, leased by the Philadelphia and Reading Company, to stop running. Fearing that it would be denied access to southern New Jersey altogether, the Philadelphia and Reading Railroad responded by acquiring the bankrupt Williamstown and Delaware River Railroad and in 1883 making an offer for the bankrupt Philadelphia and Atlantic City Railway.

The Philadelphia and Atlantic City board of directors urged that the Philadelphia and Reading Company buy the narrow gauge Camden, Gloucester and Mount Ephraim Railroad spur line as well. Although conversion of both narrow gauge lines would be expensive, the Reading system needed the Kaighn's Point terminal at the end of the spur and so acquired both lines. The Reading converted the Philadelphia and Atlantic City (1884) and the Camden, Gloucester and Mount Ephraim (1885) Railroads to standard gauge, with the latter becoming the Gloucester

Branch of the Philadelphia and Reading Company, connecting Kaighn's Point to Gloucester City and Mount Ephraim. In 1889 the Philadelphia and Reading consolidated the Kaighn's Point Terminal Railroad, the Philadelphia and Atlantic City, the Williamstown and Delaware River, the Glassboro, and the Camden, Gloucester and Mount Ephraim lines into the Atlantic City Railroad Company.

CAMDEN COUNTY RAILROAD

Although the Reading seemed to have gained access to every corner of the Camden County market, its Gloucester Branch simply ended five miles south of Camden City at Mount Ephraim in Centre Township, leaving a potentially rich area for development open to some rival company. The original directors of the Camden, Gloucester and Mount Ephraim Railroad had wanted to extend its narrow gauge line below Mount Ephraim station to Blackwood, but Brown's death in 1877 ended that possibility.

The area certainly seemed ripe for further development. Already at Chew's Landing, three miles below Mount Ephraim on the north branch of Timber Creek, three hundred residents supported Methodist and Episcopal churches, John North's general store, three blacksmith shops, a veterinary surgeon, a dentist, and a hotel. Although Brewer's large shipyard had stopped building schooners, flats, and barges at Chew's Landing because of timber exhaustion and silting on Timber Creek, the area still sustained prosperous farmers, who needed a railroad link for delivering grain, milk, and vegetables to the Camden waterfront.

Blackwood, located four miles below Chew's Landing on the south branch of Timber Creek, also had three hundred inhabitants. It was a more important place, however, serving as a crossroads stagecoach stop between Camden and Gloucester Counties. Indeed, Blackwood banked in Woodbury but traded in Camden City. It boasted three churches, a grade school, and physicians Joseph Hurff and Henry E. Branin (the latter was attending physician at the Camden County Almshouse at Blackwood and president of the Camden County Medical Society). In Blackwood also could be found four wheelwright and blacksmith shops, two hotels, the Livermore, Wilcox and Company mill, and postmistress Kate Shaw. Blackwood served the nearby hamlets of Mechanicsville, Good Intent (a largely defunct mill town), and Spring Mills. The latter was the location of the twenty-seven-acre Edward S. and Frank Bateman factory complex, which produced steel agricultural machinery and tools, including the Iron Age Cultivator. Nearby, J. C. Bradshaw operated a large general store and the post office for Spring Mills (renamed Grenloch in 1890).

MOUNT EPHRAIM TO GRENLOCH

Frank Bateman knew that for his modern industrial plant to expand (and distribute Iron Age tools nationwide), it needed a railroad connection. He discussed extension of the Gloucester Branch of the Philadelphia and Reading's Atlantic City line with railroad president Austin Corbin in 1890. Bateman formed the Camden County Railroad Company to secure a right-of-way and to procure land at cheaper prices than would have been demanded of the presumably richer Reading Railroad Company. Large area farm owners, among them the Bettle and Willets families, agreed to grade the rail bed in return for stock in the company. The Camden County Railroad line between Mount Ephraim and Grenloch opened in 1891 and was leased immediately to the Atlantic City Railroad Company of the Philadelphia and Reading system.

The company established small stations at Bellmawr, Runnemede, Glendora, Hilltop, Blackwood, and Grenloch, and erected a platform stop at Asyla for the Camden County Insane Asylum, Almshouse, and Infirmary, located below Timber Creek, just outside Blackwood.* At the Bellmawr stop, named for the Levi H. Bell family, which owned the largest horse farm in the area and granted the right-of-way to the railroad in 1890, real estate developers began to subdivide the former Marple, Browning, Glover, Budd, and Haines farmlands. By 1900 Bellmawr had a village store, hotel, and cluster of houses around the intersection of Browning Road and the Blackwoodtown Turnpike. However, Bellmawr would not incorporate as a borough until 1926.

Development of Hilltop proceeded more slowly still, and eventually failed. Philadelphia real estate speculator Moses D. Sarfaty laid out building lots at Hilltop in 1890, granted the Camden County Railroad Company a right-of-way through his development, and paid the company

---

* The complex became Lakeland Hospital in 1925, when the Camden County Board of Chosen Free-holders authorized the damming of Timber Creek to make a lake at the county hospital and asylum.

$500 to build a station there. Reading officials refused to keep the station open, however. They preferred the Asyla stop, "where a number of people get on and off our trains" and where "the superintendent of the Asylum and the Steward of the Almshouse would provide a man to open and close the station and otherwise look after it without expense to the Company."

By the time the railroad stop at Clements Bridge Road, later named Runnemede, incorporated as a borough in 1926, it had developed into a major settlement, with telephones, electric lights, and gas lines installed by 1902. Local residents speculated in real estate. General store owner Samuel J. Rowand divided his grandfather James Bettle's farm into building lots along the railroad line, advertising the area as "the highest point of land in this section, with clear, pure water [and] one of the most desirable locations in the vicinity of Philadelphia that has been opened up for building purposes." Land sold quickly. The Halyburton Realty Company of Camden City divided up William H. Rowand's farm into the Runnemede Heights development. Philadelphia house builder John H. Bowers Jr. built summer cottages and 285 single-family dwellings, and later became the first mayor of Runnemede Borough.

The Philadelphia and Reading Railroad Company's Gloucester Branch line increased accessibility to the town of Blackwood's lakeside cottage resort for summer excursionists from Philadelphia and Camden City but otherwise had slight immediate impact on permanent suburban growth. Bateman's factory benefited from the new branch line, and he built Grenloch Lake Park for his workers to picnic, boat, fish, and play baseball, and Grenloch Terrace (1893) to house his factory's foremen and executives. But the surrounding community showed little suburban development. On the other hand, the Philadelphia and Reading Railroad's main Atlantic City route through central Camden County promoted remarkable suburban expansion during the late nineteenth and early twentieth centuries.

THE READING'S ATLANTIC CITY MAIN LINE

The Philadelphia and Reading Railroad Company purchased the Philadelphia and Atlantic City line to maintain access to southern New Jersey markets and to prevent a Pennsylvania Railroad monopoly. Acquiring the narrow gauge line and converting it to standard gauge also gave the

Reading system stops and stations at prime locations west of the Camden and Atlantic line and the White Horse Turnpike for the development of a largely untapped suburban real estate market.

WEST COLLINGSWOOD

Coming out of Camden City, the Reading Railroad's main line to Atlantic City stopped first at the West Collingswood station in Haddon Township near the old Newton Burial Ground, which held the remains of the county's original settlers. Edward Collings Knight, a former executive of the Reading's archrival, the Pennsylvania Railroad, had planned the development of the West Collingswood area. His Collingswood Land Company subdivided land in the late 1870s, expecting imminent acquisition of the bankrupt Philadelphia and Atlantic City Railway. When the local company refused to sell out to the Pennsylvania Railroad and went with the Reading instead, Knight's real estate company promoted the new company's station.

Knight and his cousin Richard T. Collings, the major developer of nearby Collingswood on the Camden and Atlantic Railroad, divided up the Samuel Champion, John W. Logan, and Joseph Sheppard estates to form the developments of West Collingswood Heights and West Collingswood Extension. Located immediately below the city and with frontage on rich Newton Creek meadowlands and verdant woodlands, West Collingswood became a popular commuter suburb for Camden City's business and professional middle class. George W. Jessup located his City and Suburban Realty Company in West Collingswood, and Bayard R. and R. Wayne Kraft brought their Real Estate and Insurance, Mortgage Company of Camden City. Solicitor William J. Kraft, later Camden County's prosecutor, joined his brothers in the new Haddon Township suburban development. German American urban leader Anthony J. Kobus retired from his Camden City shoe manufacturing business and moved to the "Whitehorse Pike below City Line W. Collingswood."

OAKLYN

Advancing south through Camden County, the Reading's main line stopped next at the small Oakland station. The Philadelphia and Atlantic

City right-of-way passed through the large dairy farm of Camden County Clerk Joseph C. Hollingshead. In 1887 the Reading company opened the Oakland station to serve Hollingshead's real estate development, "Oakland the Beautiful," a community planned along Newton Creek and Lake Newton (and on the Bettle family estate, site of the former Camden and Philadelphia Race Track, which operated from 1836 to 1846). Hollingshead's lots sold well, and the Oaklyn Building and Loan Association incorporated to help middle-class workers buy lots and build houses. By 1899 the settlement was large enough to need its own schoolhouse, and by 1905 the Oakland the Beautiful development incorporated as the railroad suburb of Oaklyn.

AUDUBON

Below the Oakland station, the Reading Railroad built a large station at Audubon, replacing a platform stop on the old Philadelphia and Atlantic City narrow gauge railroad. The new commuter stop encouraged George A. Aldrich, William G. Heaney, and Charles H. Schnitzler, among others, to speculate in real estate there. Aldrich's Audubon Land Improvement Company laid out building lots in 1889, while Schnitzler and Heaney subdivided the Audubon Annex tract. The lovely rural countryside (christened in the mid-nineteenth century by the wife of ornithologist Samuel Nicholson Rhoads after a visit to her home by naturalist John James Audubon) had already attracted the likes of Kaighn's Point iron shipbuilder John H. Dialogue and Kaighn's Point lumber dealer John A. J. Sheets, who purchased farms there after the Civil War. Sheets, director of the First National Bank of Camden and the Haddonfield Mutual Loan Association, exemplified the emerging spirit of a metropolitan Camden. He sold the Philadelphia and Atlantic City Railway Company a right-of-way through his suburban property and encouraged urban residents to settle in what became Audubon Borough in 1905.

As Sheets envisaged, the railroad brought Newton Creek gristmill owner John Schnitzius, Linden Homestead and Building Association manager Heaney, Presbyterian elder and Philadelphia oil company executive John Logan, and Reading Railroad executive Oscar W. Stager to the Audubon station to lay out building lots along the railroad right-of-way. The railroad started a building boom around the Orston, Linden, and

Audubon stations, and the area's population grew from fewer than three hundred in 1890 to more than a thousand suburban residents by 1910, primarily Philadelphia and Camden City Euro-American middle-class workers (over the years, English, Irish, Polish, Ukrainian, Romanian, German, and Italian Americans). In 1904, after the street railway entered Audubon, Philadelphia realtor Harry D. LeCato speculated in Audubon real estate, advertising "High, Dry, and Healthy" building lots to urban residents.

HADDON HEIGHTS

The last stop before the Reading main line left Haddon Township and entered Centre Township was Haddon Heights, a portion of high ground located five miles from the Camden City waterfront and incorporated as a borough government in 1904. This municipality was largely the creation of Benjamin A. Lippincott, an area native who owned the family apple orchards and dairy farmland that ran parallel to the Philadelphia and Atlantic City Railway right-of-way. In 1890 Lippincott laid out building lots and persuaded the Reading company to erect a large passenger station in the center of his development. Lippincott's Real Estate Agency planned a village of Queen Anne–style cottages for urban middle-class Catholics and Protestants and encouraged the establishment of Baptist and Roman Catholic (St. Rose of Lima) churches.

Meanwhile, the Moore, Pollock and Redner Company of Philadelphia advertised Haddon Heights property. The company promised "a soil as rich and fertile as can be found anywhere; with pure, clear, cold, artesian water in whose crystal draughts lurk no typhoid germs." "Philadelphians," the advertisers knew, "will appreciate this more than anyone." By 1904, the year of incorporation, more than 500 people resided in the suburban development, and the population swelled to 1,452 by 1910, following the introduction of the trolley in 1905. Residents included Frank B. Jess, Harold E. Rogers, and other Camden City lawyers and real estate developers, along with merchant Frederick Fries and John M. Kelley, the leading Camden County waterfront real estate developer and builder.

BARRINGTON TO LAUREL SPRINGS

Crossing into Centre Township, the Reading's main line entered the historic hamlet of Clement's Bridge, stopping at the Dentdale station. After the standard gauge passed through in 1884, real estate developers advertised the area as "popular with thrifty mechanics and artisans of Philadelphia and Camden as a place of abode." Over the years, this boast proved partly true, with 51 percent of the settlers coming from Philadelphia, although only 9 percent relocated from Camden City. According to tradition, local land developers, impressed by their visit to Great Barrington, Massachusetts, renamed the railroad stop Barrington. However, fewer than eighty people had removed to the future Barrington development when the Reading Railroad opened a station in 1894. In 1903 the Public Service Company ran a trolley to Barrington, but growth remained slow. There was no post office there until 1911, and only on the eve of U.S. entry into World War I, in 1917, was Barrington's population sufficient to incorporate as a separate borough.

Down the line stood Lawnton, a flag stop for the African American community of Snow Hill, founded in the 1840s (although blacks had lived in this Free Haven enclave since at least the 1790s). In 1907 the railroad renamed the station Lawnside, and in 1926 the community of primarily African American residents incorporated as one of the very few entirely black-governed boroughs in America.

Just below Lawnton, the Reading Railroad Company built a stop at Greenland (named for the green marl soil). The Albertson family incorporated the Magnolia Villa Land Company, subdividing Chalkley Albertson's farm. (A leading Democratic state assemblyman, Albertson had helped to create Camden County, incorporate the White Horse Turnpike, and break the Republican party's monopoly over the county.) Reputedly, when they launched the effort to incorporate the place as a borough in 1915, Camden County Engineer John J. Albertson and Camden County Superintendent of Schools Charles S. Albertson named the station and post office Magnolia after the many flowering trees on their father's farm.

Below the Magnolia station, the Philadelphia and Reading's Atlantic City main line had platform stops at Somerville, Somerdale, Farm Crossing, and Laurel (White Horse), and the company developed stations at Stratford and Laurel Springs. Attorney Charles S. King purchased the Heulings Lippincott estate in 1889 and laid the groundwork for eventual development of Stratford Borough (1929). The farming and gristmill hamlet of Somerville would become the borough of Somerdale (1929). Laurel Springs was the main rail stop in the area during the late nineteenth century. The Philadelphia and Atlantic City Railway built Laurel (White Horse) station near Ephraim Tomlinson's Laurel Mills on Timber Creek in 1877. The place emerged rapidly as a resort, with the Crystal Inn, Lakeview Boarding Inn, and Laurel Springs mineral baths (Walt Whitman took mud baths here for his paralysis). Eventually, Laurel Springs replaced Lakeside, the Camden and Atlantic Railroad's development nearby at Kirkwood, as the area's leading resort.

Samuel Cord and the Atlantic City Railroad incorporated the Laurel Spring[s] Realty Company in 1889 and purchased the Tomlinson property, while the West Jersey Title and Guarantee Company purchased the adjacent Stafford farm. Cord published the *Laurel Springs Courier* to promote development of these tracts and secured a larger Laurel Springs railroad station to replace the Laurel platform stop. Cord and the Reading Railroad launched one of the most aggressive suburban advertising campaigns in county history. Laurel Springs, the place to live, "offers superior attractions and advantages for a suburban home, or summer residence, combining all the pleasure and amusements of a mountain resort, with Laurel Lake, over a mile long." "Why," the promoters asked, "do you live in Philadelphia or Camden, when you can live so much better, healthier and cheaper at Laurel Springs, in a pure atmosphere?"

CLEMENTON

Developer Theodore B. Gibbs used the same approach for his Clementon project, announcing in 1886 that "houses have recently been built for suburban homes by businessmen of Philadelphia." Gibbs purchased the Isaac Tomlinson property in 1872. The tract stood near a site on the north branch of Timber Creek that was originally founded as a glassworks by Samuel Clement in the 1820s but had long since been used as a gristmill by Ephraim Tomlinson, director of the State Bank of Camden and the largest landowner in this area. Gibbs, along with Clementon storeowner Lewis Snyder and real estate developers George A. Baghurst, Joseph Lippincott, and John R. Rowand (his charcoal mill lands became the Borough of Pine Hill in 1929), secured the Clementon railroad station in 1877.

By 1892 ten trains a day stopped at the Clementon station. "The attractions here consist of the fine surroundings, good trout and pike fishing, boating, bathing, etc.," proclaimed C. E. Howe's *Camden County Directory*. Gibbs developed a suburban town and Clementon Lake Park, incorporating a township in 1903. The developer also gained a right-of-way in 1907 from Haddon Heights to Clementon for the Camden and Suburban Railway trolley to bring excursionists from the Camden waterfront to the suburban resort park.

WILLIAMSTOWN JUNCTION TO WINSLOW

The cluster of flag stops on the main line on either side of Williamstown Junction promoted development by the Norcross, Peacock, Ware, Bodine, and Sickler families of the lower county area. Main-line railroad stops developed at Tansboro, Penbryn, Florence, Cedar Brook, Braddock, Blue Anchor, and Winslow Junction, improving the connection of Camden County's remote fruit-farming region to the Camden and waterfront market. The Williamstown Branch of the Reading system tied the Atco station, Wilton platform stop (once site of J. L. Mason's leased glassworks, producer of the world-famous Mason fruit canning jar), and the Sicklertown stop (serving the hamlet of Sicklerville) to the important stations at Williamstown and Glassboro in Gloucester County. However, little development occurred around the Camden County stops on the Williamstown Branch. Sicklerville, for instance, remained a tiny village of ten houses, two stores, and a Methodist church built on land donated by William Sickler. Paul H. Sickler ran the post office from his store, and Jacob Sickler kept the tax collector's office in the other store.

Despite the slow growth of the settlements in remote Waterford and Winslow townships (they would not really become suburban developments until the last decades of the twentieth century), the Reading system created a Camden County metropolitan corridor. This railroad system connected the new suburbs to the Camden waterfront, where Camden City was evolving from a sleepy manufacturing town of 20,000 in 1870 into a major urban industrial center of nearly 100,000 people, living in dynamic, ethnically diverse urban neighborhoods.

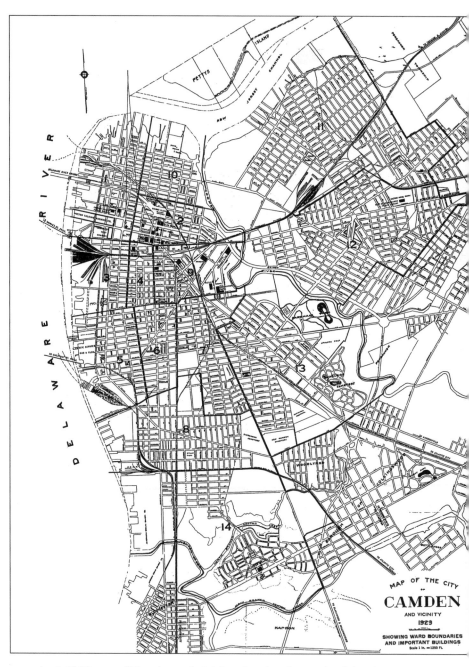

4. A 1929 map of Camden and vicinity, showing the wards of the city.
(From Paul F. Cranston, Camden County *[1931], Camden County Historical Society Collection)*

1. Evans Mill and millpond, seen here on the south branch of Cooper's Creek on the border of Delaware Township (Cherry Hill) and Haddonfield. The Kays, a pioneer tidewater planter family, once owned the mill. *(Camden County Historical Society Collection)*

2. Historic Haddonfield, one of the original colonial settlements, founded in the early eighteenth century by Elizabeth Haddon-Estaugh. *(Camden County Historical Society Collection)*

3. Haddonfield retained its early charm despite the introduction of street railways through the center of town. *(Camden County Historical Society Collection)*

4. The Camden and Philadelphia Race Track, located three miles from Camden City in present-day Oaklyn, made the area a popular entertainment center between 1835 and 1846. However, gambling, riotous behavior, and accidents— such as the collapse of the grandstands in 1846, as seen here—led to the closure of the facility. *(Camden County Historical Society Collection)*

5. Joseph Charles Delacour's drugstore and manufactory in Camden City in the 1840s. Delacour was one of the leaders in the movement to create Camden County in 1844. *(Camden County Historical Society Collection)*

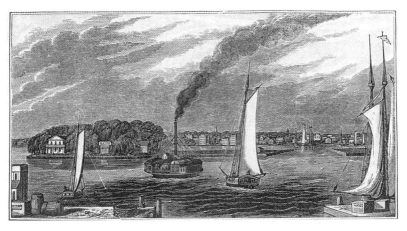

6. A steam ferry arrives at its Philadelphia terminal from Camden after passing through the Windmill Island canal in this scene from circa 1844. *(Barber and Howe,* Historical Collections of New Jersey *[1844]. Camden County Historical Society Collection)*

7. The Haddonfield and Camden Turnpike tollgate on Haddon Avenue below Euclid Avenue shortly after a fire and abandonment in 1909. During the last half of the nineteenth century, most major highways in the county leading to Camden City were operated as toll-collecting turnpikes. *(Camden County Historical Society Collection)*

8. The White Horse Tavern, once located near present-day Stratford on the White Horse Pike, long served as the social and political center for the suburban central county region. *(Camden County Historical Society Collection)*

9. The Camden and Burlington County Railroad made Merchantville (incorporated as a borough in 1874) into a favorite suburban residential neighborhood for upper-middle-class business executives and government employees working in Philadelphia and Camden City. *(Camden County Historical Society Collection)*

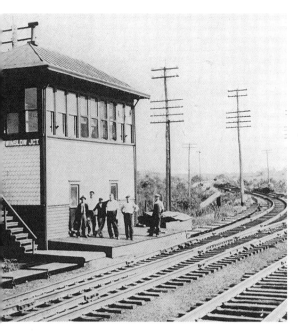

10. At remote Winslow Junction the Atlantic City Railroad main line connected with the company's branch line to Cape May County resorts and the New Jersey Southern (Central Railroad of New Jersey). The first railroad to pass through Winslow Junction was the Camden and Atlantic. This area remained a near wilderness until the late twentieth century. *(Paul W. Schopp Collection)*

11. A Pennsylvania Railroad Atlantic City Express accelerates eastbound past Divide Tower in 1922 after crossing the Delaware River on the Delair Bridge. *(Paul W. Schopp Collection)*

12. A Pennsylvania Railroad locomotive leads an eastbound freight train through the still rural Stratford countryside in 1954. *(Robert L. Long Photograph, Paul W. Schopp Collection)*

13. The middle-class suburb of Audubon under development in 1907. *(Paul W. Schopp Collection)*

14. Motorists in front of the Berlin Hotel in 1910, probably celebrating the just-completed creation of Berlin Township. The hotel had served the former Longacoming neighborhood for nearly a century. *(Camden County Historical Society Collection)*

15. The Black Horse Pike town of Blackwood and the Blackwood Theatre, circa 1930. *(Paul W. Schopp Collection)*

16. Kaighn's Point Ferry Terminal, circa 1907. George Brehm's saloon at the corner of Kaighns Avenue and Second Street sold Poth's Beer, produced at the Camden Brewery two blocks away on Bulson Street. *(Camden County Historical Society Collection)*

17. Advertised as the largest furniture store in the United States, the J. B. Van Sciver Company dominated the Camden City waterfront for nearly a century. *(Camden County Historical Society Collection)*

18. Camden County residents came to Gately and Hurley's department store at Broadway and Pine Street to shop, making Camden City the retail center of the county for nearly fifty years. *(Camden County Historical Society Collection)*

19. This rare photograph shows the boathouses at the confluence of Newton Creek and the Delaware River in 1898, just months before they were razed to make way for construction of the New York Shipbuilding Company's yard in South Camden. *(Camden County Historical Society Collection)*

20. View of the New York Shipbuilding Company's covered shipways shortly after completion, circa 1907. Also shown is the Atlantic City Railroad's Bulson Street yard to the right of the shipyard. This photograph was taken from the Camden Brewery. *(Camden County Historical Society Collection)*

21. The new Munger and Long Department Store and the old Camden County Courthouse can be seen in this 1907 view of Camden City looking north from Broadway and Mickle Street. *(Camden County Historical Society Collection)*

22. Market Street in Camden City served as a county business and government center in 1907. *(Camden County Historical Society Collection)*

23. Female employees of the William S. Scull Company, one of Camden City's oldest businesses, pack ground coffee into bags in 1907. *(Camden County Historical Society Collection)*

24. Female employees of the B. F. Boyer Worsted Yarn Mill at the corner of Delaware Avenue and Cooper Street in North Camden in the 1890s. *(Camden County Historical Society Collection)*

25. Rosario Anselmo's bakery at Fourth and Division Streets was one of the dozens of Italian American businesses, houses, shops, and social organizations that lined South Third and Fourth Streets. *(Camden County Historical Society)*

26. The Whitman Park neighborhood around Tenth and Liberty Streets was the center of the Polish American community in Camden County for most of the twentieth century. *(Camden County Historical Society)*

27. The Seidman Hardware Store on Kaighns Avenue in 1918 was one of the many Jewish-owned businesses in South Camden. *(Tri-County Jewish Historical Society Collection, Camden County Historical Society)*

28. Morris Handle's new furniture store on Kaighns Avenue above Fourth Street typified the proliferation of Jewish-owned businesses in Camden City during the early days of the twentieth century. *(Paul W. Schopp Collection)*

29. Lawnside schoolchildren, circa 1926, when the former black enclave of Snow Hill was incorporated as the African American–governed borough of Lawnside. *(Camden County Historical Society)*

30. This muddy and rutted road in Runnemede typified the still undeveloped rural Camden County countryside in 1927 and the poor quality of roads at that time. A locomotive on the Atlantic City Railroad's Grenloch Branch (the "Peanut Line") is barely visible to the right rear of the automobile. *(Paul W. Schopp Collection)*

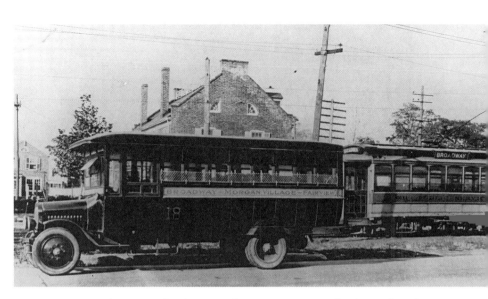

31. Motor buses met the electric trolley, circa 1920, to take shipyard workers from Morgan and Fairview Villages to the New York Shipbuilding Company's yard on the South Camden waterfront. *(Paul W. Schopp Collection)*

32. The Pusey and Jones Shipbuilding Company yards on the Gloucester City waterfront at the end of World War I. *(Paul W. Schopp Collection)*

33. Camden City native son Admiral Henry Braid Wilson prepares to celebrate Armistice Day and the naming of Bridge Boulevard in his honor in November 1929. *(Camden County Historical Society Collection)*

34. The first officials cross the footbridge suspended precariously between Camden City and Philadelphia in 1924. Seen in the background are the waterfront factories of the Victor Talking Machine Company, Camden County's second largest employer, and the smoke-covered industrial city of Camden. *(Camden County Historical Society Collection)*

35. Camden County planners hoped that the new Walt Whitman Hotel, opened in 1925, and the construction of nearly a dozen movie theaters would make Camden City an entertainment and convention center to rival Philadelphia. *(Camden County Historical Society Collection)*

36. The Broadway extension was cut from the Bridge Plaza in 1924 through the Cooper Street neighborhood to give Philadelphia and suburban residents rapid access to the Walt Whitman Hotel and the downtown Camden City business and government district. *(Camden County Historical Society Collection)*

37. Motor buses prepare to cross the new Delaware River Bridge shortly after it opened in 1926. Note that toll booths did not have a continuous roof over them yet. *(Camden County Historical Society Collection)*

38. The carefully planned upper-middle-class urban neighborhood along Linden Street was razed in the early 1920s to make way for the new Bridge Plaza. *(Camden County Historical Society Collection)*

39. Upscale housing dominated Camden City's "Society Hill" until county planners razed homes during the 1920s to build a hotel and bridge plaza that cut the city in half and isolated the remaining Cooper Street neighborhood from North Camden's other upper-middle-class residential streets. *(Camden County Historical Society Collection)*

40. The Walt Whitman Theatre, on Westfield Avenue near the East Camden–Pennsauken border, opened in 1927 and featured live entertainment and motion pictures. *(Camden County Historical Society Collection)*

41. Roosevelt Plaza, in front of the new Camden County Courthouse, was one of a number of New Deal projects during the 1930s that made Democratic Mayor George E. Brunner of Camden City the most powerful political force in the county for more than twenty years. *(Camden County Historical Society Collection)*

42. The Himmelein and Bailey Belting Manufacturing Company and brick row houses on Haddon Avenue in 1937 typified the urban working-class residential and factory landscape of Camden City. *(Camden County Historical Society Collection)*

43. Reputedly the shortest and narrowest city street in America, Fogarty Avenue housed workers from the Richard M. Hollingshead chemical works, barely visible at the end of the street in this 1926 photograph. *(Paul W. Schopp Collection)*

44. The Walt Whitman Bridge opened in 1957, connecting South Philadelphia with Gloucester City. The bridge bypassed the Camden County waterfront, rushing commuters to the suburbs or vacationers from Pennsylvania through the county to the Jersey shore. *(Camden County Historical Society)*

45. Municipal terminal and piers of the vibrant port of Camden in 1960. Note that the railroad lines still run to the site of the partially demolished ferry terminal. J. B. Van Sciver's furniture factory and retail store and the RCA-Victor and Campbell Soup companies can be seen in the upper left-hand corner, and the Camden County Courthouse in the upper right-hand corner. *(Camden County Historical Society Collection)*

46. The New York Shipbuilding Company prepares to launch the aircraft carrier *Kitty Hawk* in 1960, seen under construction in dry dock in the lower left-hand corner. *(Camden County Historical Society Collection)*

47. The Hatch Junior High School track and field team, fully integrated in 1927, eventually became all-white and then all-black as Parkside and surrounding Camden City neighborhoods underwent dramatic racial transformations throughout the twentieth century. *(Camden County Historical Society Collection)*

48. This photograph of Camden City's secondary school teachers preparing to board the train at the Broadway railroad station to attend the Business, Industrial, and Education Day at the Jersey shore demonstrates the ethnic and religious diversity of Camden County in 1958. *(Camden County Historical Society Collection)*

49. Opening of the Cherry Hill Shopping Center in 1961, the first mall on the East Coast, led to the creation of Cherry Hill Township, to the ascendance of Cherry Hill as the county's business and residential center, and, eventually, to suburban sprawl. *(Camden County Historical Society Collection)*

50. The Haddon Avenue business district in Collingswood was one of the county's most prosperous sections of suburban shops and small businesses in the early 1960s. *(Paul W. Schopp Collection)*

51. This housing development between Pennypacker Park and the Ellisburg Circle in the early 1950s represented the first stage of suburban sprawl in Delaware Township (Cherry Hill). *(Camden County Historical Society Collection)*

52. The *New Jersey,* the "Big J," makes its way up the Delaware River to its new berth on the Camden waterfront. After a battle with North Jersey forces, South Jersey won the great ship, built by (across the river at the Philadelphia Navy Yard) and served on by scores of South Jerseyans. *(Ronald S. Karafin/Image Art)*

53. OpSail 2000, one of the first events sharing the ports of Philadelphia and Camden, with tall ships berthed on both sides of the river. Pictured is Camden City Hall and the famous RCA Building. *(Photo by Curt Hudson)*

6

"THE METROPOLIS OF WEST JERSEY"

ORGANIZING A CITY

The city of Camden grew from 41,659 people in 1880 to 116,309 by 1920, making it the fifth largest city in New Jersey, following Newark, Jersey City, Paterson, and Trenton. The population became increasingly diverse with the addition of thousands of southern and eastern European Jewish and Catholic immigrants. During this era, the modest-sized, post–Civil War manufacturing town exploded into an industrial powerhouse, with some of the largest textile, chemical, shipbuilding, steel pen, food processing, and electrical industries in the United States.

On the eve of the Civil War, no one could have predicted the city's growth. City fathers did not adopt a charter until 1848 to provide a city council, building inspector, and police constabulary, nor did they plan for street layout. A young city lawyer, Thomas H. Dudley, drew up the city charter, thereby launching a career in Republican party politics that later made him U.S. consul in London during the Civil War, where he persuaded Britain to stop building ironclad warships for the Confederacy. Still, the city grew erratically without a careful street plan or adequate municipal services. Not until 1866, for instance, did the city build culverts and drain the swamps along the waterfront to prevent the flooding of city streets with every high tide on the river.

In 1871 City Solicitor Alden C. Scovel presented a new city charter "for the present and future requirements of *the metropolis of West Jersey*." In providing the framework for future growth, the new charter organized eight city wards out of the North, Middle, and South Wards created under the charter of 1848. The city annexed Kaighnsville as part of the Seventh Ward and Stockton (actually Centerville in South Camden, not to be confused with Stockton Township in East Camden) as the Eighth Ward. In general, the annexation mechanism allowed the city to grow in an orderly fashion by incorporating into the center each new urban neighborhood. Thus the city annexed parts of the former Stockton Township, now known as Stockton Town, as the Eleventh and Twelfth Wards in 1899, and Fairview as the Fourteenth Ward in 1919 (Parkside became the Thirteenth Ward in 1900). Eventually, Camden City's inability to continue such expansion into peripheral areas such as Woodlynne, Haddon Township, and Pennsauken, which had developed their own municipal governments, prevented its further growth and contributed, in the end, to its decline.

The new charter of 1871 seemed an enlightened plan to manage the city on modern business principles. The urban constitution gave the city its first professional police department, which superceded the city marshals and neighborhood constabulary. It firmly established a paid, professional fire department (founded in 1869) to replace the often-feuding neighborhood volunteer companies (Fairmount, Weccacoe, Mohawk, Independence, and Shiffler). The Camden City Board of Education (formed in 1854) reorganized the city's school districts in 1871 to conform to the new ward divisions and to construct new schools. The city built a "schoolhouse for colored Children on Mount Vernon Street" and the magnificent Cooper School in North Camden, said to be the "finest in the state." Certainly, it was the most expensive yet built in Camden County, with the cost of $30,900 double that of the standard schoolhouse. State, county, and local officials attended the dedication in 1874, and local poet Walt Whitman read a dedicatory poem.*

A public works department paved major city avenues and provided

---

*The renowned American poet Walt Whitman lived in Camden from 1873 until his death in 1892. He is buried in Harleigh Cemetery, Camden.

gas and light as a municipal service. The city government worked intimately with the Camden Horse Railroad Company (incorporated in 1866) to inaugurate a street railway system in 1871, with real estate developers to improve the waterfront, and with industrialists to organize blocks of brick row houses around their factory buildings. Such an environment encouraged industrialists (particularly from across the river in Philadelphia) to establish dozens of textile, oilcloth, shoe and leather, shipbuilding, cigar and carriage making, chemical and dye, fertilizer, machine tool, and iron forging factories in the waterfront city.

David Baird started the post-1871 boom by establishing his Timber, Spar and Piling Basin and lumberyard on the North Camden riverfront in 1872. Volney G. Bennett followed, assuming control of the Central Lumber Yard at Second and Cherry Streets four years later. In 1875 Edward L. Farr and Moses Bailey founded the Farr and Bailey Floor Oil Cloth Works at Seventh and Kaighn Avenue. John T. and Henry Bottomley incorporated the Camden Woolen Mills Company on State Street near Cooper's Creek, and the Highland Worsted Mills nearby. Jacob Loeb and Max and David Schoenfeld formed the Lace and Embroidery Manufactory on Front and Pearl Streets in 1882. The same year, Joseph Campbell, Arthur Dorrance, and Joseph S. Campbell formed Joseph Campbell and Company to can fruits and vegetables and to produce jellies and preserves. (Dorrance's nephew, John T. Dorrance, later invented the process for manufacturing condensed soup, and the company eventually became Campbell Soup.) Howland Croft and Herbert Priestly incorporated the Linden Worsted Mills in 1885 on Broadway in South Camden. (The old factory building still stood at the turn of the twenty-first century, the last structure of Camden City's golden age of textile production.) The greatest period of urban industrial and business growth in Camden County history culminated between 1899 and 1901 with the incorporation of the county's largest employers, the New York Shipbuilding and Victor Talking Machine companies.

THE DEVELOPERS

Several groups of late-nineteenth-century entrepreneurs and land speculators developed urban industrial Camden City. Just as the tidewater planter gentry had done throughout the first two centuries of the county's history, these new leaders controlled and guided urban society, government, and business. In fact, some of them were descended from the original Quaker tidewater planter families, including G. Genge Browning (treasurer of the Camden Horse Rail Road Company and president of a dye company), Howard M. Cooper (president of the Camden National Bank), and Joseph W. Cooper (president of the Camden Gas Light Company). Mostly, however, Camden County's late-nineteenth-century urban industrial developers came from a new breed of post–Civil War entrepreneurs. They saw unlimited economic opportunity for large-scale industrialization on the Camden waterfront and the chance to develop cheap farmlands into profitable suburban building lots for the urban industrial middle class.

Camden County's industrial entrepreneurs typified the late-nineteenth-century American success story, mythologized in Horatio Alger's rags-to-riches novels and embodied by steel magnate Andrew Carnegie. Thus, William J. Sewell, an Irish immigrant orphan, became the most powerful railroad executive and real estate developer in southern New Jersey. William J. Thompson progressed from tending billiard tables in a Philadelphia saloon to building Gloucester City into the amusement, entertainment, and resort center of the Delaware Valley, earning the title "Duke of Gloucester." Alfred Cramer left his family farm on Timber Creek to become a wheelwright in Camden City and amassed a fortune by speculating in Stockton Township real estate. Richard M. Hollingshead rose, according to family tradition, from mucking out horse stables to running a great chemical company that began by manufacturing a leather preservative for horse harnesses. Joseph Campbell turned his packing company, which offered "the justly celebrated Beefsteak Tomato," into an international food processing empire. Machinist Eldridge R. Johnson emerged from utter poverty, working in a little shop tucked away behind the Jacob Collings carriage factory, to organize the world's leading talking machine and recording company (selling his share in the Victor Talking Machine Company in 1927 for $28 million).

The story of Irish immigrant David Baird best portrays the entrepreneurial spirit of the age and explains how Camden County's waterfront became a great urban industrial region. Baird began his career after the Civil War by pushing handcars filled with timber for the Camden and Amboy Rail Road. By 1874 he had accumulated enough capital to form a small lumber company on the North Camden riverfront. Like many other entrepreneurs of the period, Baird found patronage and financial backing from local interests anxious to expand Camden City businesses. Baird specialized in mast and spar timber for the construction of wooden sailing vessels, and he formed a partnership with Joseph I. Morris of the Morris and Mathis Shipbuilding Company on Cooper's Point. Baird and Mathis joined ship smith John H. Tway in organizing the Tway Steel Forge and Machine Company, later the Camden Forge on Mount Ephraim Avenue, which provided the majority of forging for the nearby New York Shipbuilding Corporation during both world wars. Baird eventually bought a mansion between Cooper and Linden Streets, settling himself among the county's political, financial, and business leaders, including Secretary of the Navy George M. Robeson.

Baird's most influential neighbor was fellow Irish immigrant William Joyce Sewell, a Civil War hero. Sewell became vice president of the West Jersey Railroad and a director of the Camden and Philadelphia Steamboat Ferry Company, the Camden Horse Rail Road Company, the Camden Safe Deposit and Trust Company (South Jersey's first savings institution), and the West Jersey Mutual Insurance Company. He developed neighborhoods in Camden, Gloucester, and Cape May Counties. Sewell headed the dominant Republican party political machine in Camden City and County as well, serving in the New Jersey State and U.S. Senates. With Sewell's patronage, Baird secured a monopoly on contracts to provide poles to string telephone, telegraph, and electric wires in the city and immediate suburbs. Sewell also helped Baird obtain U.S. War Department timber contracts during the Spanish American War. In return, Baird took care of local politics for Sewell, becoming the First Ward's Republican party chief, a representative on the Camden County Board of Chosen Freeholders, and Camden County sheriff. He also sat on the State Board of Assessors, which held responsibility for levying taxes on Sewell's railroad and real estate properties.

Baird, Sewell, and their fellow Irish entrepreneurs—among them, Edward Ambler Armstrong, utilities developer Joseph J. Burleigh, and house builder and realtor Edward N. Cohn—developed North Camden's working- and upper-middle-class neighborhoods. At the same time, John F. Starr Jr., a real estate developer, Benjamin C. Reeve, president of the Camden Horse Rail Road Company, and John F. Starr Sr., president of the First

National Bank of Camden, formed the Camden Land and Improvement Company in 1884 to develop properties below those of the Baird-Sewell syndicate. The Starr enterprise sold lots on Market Street and on Bridge and Kaighns Avenues, and made major land sales to the expanding Victor Talking Machine and Esterbrook Steel Pen companies.

Reeve, Burleigh, Baird, Armstrong, and Browning, among others, formed a syndicate that took over the Camden Horse Rail Road in 1889 and organized the New Camden Land Improvement Company in 1892 to develop the Wood Lynne amusement park on the Charles M. Cooper estate below Newton Creek. The horse railroad syndicate merged with its bitter rival, the West Jersey Traction Company, in 1896 to form the Camden and Suburban Railway Company. The trolley syndicate developed part of Wood Lynne Park (which lasted until 1914, when it was destroyed by a fire) into a housing development, leading to incorporation of Woodlynne Borough in 1901.

All along, Cohn bought large tracts from Starr to develop North Camden neighborhoods. The city's largest late-nineteenth-century real estate developer, Cohn financed house building for the working middle class through the North Camden Building and Loan Association, created in 1875 by Sewell, Starr, and Baird, which enabled smaller homeowners and lot buyers to invest in a cooperative mortgage lending organization. In this fashion, Cohn and his partners, George Holl and Joseph E. Roberts (president of the West Jersey Railroad Company), sold lots and built blocks of two- and three-story brick and frame row houses and modest single-family dwellings from Cooper's Point to Pearl Street. They sold or rented to carpenters, sawyers, and ship fitters who worked for the Baird Spar, Mast and Timber Yard and for Morris and Mathis, Samuel W. Tilton and Son, the Rilatt Brothers, and other small North Camden shipyards and factories.

Cohn rented some of these houses to employees of North Camden textile and paper mills and local match, box, cigar, and printing factories. Cohn also bought property from Starr around the Liberty Park station on the Camden and Atlantic Railroad line in South Camden, where he developed housing along Liberty, Mechanic, and Atlantic Streets and Kaighns Avenue. He sold first to middle-class Irish, German, and African Americans and later to Polish, Russian, and Austro-Hungarian immigrants, who arrived in Camden City in the last decades of the century to work in South Camden's booming industries.

ORIGINS OF CAMDEN'S URBAN ETHNIC NEIGHBORHOODS

British American Protestants, many related to the original founders of the county, created urban industrial Camden County, but a Catholic, Jewish, and Protestant urban working middle-class built the city. During this era of large-scale industrialization and urban growth (1865–1920), Camden City became an increasingly rich collection of ethnic neighborhoods. These included an earlier population of Western European, African, Irish, and German Americans and later groups of Austro-Hungarian, Italian, Polish, and Russian Americans, along with small clusters of Greek, Lithuanian, Slovak, Armenian, and Chinese Americans.

For most of this formative period, many different ethnic groups lived together in the same city neighborhoods. Only the Cooper Street area of North Camden remained predominantly Anglo-American Protestant. Most other sections of Camden City contained African, English, Polish, Irish, and German Americans close to each other on streets of brick row houses, stores, and corner shops. Unlike neighborhoods in most other large New Jersey cities, the ones in Camden City never divided into clearly defined Little Italys, Polands, or Russias, or formed ethnic ghettos. Yet different ethnic groups concentrated in their own cultural enclaves, often around a Catholic parish church and school, "colored" school, or Jewish community association.

AFRICAN AMERICANS

Camden County's African American community was as old as that of the white tidewater planter founders, who had brought blacks to the county as slave labor. The first African American residents were scattered about the rural county, working in the houses and fields of the tidewater planters. But in the 1830s an urban black community formed after Richard Fetters bought the former Charity Kaighn estate and sold building lots to Philadelphia middle-class blacks in the area bounded by Third, Line, and Cherry Streets and the Delaware River. This neighborhood included the city's first black churches: the Macedonia African Methodist Episcopal Church (founded circa 1832), located on Spruce Street, and the Union AME Church on Mount Vernon Street (1855). The Fettersville neighborhood contained the original West Jersey Orphanage for Colored Children and the John Greenleaf Whittier Colored School for Boys and Girls on Chestnut Street.

Just below Fettersville, Benjamin Vandyke, Daniel Wilkins, and other Philadelphia middle-class African Americans founded Kaighnsville (1838). This black settlement became part of Centerville, the largest and most successful African American urban neighborhood in Camden County history. It extended from Kaighns Avenue south to Ferry Avenue and from Ninth Street west to the river. Centerville (later called Stockton) was a creation of the Kaighn's Point Land Company, which purchased the Dr. Isaac Mulford and Isaac W. Mickle estates in 1849, a vast tract that extended from Line Ditch to Newton Creek and from the future Evergreen Cemetery to the Delaware River.

In the 1840s Dempsey D. Butler, a prosperous African American merchant from Philadelphia, opened a general store on Kaighns Avenue, purchased lots, built boardinghouses, a Masonic hall, churches, a cemetery, and schools for black residents, becoming in the process the wealthiest black in Camden County. The African American community formed the Kaighns Avenue Baptist Church and Scott's African Union Church. A few streets below Kaighns, on Central Avenue in the heart of Centerville, black residents formed Bethel African Methodist Episcopal Church and other chapels. This South Camden section was home to William F. Powell, principal of the Mount Vernon (Colored) School, who was named by President William McKinley in 1897 to serve as minister to Haiti. Also residing here was Peter D. R. Postels, a Civil War veteran (Colored Volunteers U.S. Cavalry, Company M, Second Regiment), a leader of the Republican party in the Eighth Ward and a Camden County freeholder in 1882–83. Meanwhile, the Kaighn, Clement, Mickle, and other Quaker pioneering white families founded the West Jersey Orphanage for Destitute Colored Children in the neighborhood.

The population of the South Camden neighborhood between Kaighns and Central Avenues included 1,142 blacks and 4,663 whites in the 1880s, living in a dynamic multicultural community. It even housed Camden County's first Chinese Americans in the 1890s, with Sing Wah, Gee Wah, Sam Wah Lee, and Fong Toon operating laundries there. By 1895, however, racial discrimination and violence directed against the Chinese and African Americans convulsed the neighborhood. Postels left, settling near

Berlin in remote Waterford Township, and other blacks from the neighborhood followed. "Colored grocer" John Saddler and "colored farmer" Isaac H. Saddler left Centerville for rural Camden County, organizing Saddlertown in Gloucester Township. Centerville preacher Isaac Hinson joined Saddlerton residents James and Charles Fussell in developing Fusselltown in Haddon Township (present-day Oaklyn).

IRISH AMERICANS

Camden County's Irish heritage was as old as that of its African Americans. Scottish (Ulster) Irish Protestants helped found the county, while Irish Catholic indentured servants came over on the earliest boats. During the American Revolution, patriots of Irish ancestry contributed mightily to the anti-British war. The main influx of Catholic Irish immigrants arrived in the county during the 1830s and 1840s to work on the Camden and Amboy Railroad and in Starr's Camden Iron Works, forming Camden's first urban Irish neighborhood below Bridge Avenue on Stevens and Benson Streets.

The arrival of Irish immigrants coincided with antiforeign ("nativist") political and Protestant religious revival movements, which led in 1844 to violent anti-Catholic and anti-Irish rioting in Philadelphia. In Camden, the pastor of the First Presbyterian Church, Reverend William McCalla, launched a hateful anti-Catholic campaign. "His address was replete with invective against the Church of Rome," Isaac Mickle observed, and was filled, "I guess, with not a little of intolerance." Undoubtedly, McCalla's invective contributed to the defiling of the Catholic mission of St. Mary in Gloucestertown in 1846 and, more seriously, to the partial burning in 1852 of Starr's Hall in Camden, where Catholics held mass. Nevertheless, parish priest Edmund Q. S. Waldron of Philadelphia successfully established St. Mary's Roman Catholic Church in Gloucester (1849) and St. Mary's parish in Camden (1855), where Father James Moran built St. Mary's Church at Fifth and Taylor Streets (1859).

Irish American support for the Union and the heroic service of Irishmen in the Civil War removed some of the animosity toward Camden's Irish Catholics. There was little controversy in 1864 when Father Patrick Byrne moved St. Mary's parish to Broadway and Market Street and built the magnificent Cathedral of the Immaculate Conception (1866). Few took notice when Irish Catholics established a mission on Van Hook Street (1885) and opened the Church of the Sacred Heart at Ferry Avenue and Broadway (1886). John J. Burleigh, an Irish Catholic railroad, telegraph, and telephone entrepreneur, faced no discrimination when he moved to the exclusive Protestant-dominated borough of Merchantville and helped establish a Catholic mission there. However, labor strikes in Camden, organized in part by Terence V. Powderly, the Irish American founder of the Philadelphia chapter of the Knights of Labor, resurrected anti–Irish Catholic sentiment. (Peter J. McGuire, the reputed Irish American founder of Labor Day, resided in North Camden in the 1890s.) Moreover, Protestant temperance reformers blamed the Irish American racetrack and saloon promoter William Thompson of Gloucester City for causing debauchery and drunkenness among the Philadelphia and Camden County working class. The American Protective Association, the Patriotic Order Sons of America, and the Sons of St. George organized to protect Camden from a feared Irish Catholic onslaught.

GERMAN AMERICANS

German Americans faced far less discrimination than their black and Irish neighbors. Although, according to tradition, woodcutters Xaverius, Ignatius, and Sebastian Woos held the county's first German Catholic mission services secretly in the remote southeastern woods of Waterford Township in the 1760s, it helped that most early German American residents were hardworking Protestant craftsmen and mechanics. In Camden City, they settled in the Middle Ward to work for the railroad or in nearby shops and factories, and they adopted American institutions, forming the Mozart Lodge and joining the Masons and other acceptable organizations. Still, Camden County's first German American urban community wanted to preserve its own language and culture. The Fackler, Beck, Bauder, Hertlein, Dauer, Roedel, Schlorer, and Schneider families organized Trinity German Evangelical Lutheran Church at Fourth and Pine Streets in 1853 (moved later to Fifth and Stevens) to teach "Luther's Catechism" in German. In 1854 Reverend Adam Hinkle met with German residents at Louisa Moushe's house at Third and Cherry Streets to found Emanuel United Brethren (Lutheran) Church. Wealthy Philadelphia philanthropist John Warner agreed to build their church so long as the congregation held services in German and opened the place to the poor people of Camden City. Meanwhile, Alexander Schlesinger came to Camden from Philadelphia in 1883 and published the German-language newspaper *Tageblatt,* promoting German American settlement of the new Liberty Park neighborhood along the railroad in South Camden.

Camden County's urban German Catholics attended mass with Irish Catholics until Father Byrne moved the parish out of the German-Irish neighborhoods of the Middle Ward during the Civil War. In 1867 German Catholics met at Fourth and Spruce with Father Joseph Thurnes at the home of Anthony Kobus, Camden City's leading shoe manufacturer, where they organized Saints Peter and Paul German Catholic Church. They purchased the Second Baptist Church at Third and Line Streets in 1868, built a school in 1883, moved to their own church at Spruce above Broadway, and built the convent for the School of the Sisters of Notre Dame in 1890.

Saints Peter and Paul became the center of the most prosperous German neighborhood in Camden County. Here, Kobus, Valentine and Anthony Voll, Anthony J. Oberst, and other church leaders created German cultural and business organizations, including the Camden Turnverein (athletic club) at Fifth and Pine Streets. Kobus and Oberst (a real estate and insurance agent) formed building and loan associations (Central, German Centennial, Greater Camden, and Union), with offices at Fifth and Pine Streets, to assist German and Irish American (and later Italian and Polish American) middle-class families in buying houses in the neighborhood. Also sponsoring the social and religious events at Saints Peter and Paul were German American wagon makers Theodore and William H. Tiedeken and stove and heater merchant Frederick Klosterman.

Meanwhile, German American craftsmen and shopkeepers from Philadelphia moved to the Cramer Hill, Wrightsville, Rosedale, and North Cramer Hill developments (what would become the Eleventh and Twelfth Wards of East Camden). The Bachman, Buren, Hettel, Reninghaus, Stadtler, Stoeckle, Schwartz, and Tiedeman families organized Christus German Evangelical Lutheran Church (1887) in the Cramer Hill and Rosedale neighborhoods. German Americans filled skilled positions as carpenters, car builders, coach makers, and machinists at the Pennsylvania Railroad Company's Pavonia Car (Shops) Works, established in East Camden in 1888. German Americans dominated the Cramer Hill business community:

Henry W. Dorward ran the Rosedale grocery and Otmar E. Schmid the North Cramer Hill coal business; William Schmid became postmaster at the North Cramer Hill post office at Pavonia station; and Frederica Rugart operated a Cramer Hill German American beer hall.

POLISH AMERICANS

German-speaking Polish Catholics were among the first of the new immigrants to define a neighborhood in Camden. They had been moving across the river from Philadelphia at least since the early 1880s to work in the leather tanning, morocco, oilcloth, iron, and shipbuilding industries on the Camden waterfront. They settled among the Germans, living between Fourth and Fifth Streets below Spruce to Liberty Streets. At first, these Polish Catholics worshiped at Saints Peter and Paul Roman Catholic Church on Spruce Street or at St. Stanislaus Roman Catholic Church in Philadelphia, where most had settled originally. As more Polish American families moved to Kaighns Avenue, to Liberty, Mechanic, and Van Hook Streets, and east toward Ninth Street and Haddon Avenue, establishment of a Polish Catholic parish seemed desirable.

Camden Polish American Catholic leaders gathered at the Kaighns Avenue home of mill worker Joseph Wojtkowiak in 1891 and organized the St. Joseph's Society of Camden, an offshoot of the Philadelphia Polish Catholic church. The group incorporated the St. Joseph's parish building committee on 24 October 1892, with Valentine Pepeta, a lay trustee at Saints Peter and Paul, as president. Mechanic Street clerk Adalbert Mazur became vice president, saloon proprietor Theodore Walter, treasurer, and morocco finisher and meat dealer Valentine Meksa, financial secretary. Sycamore Street laborer John Rozycki and mill worker Vincent Michalak joined Wojtkowiak as director of the St. Joseph's Polish Catholic Church building committee, and Jacob Slomkowski served as recording secretary. Pepeta, Walter, Slomkowski, and several others moved to East Camden, forming St. Joseph's mission and holding a mass at Wright's Hall on Howell Street in 1892. The rest stayed to build St. Joseph's Church at Tenth and Liberty Streets.

Reverend Michael Baranski held St. Joseph's first mass in 1893, and a parish school opened at Tenth and Liberty in 1896. Community support services developed around the church. Mazur and Baranski organized the

Kosciuszko Building and Loan Association in 1896 and the Kazimir Pulaski Building and Loan Association in 1910, helping Polish American working families to purchase lots in the still undeveloped Liberty Park farmlands. Polish residents bought or rented between Ninth and Twelfth Streets below Kaighns, along Liberty, Mechanic, and Van Hook Streets, and on Thurman, Rose, and Louis Streets in the Liberty Park neighborhood of South Camden. Between Everett and Thurman Streets were founded the First Polish Baptist Church and the Polish National Catholic Church of the Resurrection of Christ. Some Polish shipyard workers moved to "Sweet Potato Hill," a farm being developed as part of Morgan Village by the New York Shipbuilding Company (founded on the South Camden riverfront in 1899).

ITALIAN AMERICANS

Destined to become the largest ethnic community in Camden County, Italian Americans formed urban neighborhoods gradually. The first Italians to cross the river from Philadelphia worked on the Philadelphia and Atlantic City Railway in 1876–77 and as berry pickers and farm labor in the extreme southeastern corner of the county. Italian Catholic priest Michael DiIelsi held mass for these rural Italians in 1886 at Laurel Springs and Berlin mission churches near the railroad stops on the Philadelphia and Atlantic City main line. Meanwhile, some railroad workers probably settled in Camden City between Third and Fourth Streets below Benson in the late 1870s and early 1880s, a section that had served as home for railroad employees since the 1840s. Fruit pickers, such as Antonio Mecca and Frank Errichetti, moved to Camden City to sell fruit from carts or stands. During the 1890s Italian grocers, barbers, bakers, junk dealers, and laborers joined the German Catholics between Third and Fifth Streets below Stevens. The Italian American community grew rapidly, forming the Sons of Italy, Dante Alghieri, Societa Cavalieri Di Colombo, and other civic clubs and organizations. Father DiIelsi traveled to the city from the lower county to hold mass at Third and Line Streets.

Father DiLesi organized the parish and school of Our Lady of Mount Carmel in 1903 at Fourth and Cherry Streets. Lay trustees included Mecca, now a liquor store proprietor, barber Thomas Auletto, junk dealer and liquor store owner Nicholas Viggiano, and druggists Giacinto Capuano,

Gennaro Grassi, and Francesco Travascia. South Fourth Street grocer Antonio Saponaro was the groom at the first wedding mass celebrated at Our Lady of Mount Carmel Roman Catholic Church, built at Fourth and Spruce Streets.

The founding of Mount Carmel Church stimulated formation of a vibrant South Fourth Street Italian neighborhood. Mecca opened a funeral home and real estate office at Fourth and Division Streets in 1906, organized the First Italian Republican Club, and joined Frank Viggiano and Joseph Lamaina in forming the Camden First Italian Building and Loan Association. Pine Street liquor merchant Antonio DiPaolo and junk dealer Louis Bantivoglio incorporated the Camden Italian-American Building and Loan Association and the First Italian Bank (which merged with the Victory Trust Company after World War I). Benjamin DiMedio organized the Camden Mill Works at Fourth and Divison. Rocco Palese, whose family established grocery and bottling businesses at the corner of Third and Spruce Streets and on Kaighns Avenue, became interpreter for the Camden County Court and probably the first Italian American attorney in Camden City. Another Italian enclave developed on Line Street between Second and Fourth, anchored by Rocco Fanelle and Sons junk dealers, Campanale's Grocery, the First Italian Baptist Mission, the South Camden Bocci Club, and the Camden Italian Bakery.

JEWISH AMERICANS

Camden County's first Jewish urban community evolved more slowly and was more poorly defined than the Irish, German, Polish, and Italian Catholic communities. Immigrants who came from different provinces of a country usually shared common cultural and national roots. The original Jewish American residents of Camden County, however, arrived from Poland, Germany, Austria-Hungary, Lithuania, Russia, and other places, and held only the Jewish religion and cultural traditions in common. Newly arrived Polish and Italian Catholics settled close to established and familiar Irish and German Catholic neighborhoods and created similar civic and social organizations, which made adjustment to American urban life easier. From the beginning, however, Camden County's first urban Jewish community lacked a central location and scattered here and there in South and East Camden.

Jewish immigrants from central and eastern Europe filtered into Camden County's most rural southeastern corner from New York City and migrated to Camden City from Philadelphia after 1880. During the late nineteenth century, Jewish shopkeepers, tailors, and shoe store proprietors of Russian, Lithuanian, Austro-Hungarian, and Polish ancestry lived and worked on Kaighns Avenue and Sycamore and Baring Streets. German-speaking Jewish families resided on Ferry, Newton, and Mount Ephraim Avenues and Broadway below Spruce Street, and managed dry goods, liquor, and clothing businesses there. By 1892 Camden Jewish residents operated (Shomra) Synagogue and "schul" on Liberty Street, Congregation Sons of Israel at Eighth and Sycamore Streets (just above Kaighns Avenue), the Hebrew Ladies Aid Society on Baring Street, and Congregation Ahavzedak at Fourth and Arch Streets. Camden City's Jewish pioneers purchased a Hebrew Burial Plot at the New Camden Cemetery on Mount Ephraim Avenue, consecrated it, and recorded their first burial in 1892.

Isidore Samuel Siris opened a dentistry office and Hyman Caplan a junk business on Newton Avenue, while scrap dealer David Levin, bottler Isaac Feldman, tailor Herman Budman, grocer David Rosen, and the Berman family located businesses on Baring Street, all prior to 1900. During the late nineteenth century Kaighns Avenue's Jewish community included dry goods merchants Solomon Goldstein, Otto Praissman, and Abraham, Morris, and Hyman Lichtenstein. The most successful Jewish businessmen located on Broadway. Dry goods merchants Joseph and Max Plotka and Abraham Feldman and Sons, jeweler Harry Nurock, and furniture store proprietors Abe and Nathan Fuhrman, Lewis Nelson, and Samuel Heine operated there. Heine's Imperial Home Furnishing Company advertised goods "from garret to cellar, head to foot, cash or credit."

Building supply dealer and realtor Isidor Green settled Jewish families in the Liberty Park section of South Camden along the east side of Mount Ephraim Avenue, offering building lots on "easy terms." At the same time, Meyer and Harry Teitelman developed a Jewish-owned real estate and contracting business at the corner of Mount Ephraim Avenue and Pear Street. Meyer Teitelman organized the Pleasant Hill Real Estate Company and advertised twenty-by-one-hundred-foot building lots for $75 each in Pleasant View Heights in the 300 block of Kaighns Avenue. The Teitelmans developed a network of businesses, including the Union Bottling Company with liquor dealer Joseph J. Weitzman and the Friendship

Building and Loan Association with junk dealers Morris Heine and Samuel Mackler. The Varbalow family, with roots in the rural Jewish agricultural community at Hammonton, Atlantic County, established a real estate business on Ferry Avenue. Building contractor Harry Varbalow and liquor dealer Kolman Goldstein formed the Guarantee Building and Loan Association (1886) and the Guarantee Realty and Guarantee Mortgage and Title Insurance companies. Hyman and Joseph Varbalow became partners in the Abraham E. Wessel and Sons shoe company.

The Varbalows and other South Camden Jewish families started to relocate to East Camden during the first decade of the twentieth century, settling on Federal Street between Twenty-fourth and Thirty-seventh Streets. The Hermann family left their tailor shops on Kaighns Avenue and clothing stores on Broadway for East Camden, where they helped establish the Beth Israel congregation at Twentieth and High Streets. Founders of the East Camden Jewish neighborhood included dry goods merchants Morris Tomar and Louis Kotlikoff and shoe store owner Adolph Newmeyer. Further east, toward Merchantville, Samuel Kotlikoff opened a dry goods store, Samuel Zeff a liquor store, and Edward P. Tomkins and his son a shoemaking business.

PARKSIDE

While a Jewish community formed in East Camden, a new generation of American-born Jewish professionals began to settle in the Parkside neighborhood. They included attorneys Benjamin Natal, Carl Kisselman, and Jacob L. Furer and realtors Nathan Obus, Morris Handle, and Raymond L. Siris. Located between the older South Camden Jewish neighborhoods and the more recent East Camden Jewish community, and linked in 1903 by the new Baird Avenue Bridge over Cooper's Creek, Parkside became Camden County's first truly diverse urban neighborhood. By 1915 it held every ethnic group, with the notable exception of Camden's African American community. Annexed as Camden City's Thirteenth Ward in 1913, Parkside contained middle- and upper-middle-class German, Irish, English, Polish, and Russian Americans residing in upscale brick row and single-family houses on streets carved out of the former Cooper plantation along Cooper's Creek (renamed Cooper River in 1911). (The former plantation house, Pomona Hall, is now home to the Camden County Historical Society.) Here, Protestants, Catholics, and Jews established a single urban neighborhood that was closely linked to the developing inner suburbs of East Camden and Pennsauken and the townships of Delaware, Haddon, and Gloucester.

The development of Parkside exemplified Camden County's turn-of-the-century experience in building urban neighborhoods. The Diocese of Newark purchased one of the first tracts north of Harleigh Cemetery along Haddon Avenue before 1900 to establish the Convent of the Order of Perpetual Rosary and, later, Our Lady of Lourdes Hospital. Local development started in earnest when a group of Irish Catholic and Protestant developers, including John M. Kelley, Patrick J. Farley, David Baird, and Cooper B. Hatch, incorporated the Parkside Land Company in 1901. Hatch's Fairview Brick Works and Hiram E. Budd's City Line Brick and Lumber Company provided building materials for the project, and the board of directors of Budd's company bought the first lots and built houses on Baird Avenue. David Baird's business partner T. Yorke Smith (director of the Broadway Mechanics and Trust Company and the Broadway Building and Loan and the North Camden Building and Loan associations), incorporated the Forest Hill Realty Company to develop the land between Baird and Park Avenues nearest Cooper River. Smith sold the property to the city to develop an athletic field, Camden High School (1916–18), and Forest Hill Park, a Progressive Era playground and forerunner of the Camden County park system.

Parkside developers promised buyers that city water, sewer, and traction lines would soon enter their Princess, Belleview, Kenwood, Wildwood, and Ormond Avenue neighborhoods and assured prospective homeowners that streets would soon be paved. Services developed slowly, however, and it took the incorporation of the Parkside Trust Company to improve the development. The company's directors included Alfred L. Sayers, Camden's street commissioner, William C. Coles, a lumber company president, Leon A. Goff, a patent medicine tycoon and developer of the Goff Building in downtown Camden, and Theodore T. Kausel, superintendent of the Castle Kid Company. Kausel, a German American, formed a real estate partnership with Teresa C. Walsh, an Irish American, and the firm of Kausel and Walsh promoted settlement of middle-class Irish, German, and Polish Americans in the neighborhood between Belleview and Haddon Avenues and along Princess Avenue.

Early Parkside German American residents included the Schoenroth, Valentine, Detweiler, Wendkos, Wenderoth, Nowyck, and Oberst families. The city's first Polish American attorney, Peter Stanislas Gulcz, moved from "Polaktown" in the Liberty Park section to Ormond Avenue, Parkside. Soon Jewish professionals Natal, Handle, Hechter, and Siris settled in Parkside. Anglo-American Protestant families located nearby as well, including William Sitley, manager of the grain elevator at Sixth and Chelton, and clerk William Cahill, father of the future Camden prosecutor and governor of New Jersey William T. Cahill (1970–74). Up-and-coming Camden County lawyers, such as Walter R. Carroll, and second-level political and economic leaders resided here as well. Among the latter were Arthur Armitage, the education secretary for the Camden Young Men's Christian Association, and later the founder of the College of South Jersey in Camden (now Rutgers University, Camden) and the mayor of Collingswood. Albert Austermuhl, secretary of the Camden City Board of Education, and Frank S. Albright, personal secretary to Camden City's Progressive Era reform-minded mayor, Charles Ellis, became Armitage's neighbors in Parkside. In the years ahead, this ethnically diverse middle- and upper-middle-class neighborhood provided leaders for the Greater Camden Movement that flourished with the county in the first decades of the twentieth century.

7

"GREATER CAMDEN'S GATEWAY TO NEW JERSEY"

THE GREATER CAMDEN MOVEMENT

The concept of Camden County as a single entity, encompassing waterfront city and rural suburb in a metropolitan community, developed during the last decade of the nineteenth century and through the middle decades of the twentieth century. Camden County's Progressive Era reformers, New Era businessmen, New Dealers, and World War II industrial and social planners promoted this vision, and groups of closely associated Camden City business and civic leaders joined Philadelphia and Camden County suburban real estate, trolley, and railroad developers to create the Greater Camden Movement.

In the process, they made Camden City into the cultural, economic, and business center of the county, and its population grew to well over 125,000 by the end of World War II. They connected the developing suburban municipalities to the urban waterfront by railroad, street railway, and an ever-improving system of paved automobile and motor bus roads. The Greater Camden Movement achieved its highest moment in 1926 with the dedication of the Delaware River Bridge between Philadelphia

5. The Greater Camden Movement's vision of a metropolitan Camden County road network connecting the riverfront cities with the suburban countryside. (Camden First, *June 1925. Camden County Historical Society Collection)*

and Camden (the present-day Benjamin Franklin Bridge). Shortly thereafter, however, the Great Depression undermined the Greater Camden Movement, and New Deal regional planners and returning prosperity during World War II never brought about complete recovery.

CAMDEN COUNTY PROGRESSIVES

Between the founding of Woodlynne Borough in 1901 and the opening of the Delaware River Bridge in 1926, a generation of local Progressive businessmen organized Camden County's urban landscape and built middle-class suburban communities. They were part of an early-twentieth-century national reform movement that developed in response to the dramatic social changes brought about by large-scale industrialization and the influx of millions of new Catholic and Jewish immigrants. Led for the most part by Protestant businessmen and professionals, the Progressive movement sought to create a stable, efficient, and prosperous middle-class society by reforming social, political, and economic institutions.

Camden County's Progressive Era industrial, business, and financial leaders exemplified the national movement. For instance, Theodore Thomas Kausel, a Merchantville businessman and member of the Camden City Planning Commission, advanced "Camden's progressiveness as a business city." Realtor Kausel put together an efficient organization to develop the Parkside neighborhood, including the Parkside Trust Company and the American Building and Loan Association. He was instrumental in Camden's annexation of Parkside as the city's Thirteenth Ward and in the efforts to improve municipal services there, working with Alfred Leon Sayers, who was Parkside Trust Company's president and Camden City's street commissioner and director of the Camden County Board of Chosen Freeholders.

Big businessmen, such as Eldridge Reeves Johnson, provided the economic framework to organize Camden County. Johnson made his Camden-based Victor Talking Machine Company into one of the world's largest producers of recording, radio, and motion picture machines, eventually merging in 1929 with the Radio Corporation of America. He used his wealth and economic position to advance the Greater Camden Movement, organizing citizens' committees for good government, a modern chamber of commerce, a community hotel, and the Delaware River Bridge. He also donated funds for public libraries, playgrounds, and civic improvements.

Camden businessman William Leonard Hurley more closely fit the middle-class image of the Progressive reformer. Hurley assumed sole ownership of the Gately and Hurley Department Store on Broadway and Pine in 1904, eventually developing an efficient system of smaller businesses along Broadway and a retail empire with seven department stores throughout New Jersey, Pennsylvania, and Delaware. Hurley organized the Endowment Building and Loan Association to finance middle-class homebuyers in the neighborhoods close to his stores. He joined Progressive Camden lumber merchants Volney G. and Killam E. Bennett and retail merchant George A. Munger to incorporate the Central Trust Company, advertised as "the most acceptable small bank known," catering to "women's accounts" for "a true and accurate" management of the middle-class Progressive household. They announced Saturday evening hours for workers unable to bank on weekdays.

As president of the Camden Board of Trade, Hurley proposed lower utility and trolley rates and promoted urban planning and the development of better automobile roads and bridges. Indeed, Hurley owned the first motorcar in Camden City and became the county's leading advocate for the construction of a system of good city streets and county roads. Hugh Morgan Hatch, Pennsauken Township's collector of taxes, supported better roads as well, because they aided business. Hatch and J. R. Mick formed the New Jersey Automobile and Supply Company, Camden County's exclusive agent in 1908 for Buick, Cadillac, Hupmobile, and Ford models. Other Camden County leaders joined the Progressive movement for personal advantage as well. Fourth Ward Republican party boss Benjamin F. Sweeten, Camden City Mayor Cooper B. Hatch, and Camden County Sheriff William Penn Corson supported road improvements to attract paving contracts for their construction companies.

John Martin Kelley formed one of the largest Progressive Era real estate, banking, and building and loan businesses in Camden County history. His business partners included other leading Irish Catholic Progressives, among them Hurley, Thomas O'Brien, and William C. A. Costello of Gloucester City. Costello and O'Brien were directors of the Bishop Bayley Building and Loan Association, the Catholic Lyceum, and the J. R.

Quigley Lumber, Mill Work and Builders Supply Company of Gloucester City. Between 1901 and 1926, Kelley, O'Brien, and Costello built middle-class housing in Camden City and Gloucester City and along the White Horse Pike suburbs, including Stratford. They constructed concrete slips, shipways, and piers in Gloucester City for the Pennsylvania and New Jersey Shipbuilding companies, which consolidated during World War I as the Pusey and Jones Shipbuilding Company. After the war, Kelley led the Greater Camden Movement in promoting a community hotel, a network of urban and suburban highways, and the Delaware River Bridge. Costello became secretary of the Delaware River Joint Bridge Commission. Meanwhile, Kelley built the entire Camden City conduit system for the Public Service Corporation, which in 1907 consolidated all southern New Jersey gas, utilities, and traction companies into a government-regulated system designed to improve efficiency and lower rates. Kelley also installed twenty-five miles of modern sewer systems in Oaklyn, Pennsauken, and East Camden to improve health in these neighborhoods.

World War I

World War I (1914–18) slowed the Greater Camden Movement's efforts to develop urban public playgrounds, better housing, improved schools and public services, and safer, more efficient trolley, rail, and automobile systems. Yet the war gave Camden County Progressives the organizational tools they needed to advance the Greater Camden concept. It led to centralization and consolidation of businesses and public institutions to meet production needs and to guide social organization. Government agencies and private businesses formed corporate partnerships. The U.S. government pressed J. B. Van Sciver to stop building furniture and employed the Van Sciver Corporation's Hainesport Mining and Transportation Company and his Knickerbocker Lime Company to supply sand, gravel, and concrete to build the Emergency Fleet Corporation shipyard across the Delaware River on Hog Island. The War Industries Board guided the conversion of the Victor Talking Machine Company to war production. Instead of making Victrola record players and records, the big Camden corporation reorganized and expanded to produce aircraft and rifle parts and other war goods. Federal war-contracting policy contributed to reorganization and expansion of Howland Crofts Sons and Company textiles, Farr and Bailey Oil Cloth Company, Esterbrook Pen, and Kind and Landesmann Edible Gelatine Manufacturing Company. Government contracts also led to the expansion of Camden Forge, which became the primary supplier for the warships built at the big New York Shipbuilding Corporation of South Camden and the Pusey and Jones Shipbuilding Corporation of Gloucester City.

The Emergency Fleet Corporation collaborated with the New York Shipbuilding and Pusey and Jones Shipbuilding companies to build housing for thousands of shipyard workers. The government and New York Shipbuilding purchased the Kelley-Smith tract and the Samuel Cooper farm from Kelley's Fairview Land Company and hired noted New York architect Electus D. Litchfield to plan Yorkship Village. Employing the British "garden city" concept, intended to relieve overcrowded industrial cities, Litchfield designed more than a thousand dwellings of brick and stucco around a concentric circle of streets that radiated out from a central square. He placed his garden village on the rich farmland that lay between the north and middle branches of Newton Creek below the city and west of Mount Ephraim Avenue in Haddon Township. "We did not expect to create a new Utopia," Litchfield explained, "but we did have to produce a community for the development of a true American citizenship."

Developers advertised "Yorkship Village: The Ideal Place to Live[,] Immediate Possession" and only a five-minute trolley ride "or hour stroll" to the shipbuilding plant at the confluence of Newton Creek and the Delaware River. Unable to maintain municipal services, Haddon Township ceded the wartime village (renamed Fairview) to Camden City in 1918, which annexed it (and the earlier Morgan Village development) as the Fourteenth Ward in 1919. Although less elaborate, the 145-acre Noreg Village, created by Norwegian shipbuilder Christoffer Hannevig below Gloucester City at the mouth of Big Timber Creek for his Pusey and Jones Shipbuilding Corporation employees, became the center of the borough of Brooklawn, incorporated in 1924.

During World War I, federal, state, and county governments established organizations in Camden County to raise money through the Liberty Loan Bond, Red Cross, War Saving Stamps, and other patriotic drives. They created local agencies to draft 16,268 Camden County men for military service, enroll volunteer women for war duty, and strictly ration scarce coal supplies and foodstuffs. Camden's mayor at the time, Charles H. Ellis (1905–23), appointed two hundred Camden businessmen to a Public Safety Committee in 1917 to safeguard property and ensure law and order.

The leaders of these wartime organizations embodied the Progressive Era ideals of the Greater Camden Movement. Andrew Blair Frazee Smith, for example, of the Smith-Austermuhl real estate and insurance firm, served as a coal-rationing commissioner. The great-grandson of Camden City neighborhood founder Richard Fetters and the son of Camden County Sheriff Richard F. Smith (1884–87), he attended the venerable Cooper School in North Camden, belonged to the elite Tavistock Country Club, and was a director of the Progressive-model Central Trust Company of Camden. Elmer Ellsworth Long served as Camden County chairman of the Liberty and Victory Loan and Red Cross committees. Long built the Munger and Long Department Store on Broadway and Federal, and held interests in the Hurley, Van Sciver, Bennett, and other business enterprises. He served as director of the Merchants' Trust Company and of the Stockton Building and Loan Association, and he developed the Camden Young Men's Christian Association to provide urban recreation and playground facilities.

THE WALT WHITMAN HOTEL

The end of World War I brought a period of demoralization to Camden County. A terrible influenza epidemic raged through the Delaware Valley in October 1918, killing hundreds each day. Hospitals filled to capacity, and the Haddon Avenue Armory became an emergency ward. Camden County schools and public places closed for a month. Meanwhile, the New York Shipbuilding Company and other firms laid off workers as the demand for war production stopped. Unemployment exacerbated growing social unrest, stimulated by a local red scare (part of a nationwide reaction to the Bolshevik Revolution of 1917 in Russia). Russian American Jews suffered arrest for their alleged participation in the violent protest against the doubling of trolley fares and the call for a general strike that rocked

Camden in late 1919. "This Bolshevist method cannot be tolerated here," Mayor Ellis declared, while Camden City Solicitor Edwin G. C. Bleakly wanted Russian-born agitators "shot first, and [sent] out of the country as corpses."

Camden County leaders turned instead to the type of crusade and fund-raising drive that had united the county behind the war, and they joined these efforts to the postwar Greater Camden Movement. The grand project to stimulate recovery and optimism included construction of a bridge between Camden and Philadelphia and a community hotel on the Camden side of the bridge entrance. The undertaking would require a countywide network of wide paved boulevards and highways, emanating from the bridge and leading east and south through the county's suburban communities to the Atlantic shore. The result would be "Greater Camden's Gateway to New Jersey."

The gateway idea appeared soon after World War I. In 1920 Eldridge Johnson, president of the Victor Talking Machine Company, offered to put up the first $100,000 for a hotel to house the newly organized Camden County Chamber of Commerce, for which he served as a director. Fellow director J. David Stern bought the Courier Publishing Company in 1919 to publicize and promote the Greater Camden hotel project. In 1924 the Camden County Chamber of Commerce incorporated the Community Hotel Corporation with an executive committee led by many of the leaders of the prewar Progressive business organizations. These included department store owners W. Leonard Hurley and George A. Munger, lumber merchant Volney G. Bennett, insurance and real estate agents Leon E. Todd (East Camden), David Baird Jr., and Charles W. Austermuhl, and Camden Lime Company executive Frank Hineline.

The Community Hotel Corporation used the principles (and leaders) that had guided Camden County during World War I in organizing fund-raising drives, local draft boards, and food- and coal-rationing programs. The community corporation formed neighborhood teams to collect $1.25 million in public subscriptions to build an eight-story brick and stone community hotel. To give the project a local identity, the Community Hotel Corporation named their building the Walt Whitman Hotel, after the Camden poet who had once called his adopted home "the city invincible." Every ethnic neighborhood fielded a Greater Camden campaign team for the hotel subscription. Attorney and Liberty Park realtor Peter S. Gulcz led the Polish American contingent. Meyer Wessel captained the Jewish team, and Antonio DiPaolo the Italian American campaigners. Dr. Clement T. Branch, the first black elected to the board of education, mobilized the African American community.

With the Greater Camden spirit fully engaged, the Community Hotel Corporation easily raised the necessary funds and secured a city ordinance to open New Broadway past the Walt Whitman Hotel from the courthouse on Market Street to the proposed bridge entrance. The corporation purchased and demolished the magnificent Hussong, Truscott, and Hanford mansions on Cooper Street, beginning the destruction of Camden's most historic and once wealthiest neighborhood. The Walt Whitman Hotel opened in 1925 just as the final stage of construction began on the 9,750-foot-long suspension bridge (from plaza to plaza) that would at last connect Philadelphia to Camden.

DELAWARE RIVER BRIDGE

The idea of a bridge between Philadelphia and Camden had agitated the county since the early nineteenth century, when Edward Sharp bought part of Windmill Island and developed Bridge Avenue. Sharp's scheme, and several others over the years that sought to build a bridge to Windmill Island in the middle of the river, failed. When the U.S. Army Corps of Engineers dredged the island at the end of the nineteenth century, dreams of an island bridge ended. In 1915 the Camden County Board of Chosen Freeholders, prompted by the Greater Camden Movement, authorized $5,000 to study the feasibility of a Delaware River bridge across the open river between the cities.

Innovations in the engineering of suspension bridges encouraged further study. Moreover, the inability of the ferry lines to handle the large number of Philadelphians coming to work in Camden's war industries during World War I demonstrated the urgency of building a bridge to Philadelphia. The postwar weekend motorcar excursionists who jammed the ferries from Philadelphia on their way to the Jersey seashore provided the final impetus for New Jersey and Pennsylvania to form a Joint Bridge

Commission and gain legislative funding for the bridge. Construction began in 1922 and eventually cost $40 million. The 1.82-mile-long span opened to motor traffic and pedestrians on 1 July 1926.

A New Era of Business

President Calvin Coolidge's dedication of the Delaware River Bridge ushered in a period of frenzied business expansion in Camden County. Greater Camden spokesman William Leonard Hurley introduced the Hurley Plan for a second bridge to connect Gloucester City to South Philadelphia. The local Republican party organization, led by David Baird Jr. and Elizabeth Croty Verga (former private secretary to Baird's father), endorsed the Coolidge administration's claims that America had entered a new era of business progress and prosperity. They announced that the county "should be able to erect an economic structure that will work a new era in [business and] governmental efficiency." Meanwhile, urban Progressives organized the Non-Partisan Commission Government League to change the old council form of city government to a five-member commission. At the same time, Camden real estate speculator J. Robley Tucker proclaimed a "New Era of real estate [and] unsurpassed opportunities for Investors, Developers, [and] Builders." Tucker arrived in the county without a dime in the early 1920s, persuaded the Camden banks to lend him money, and bought real estate in Camden City, in Voorhees and Delaware Townships, and at the entrance to the newly paved White Horse Pike. He became an instant millionaire.

Camden bankers encouraged metropolitan speculators like Tucker. Caught up in the New Era spirit, they formed larger firms and built magnificent stone bank buildings. In 1927 the First National State Bank of Camden merged with the Camden National Bank and erected the First Camden National Bank and Trust Company Building at Broadway and Cooper. The Central Trust Company combined with the Camden Safe Deposit Company and constructed the Bank of New Jersey on Broadway and Market, and the American National Bank erected a building at the corner of Broadway and Kaighns Avenue. They extended easy credit to Newton B. T. Roney for Camden County and Miami Beach, Florida, real estate ventures. Camden bankers loaned money to Walter E. Lorigan and

William L. Hurley for real estate development on Westfield Avenue. They provided capital for Burleigh B. Draper to speculate in Marlton Pike properties (made most desirable by the direct link to the Camden bridge), for Harvey K. Partridge to buy Parkside land, for Frederick S. Fox to purchase White Horse Pike properties, and for dozens of other local entrepreneurs.

Businesses rushed to invest in Camden County. The $1 million Stanley Movie Theatre opened in February 1926 at the corner of Broadway and Market Street. New York Mayor Jimmy Walker led the gala dedication ceremony. Realtors Louis Tarter and Meyer Weinberg developed the Lincoln Theatre at Seventh and Kaighn Avenue "exclusively for Negroes." The Woolworth Company built a large department store on Westfield Avenue in East Camden. In 1927, near the Camden Convention Center, Sears, Roebuck and Company opened a store on the concrete highway that ran directly to the Delaware River Bridge and connected the city to the suburban county along the planned tree-lined Cooper River parkway. Development of Camden's waterfront—with a new Reading Railroad terminal at the old Dialogue Shipyard property on Kaighn's Point, a municipal pier at the foot of Spruce Street, and a $2 million Camden Marine Terminal at the foot of Beckett Street—brought more business to the county. The Brown-Boveri Company purchased New York Shipbuilding Corporation and planned for expansion. The Garland Steamship Company and Quaker City Line opened maritime service directly from Camden to Pacific coast ports. Upriver, the Crew Levick Company, a subsidiary of Cities Service Oil Company, erected a tank farm, refinery, and tanker ship port on Petty's Island in Pennsauken Township.

Perhaps the most ambitious and successful enterprise was dedicated at the end of the decade. The Central Airport in Pennsauken stood at the intersection of Crescent Boulevard, Kaighns Avenue, and Bridge Boulevard.* Volney G. Bennett, J. Edward Fagen, Frank O. Stem, and other local aviation enthusiasts envisaged an airport in Camden to complement the opening of the Delaware River Bridge. Stem actually operated an airport on State Street in North Camden, from which he hoped to rush arriving mail, passengers, and packages across the bridge to Philadelphia with

---

*Bridge Boulevard was renamed Admiral Wilson Boulevard in 1929, after Camden native Henry Braid Wilson, who commanded the U.S. Navy Atlantic Squadron troop convoys during World War I without the loss of a single life.

his Camden Yellow Cab Company. The presence of tall factory chimneys that spewed smoke over the airfield prevented the establishment of a major airport in North Camden, however. Nicholas S. Ludington, president of Transcontinental Airways, and Haddonfield real estate entrepreneur J. William Markeim selected instead the flat open fields on the Pennsauken–Camden City boundary at the end of Admiral Wilson Boulevard to build an international airport. Ludington's Central Airport proved immensely profitable, even during the Great Depression. It received all local airmail deliveries, and at its peak in 1933 more than a hundred airplanes arrived daily, including transcontinental flights. Central Airport served as Philadelphia's international airport and airmail terminal until the opening of Philadelphia International Airport in 1940, and an autogiro airmail service linked Central Airport and the roof of the main post office in Philadelphia at Thirtieth and Market Streets.

Older county businesses also flourished during the New Era of business progressivism under Coolidge and, later, Herbert Hoover. The Victor Talking Machine Company expanded into the movie business, opening studios and producing some of the first "talking" motion pictures. Success led to a merger with the Radio Corporation of America in 1929, forming the RCA-Victor Corporation. The company stimulated development of a booming motion picture and theater industry in Camden County during the late 1920s. Joseph and Samuel Varbalow of East Camden and Philip Kalikman of Gloucester organized the Gloucester City Amusement Company, which managed the Walt Whitman Theatre on Westfield Avenue in Pennsauken and the Stanley Theatre on Broadway, the largest motion picture theater in the world. Camden's movie moguls—Louis, William, and Abraham J. Rovner and realtor Morris Handle—developed the Garden and Lyric theaters in Camden and the suburban Runnemede Theatre, among others. The local motion picture industry reached its peak in 1933, when the RCA-Victor Company produced automobile speakers for the innovative Automobile Drive-in Theatre, established by Camden chemical company magnate Richard M. Hollingshead on Admiral Wilson Boulevard at the Airport Circle.

Camden County government caught the New Era spirit as well, expanding the Greater Camden Movement to include development of a system of county highways, bridges, and public parks. The county opened

Crescent Boulevard (State Route 130) and other roads to connect with the network of state highways planned to move bridge traffic from Philadelphia through the county to the Jersey shore or north toward Trenton and New York City. The county also improved Browning Road, leading to the new Camden County Vocational School in Pennsauken, which opened in 1928. Newly paved and widened roads and new bridges connected the northern and eastern parts of the county to the expanding Lakeland Hospital complex near Blackwood and the Gloucester County border. Between 1926 and 1929 the county funded a new tuberculosis hospital, workhouse, almshouse, infirmary, power plant, isolation building, and nurses' quarters, and built an addition to the mental hospital. Still, county road builders frustrated Blackwood developer Frank Pine's dreams of completing the Black Horse Pike to the shore.

BERLIN BOROUGH

Dr. Frank Ott Stem, coroner of Camden County, physician in charge of the Camden County Insane Asylum (1921–40), director of the Camden County Almshouse and General Hospital at Lakeland, and mayor of Berlin Township (incorporated in 1910), had no trouble getting the roads he wanted. The county's most ambitious road-building project during the 1920s connected Berlin to Cedarbrook, Gibbsboro, Erial, Blackwood, and Haddonfield. Extension of the Haddonfield-Berlin Road and construction of new bridges over Timber Creek in 1927 became the county's most expensive projects during the New Era period. Development of Berlin's county road network coincided with Stem's incorporation of the Camden Yellow Cab Company, the American Auto Association of Southern New Jersey, and the Camden County Beverage Company (Camden Brewery) and his affiliation with the South Camden Trust Company and the creation of Berlin Borough in 1927.

A powerful county Republican leader, Stem pushed for creation of the new borough to persuade upper-middle-class and business folk to invest in his upscale neighborhood. Under township government, Stem's suburban neighborhood bore the tax burden for schools and public services for the surrounding area, which was populated by Italian and African

American working-class and poorer farmers. Creation of the new borough immediately attracted the attention of Greater Camden's urban middle-class leadership. A few days after incorporation, the borough received a county park site from the Camden County Park Commission (on which Stem served as a charter member and treasurer [1927–40]), making the remote borough an integral part of the Greater Camden and New Era development plans.*

CAMDEN COUNTY PARK COMMISSION

Camden County embraced the idea of a county park system as part of the Greater Camden Movement after World War I. Eldridge R. Johnson, E. David Stern, William L. Hurley, Volney Bennett, and other bridge, community hotel, and civic center organizers advanced the notion that county parks, picnic areas, and playgrounds would attract more convention business to the city. The county organized a park commission in 1926 and hired Bridge Boulevard architect and Camden City planner Charles W. Leavitt as consulting engineer to develop a countywide public park and playground system. The commission acquired land along the Cooper River in Camden City and Delaware Township, as well as Silver Lake, the Hopkins and Evans millponds, and swimming holes in Haddonfield Borough. The park commission developed Mountwell Park (1928), Berlin Park (1929), and Camden Park (1931), the latter adjacent to Farnham Park (formerly Forest Hill Park, renamed in 1921 in honor of city engineer Levi Farnham) and near Camden High School on Park Boulevard. County planners also acquired Gloucester City riverfront property and prepared to raze the historic Hugg's Tavern to make room for a public playground and swimming pool. Leavitt opposed the purchase of some of these sites because they simply enhanced the nearby property values of park commissioner Stem and state senator Joseph F. Wallworth and failed to meet the best interests of the Camden County public. The park commission therefore fired the brilliant engineer and so lost the vital support and

---

*Similarly, Greater Camden business leader Frank Middleton led the movement to separate the Haddonfield Country Club from the borough of Haddonfield, which banned alcohol and Sunday golf, transforming it into the Tavistock Country Club and the borough of Tavistock in 1921.

financial backing of his patron, Eldridge Johnson, president of the Victor Talking Machine Company.

Minor political controversies could not dampen the New Era–Greater Camden spirit, however, and celebrations of the county's historic heritage during the 1920s reflected that optimism. In 1923 Gloucester City celebrated the three hundredth anniversary of the first European settlement in the Delaware Valley at Fort Nassau. It was "the biggest affair of the kind ever held in South Jersey," claimed a local newspaper, with a riverfront banquet celebration for the governors of Delaware, Pennsylvania, and New Jersey. Not to be outdone, Camden City organized a centennial celebration in 1928. T. Yorke Smith, city commissioner of revenue and finance and a county park commissioner, requested that his Cooper Street neighbor Charles S. Boyer write a historical chronology of Camden City. Mill owner Boyer, president of the Camden County Historical Society, published *Span of a Century* in 1928 to commemorate the city's first hundred years. Meanwhile, Boyer, Smith, Bennett, Hurley, Draper, and other Greater Camden promoters organized the South Jersey Exposition at the Camden Convention Center on Haddon Avenue. An earlier commissioner of revenue and finance, Melbourne F. Middleton Jr., had purchased the inactive Camden Iron Works in 1925 for conversion to the Civic Center, planned by Charles Leavitt, and he sold the remainder of the site to Sears, Roebuck and Company. The exposition celebrated "the industrial and agricultural resources of intelligent, dependable house-owning labor to be had [in Camden County]."

THE DEPRESSION OF 1929

Such celebrations would shortly be obscured by dark economic times. The stock market collapse in October 1929 ushered in the worst depression in modern American history. At first, Camden County seemed unperturbed. "The fundamental basis of American business is sound and general business conditions throughout the country are good," announced Frederick L. Holman, president of the Merchantville Trust Company and the Republican mayor of that borough. Republican Congressman Charles A. Wolverton, a native of North Camden who moved to Merchantville in 1930, insisted that Camden County would not suffer the dislocation seen in other counties because it enjoyed a diverse economic base. The county had large agricultural, food processing, cigar making, shipbuilding, licorice, leather, textile, ink pen, radio, talking machine, and chemical industries, along with more than two hundred smaller businesses. Should one fail, others would pick up the slack and keep the county's 27,000 wage-earning residents fully employed.

BANKING COLLAPSE

The Camden Chamber of Commerce urged county residents to place their trust in local financial institutions, assuring them that "there has never been a bank failure in Camden's history." Nevertheless, Camden County banks failed, one by one, in every township, borough, and city. They had joined the boom in local and Florida real estate and the margin buying in the stock market that swept the nation during the New Era of American business. Camden banks readily lent money to realtors Roney, J. R. Tucker, and other speculators, all of whom went bankrupt when the market crashed. Even older, established real estate firms failed. Ephraim Tomlinson, secretary of the Camden Safe Deposit and Trust Company and president of the Camden Land and Improvement Company (founded in 1884), warned that the venerable real estate company had to take the best offer for its Market Street properties. Such an offer, "if one was forthcoming, could not be ignored owing to the urgent need for moneys to pay taxes in arrears on other properties belonging to the Company and in order to as promptly as possible get the Company out of its present difficulties."

Such failures reverberated throughout the county, stopping real estate investment in Delaware and Voorhees Townships, in White and Black Horse Pike communities, and in the city. Fading confidence forced a run on Camden County banks. County prosecutor Clifford Baldwin threatened to lock up anyone spreading rumors that a bank might close its doors. Small suburban banks seemed most susceptible to failure. The collapse of suburban real estate development, a declining tax base, unemployment, and bankrupt local governments dried up deposits. The First National Bank and Trust Company of Blackwood went into receivership. The Mount Ephraim National Bank, Haddon Heights Bank and Trust Company, Westmont National Bank, and Woodlynne National Bank all failed. Local residents defaulted on mortgages and lost their houses and properties. By

1930, 79 percent of the houses in the tiny Black Horse Pike neighborhood of Runnemede were vacant, and one developer committed suicide.

More affluent suburban towns confronted banking troubles as well. The Haddonfield Safe Deposit and Trust Company, the Merchantville Trust Company, and the First National Bank of Merchantville closed their doors. The Collingswood Trust Company failed "after a desperate scramble among the town's reputed money-men to save it." Camden City banks struggled too. Many shut their doors, reorganized, or combined with healthier banks. The West Jersey Trust Company absorbed the South Camden and the Victory Trust companies, and the Broadway Merchants Trust Company merged with the Camden Safe Deposit and Trust Company. When banks reopened, they followed the Hoover administration's policy of doing business only with financially sound investors or fully employed depositors. Camden banking customers were warned to give advance notice for withdrawals.

CAMDEN COUNTY EMERGENCY RELIEF ADMINISTRATION

The administration of Herbert Hoover expected state and local governments and private businesses to provide relief for the unemployed. Camden County tried, forming an Emergency Relief Administration to coordinate municipal relief directors in every borough and township. Municipalities opened food stations in firehouses and public buildings. Runnemede Borough set up a tent city for its dispossessed homeless. But local governments soon faltered in their efforts to assist the 40,741 Camden County residents on relief by June 1933. Unable to raise revenues, municipalities paid their employees in promissory notes known as scrip. In 1936 only six out of thirty-six Camden County municipalities met tax and relief obligations. The county took Bellmawr, Runnemede, and Laurel Springs Boroughs to court to collect back taxes, and the State of New Jersey placed Delaware and Voorhees Townships under the purview of the State Municipal Finance Commission.

The borough of Haddonfield slipped $2.4 million into debt, stores on King's Highway boarded up their windows, and junk littered the streets. Eventually, the borough's commissioner of revenue and finance, Alfred E. Driscoll (a future governor of New Jersey), refunded bonds, reduced interest on loans, and pulled Haddonfield out of financial chaos. Nearby

Pennsauken Township found a financial savior in its treasurer, W. Leslie Rogers, president of the Lesmer Insurance Agency. Rogers raised revenues by attracting real estate investors and expanding businesses, including Rundle (Sanitary Bathroom Ware) Manufacturing, Crew Levick Oil, and Kieckhefer (Fibreboard) Container, companies already established in the township before the Depression. Rogers thus developed the soundest corporate and residential tax base in the county. In Camden City, Freeholder George E. Brunner of the Fourteenth Ward organized a nonpartisan political coalition that would defeat the faltering Hoover Republicans in city government and reorganize city finances.

Nevertheless, local government simply could not deal with relief during the early 1930s, by default leaving much of the burden to voluntary organizations. The Wiley Mission Methodist Episcopal Church, for example, dispensed poor relief to Camden's unemployed "without regard to race, color, or creed." Social worker Mary Walsh Kobus (later elected to Camden City government with Brunner on a nonpartisan ticket) managed the *Courier-Post* relief fund, while the Gloucester City Amusement Company contributed half the proceeds from the Walt Whitman Theatre for unemployment relief. The Camden Diocese scheduled the first football game between Camden Catholic High School and Camden High School to raise money for the needy. Camden County business and civic leaders William J. Strandwitz (a South Camden manufacturer of wire-stitching [staples] machines), Walter Keown (a Haddonfield attorney), and Walter J. Staats (a Camden civil engineer) headed the Citizen's Relief Committee. The Freihofer Baking Company of Camden donated bread to the hungry.

Camden County retained faith in the Hoover administration's ability to overcome the Depression through limited federal intervention, county emergency relief agencies, and local voluntarism. During the presidential campaign of 1932, Camden County Republican leader David Baird Jr. warned that the Democratic candidate, Franklin D. Roosevelt, would interfere with local government if elected. Baird suggested that Camden County organize its own recovery, beginning by merging all local municipalities into the Greater Camden system to coordinate taxes, public services, and banking policies. Though the fiercely independent suburban communities balked at this idea, Camden County gave Hoover and the Republican party a seven-thousand-vote margin over Roosevelt. The suburban boroughs of Haddonfield, Collingswood, and Merchantville continued to vote against FDR in 1936, 1940, and 1944, although Camden City's dominant Democratic party eventually swung the county vote to Roosevelt and support for the New Deal.

THE NEW DEAL

The Depression gradually eroded the local Republican party machine, which had dominated local politics since the Civil War. Indeed, a political revolution of sorts occurred in the county's urban neighborhoods during the 1930s. Camden County Democratic party leader Edward J. Kelleher of Audubon, along with Brunner, Kobus, and a Nonpartisan/New Deal urban political coalition, organized female, Jewish, Italian, eastern European, and African American middle-class voters, particularly in South Camden's wards. The "New Deal Non-Partisan League" won a stunning election victory in 1935 over the entrenched North and East Camden Republican city machine, with Brunner and Kobus winning seats on the five-member city commission. Brunner used his position as director of the city's parks and playgrounds to secure money from the Roosevelt administration's massive federal program of social and economic relief and recovery, known as the first New Deal.

The New Deal made an immediate impact on Camden County. The Civil Works Administration (CWA) provided funds to hire unemployed county workers for development of the park system, while the Public Works Administration (PWA) gave the Delaware River Joint Commission an $11.9 million loan/grant to begin construction on a high-speed commuter rail line across the Camden-Philadelphia bridge. Work started in 1934, and the service opened for business in June 1936. At the same time, the Roosevelt administration declared a national bank holiday, which allowed the reorganization of local banks in Camden City, Clementon, Collingswood, Merchantville, Haddonfield, Haddon Heights, and elsewhere. In August 1933 the blue eagle of the National Recovery Administration (an agency later declared unconstitutional) appeared in the windows of five hundred Camden County businesses, signifying that they adhered to federal wage and price guidelines. Better still, the Roosevelt administration repealed Prohibition in 1933 and released from jail local bootleggers and violators of the ban on alcohol. On 7 December 1933, Camden City issued 197 saloon licenses. Although Gloucester City authorized Sunday liquor sales, Collingswood and Haddonfield upheld their antiliquor option of 1873, and the mayor of Woodlynne resigned after the borough council allowed liquor sales.

Despite some corruption, most notably in the CWA parks program, the New Deal improved the county's infrastructure. The Works Progress Administration (WPA) hired eleven thousand unemployed locals, spent $3.5 million rebuilding county roads and bridges, and put nearly $1 million more into public parks and playgrounds. The WPA constructed swimming pools in Gloucester City, Collingswood, Haddon Heights, Pennsauken, and South Camden. The one in the latter community, located at Ninth Street and Ferry Avenue in the "heart of a large portion of the City's colored population [and] graced only by shanties and rubbish," benefited "our Negroes." Cleanup of the Cooper River by the Civilian Conservation Corps (CCC), yet another New Deal agency, allowed the county to hold its first intercollegiate sculling (rowing) regatta in 1939, a tradition that continues to the present. Meanwhile, the PWA built the Lower Camden County Regional High School in Lindenwold, and the WPA constructed athletic fields and facilities for Collingswood High School, Audubon, and other suburban communities. The PWA spent $3 million on low-cost housing projects, including Westfield Acres for whites in East Camden and Branch Village "for Negroes" at Tenth and Van Hook in South Camden (named for Dr. Clement T. Branch, the first black to sit on the Camden Board of Education, in 1920).

SOCIAL CHANGE ON THE EVE OF WORLD WAR II

CAMDEN COUNTY'S ETHNIC GROUPS

Although the New Deal failed to pull Camden County completely out of economic depression, it contributed to some social advances for nonwhites, women, and the working class during the 1930s. Camden's eleven thousand urban blacks, who composed 10 percent of Camden City's population in 1930, had long remained a silent community in the face of ongoing discrimination and growing segregation. Patiently, Camden's African Americans organized religious, fraternal, and recreational facilities, including the Frances Harper Branch of the YWCA for "colored women" at 822 Kaighns Avenue. However, aggressive inclusion of the city's African Americans in Brunner's Non-Partisan/New Deal coalition revived the long silent minority and weaned many Camden blacks away from traditional allegiance to the party of Abraham Lincoln. The New Deal and the Brunner administration hired hundreds of African American city (and county) residents for the city's Department of Public Works and for the National Youth Agency, the WPA, and the CCC. Nearly half of the blacks on Saunders Street in East Camden, for instance, worked for the WPA.

Heuston Mincy, a laborer in the Philadelphia Navy Yard, helped to organize the Second Ward Colored Citizens Club in the small black urban enclave that formed around the Powell School at Tenth and Linden Streets, and the organization secured a "colored" playground at Eleventh and Linden. Walter L. Gordon, principal of the Mount Vernon (Colored) School and a resident of the East Camden black enclave bounded by Mitchell and Saunders Streets, helped obtain the Catto School playground at Thirtieth and Saunders. The Eighth Ward Colored Democratic Club organized black voters for Brunner and the New Deal in Camden City's oldest urban neighborhood, which surrounded the Charles Sumner (Colored) School at Eighth and Van Hook Streets. The black Democratic party organization in the Eighth Ward was instrumental in the development of a playground at the corner of Philip and Central, a pool and recreation facility at Ninth and Ferry, and Branch Village, the first low-cost housing project for city blacks financed by the federal government. In addition, the WPA established a warehouse in the neighborhood and hired several hundred Eighth Ward African Americans to work there.

Camden's first African American attorney, Robert Burk Johnson, physician Ulysses S. Wiggins, Reverend George E. Morris, stenographers Beatrice F. Morris and Wilda R. Townsend, and Reverend William J. Townsend, pastor of the Macedonia AME Church, organized the Colored Democratic Club and the Camden County Colored League for Good Government. Wiggins and Johnson sat on the Camden Board of Education and obtained playgrounds at Eighth and Chestnut Streets for the John Greenleaf Whittier (Colored) School and at Fifth and Mount Vernon for the Bergen (Colored) School. Lawnside native Dr. Howard W. Brown, a Howard University graduate with a degree in education from the University of Pennsylvania, served as a director of the Hunton Branch YMCA and principal of Whittier School (1919–46). Pine Street physician Howard E. Primas served on the Camden Housing Authority and secured government housing at the Chelton Terrace development for the African

American shipyard and war workers who flooded into Camden during World War II. In the suburbs, George H. Bennett organized black Republicans in support of Haddonfield attorney Alfred Driscoll for governor, while R. B. Johnson became solicitor for Lawnside, the black-governed neighborhood on the White Horse Pike (incorporated as a borough in 1926).

Camden County's ethnic urban neighborhoods became more active in county affairs during the Depression and New Deal, particularly in the organization of labor. Eastern European and Jewish American women constituted much of the workforce in the restless cigar and textile industries in South Camden, and the International Ladies Garment Workers Union local had its office at 621 Kaighns Avenue, the address as well for the Camden Talmud Torah School and the Federation of Jewish Charities. Camden's Jewish community expanded the YMHA and YWHA and built Beth-El Synagogue on Park Boulevard. Meanwhile, leaders of Camden's Jewish neighborhoods began to hold public office as well. Isadore Hermann headed the city tax and title bureau, Joseph Varbalow served as judge of the city district court, and Edward Praiss sat on the Camden County Park Commission.

Among Italian Americans in local government were attorney Anthony Marino, who served as freeholder from the Third Ward, and Ventorino Francesconi, who was elected freeholder from the Fourth Ward and became clerk of the Board of Tax Assessors. Camden Iron and Metal Company president Louis Bantivoglio represented Camden City's Fifth Ward.* Vincent Canzanese served on the city's alcohol beverage commission, and his brother Vincenzo worked for the Department of Public Works. Attorney Vincent Sarubbi became county clerk, and Rocco Fanelle was fire captain.

There were signs during the months before World War II that the city's Italian Americans might migrate to the suburbs. Grocer Peter Sarubbi, realtor Anthony Malatesta, South Jersey Bottling Company president Vito Moles, and attorney Rocco Palese formed the Italian American Building and Loan Association to sell properties in the urban fringe and suburbs. Palese and Moles took up residence in the exclusive Parkside neighborhood, and Joseph V. Bantivoglio moved across Cooper River to Baird

---

*Each city ward sent a representative to the unwieldy thirty-eight-member Camden County Board of Chosen Freeholders until it was reorganized in 1939 with seven members elected from the county at large.

Boulevard in East Camden. Meanwhile, other urban Italians looked for new homes along the White and Black Horse Pikes. Joseph Gaudio, who ran Gaudio Brothers wholesale produce stores on Kaighns Avenue and Broadway, moved to Haddon Township before World War II, and members of the Fanelle family began to relocate in Collingswood, Haddon Heights, Audubon, Bellmawr, and Stratford.

The Polish American community, for the most part, remained in the city. Arthur Bruno Strenski arrived as parish priest in 1934 to revitalize "Polaktown," building St. Joseph's High School. Bronislaw Piontkowski took over J. Lukens Anderson Real Estate Company and sold and rented three thousand houses to Polish American families in the city and Mount Ephraim suburbs, offering financing through the Jan Sobieski Building and Loan Association and the Mount Ephraim National Bank. On the eve of World War II, the Polish neighborhood in the Thirteenth Ward elected truck driver Anthony Budniak to the Camden County Board of Chosen Freeholders. Funeral director Stanley Ciechanowski represented the Seventh Ward, and Dr. Henry Wisniewski sat on the Camden Board of Education.

WOMEN

The New Deal era also saw a more active role for women in Camden County politics. Mary D. Guthridge of Mount Vernon Street served as the first woman on the Camden County Board of Chosen Freeholders, representing the Seventh Ward of Camden City. Also from the Seventh Ward, Martha Kemble, a justice of the peace and deputy director of public works, filled out the term of Frank B. Hanna as city commissioner in 1934. In May 1935, as part of the Brunner nonpartisan coalition, Mary Kobus became the first woman elected as a city commissioner, and she also served as director of public safety. The first female graduate of South Jersey Law School in Camden (now Rutgers Camden Law School), Kobus directed the women's division of the Camden County Red Cross during World War I and served as Camden City's movie censor and president of the Camden Board of Education, among other posts.

President Franklin D. Roosevelt appointed Emma E. Hyland as the first female postmaster in Camden City in 1934. Hyland had headed the Camden County Women's Democratic Club and county organization since

1923. Dr. Jennie S. Sharp, cofounder of the Young Women's Christian Association in Camden (1905), served as president of the Camden Board of Education and head of Cooper Hospital's gynecological department. Other Camden County women directed municipal relief committees during the Depression in Barrington, Haddon Township, Magnolia, Pine Hill, and Somerdale, and they served as principals of twenty-six of Camden City's forty-four schools (following the tradition of Clara S. Burrough, the first principal of Camden High School, 1918–32).

Labor Unrest

The New Deal stimulated Camden County labor activism. A conservative collection of craft unions had maintained a tranquil and docile workforce, to the extent that the Camden Chamber of Commerce could boast in 1929 that the county had never suffered a long strike. But economic depression and unemployment, combined with growing agitation by socialists and more radical union organizers from the Congress of Industrial Organizations (CIO), unleashed the most violent decade of labor unrest in Camden County history. Female employees of the Congress Cigar Company at Ninth and Liberty Streets went out on strike in 1933, causing riotous conditions in South Camden. John Green organized the Camden local of the Industrial Union of Marine and Shipbuilding Workers of America and unionized New York Shipbuilding Corporation, leading to a three-month strike in 1935. The United Cannery, Agricultural, Packing and Allied Workers Union organized a strike among 1,500 of nearly 4,000 workers at the Campbell Soup Company in 1934. A strike and bomb blast at Davis and Copewood Streets rocked the Radio Condenser Company (founded at Third and Federal Streets in 1919 by Russell E. Cramer Jr.). The United Electrical Radio and Machine Workers closed down RCA-Victor Corporation, which employed 6,700 men and 2,000 women, for a month during the summer of 1936. Union picketers around the big RCA plant, characterized as anarchists and communists by the local press, were attacked by strikebreakers and city police. Intervention by Labor Secretary Frances Perkins, the first woman to hold a Cabinet post, led to arbitration by the National Labor Relations Board.

The intensity of the local labor agitation arose in part from the failure of the New Deal to pull the county out of economic depression. It took American rearmament in the face of Japanese, German, and Italian aggression throughout the world between 1937 and 1940 to restore full employment in Camden County. Shortly after the Japanese invasion of China in 1937, the Roosevelt administration began a naval expansion program that brought warship contracts to New York Shipbuilding Corporation in South Camden. The assignment of the 35,000-ton "Battleship X" (the *South Dakota*) contract to the local yard in 1938 ended the Great Depression in Camden County.

8

"DETERIORATION IN THE LIFE AND BUSINESS OF THE CITY"

WORLD WAR II

Battleship X marked the first of twenty-five major naval contracts acquired by the New York Shipbuilding Corporation during World War II. Employment at the big South Camden works peaked at 33,000, including 3,000 female welders. Camden Forge received a $3 million government defense grant to retool so that it could provide forgings for warships, while RCA-Victor obtained top-secret contracts to develop radar, sonar, and proximity fuses. The Camden County Vocational School in Pennsauken, once closed during the Depression, now instituted a War Training Program to prepare county residents to work in the expanding local defense industries. Central Airport, closed in 1940, reopened as a naval aviation training center. In early 1941 the federal government spent $1.5 million to build five hundred units of defense housing for shipyard workers on the Black Horse Pike in Audubon. Called Audubon Village, the project was incorporated as a borough after the war by the Audubon Mutual Housing Corporation, with all residents becoming members of the corporation rather than owning individual houses.

The attack on Pearl Harbor in December 1941 mobilized county de-

fense operations. In the months following, every city ward, suburban borough, and township set up air raid watch stations and held blackout drills.
Camden County organized the Civilian Defense Council to conduct air
raid drills, war bond campaigns, and salvage drives, which collected scarce
materials such as rubber tires and scrap iron. The Camden City District
Council even dug up the old iron trolley rails that had been paved over by
WPA workers after the last streetcar ride in 1937. The county also divided
itself into draft board districts to contribute manpower to the war effort.

The Office of Price Administration (OPA) opened headquarters in
Camden under the direction of Voorhees Township insurance agent
Harry F. Roye, a former administrator in the New Deal National Youth
Agency. OPA organized the county into seven district rationing boards to
monitor the use of scarce foodstuffs, gasoline, scrap metal, and war matériel. District Board No. 1 regulated rationing in Camden City and Woodlynne, No. 2 in Merchantville and Pennsauken, No. 3 in Haddonfield,
Delaware Township, Lawnside, Magnolia, Tavistock, Hi-Nella, and Somerdale, No. 4 in Collingswood and Haddon Township, No. 5 in Gloucester
City, Brooklawn, Mount Ephraim, Bellmawr, and Runnemede Boroughs
and Gloucester Township, No. 6 in Audubon, Haddon Heights, Oaklyn,
and Barrington, and No. 7 in Berlin, Winslow, and the most remote southeastern sections of the county. OPA rigorously enforced gas, food, and
critical materials rationing, although Vineland automobile dealer Eugene
Mori received a special exemption in 1942 to build the Garden State Race
Track in Delaware Township to entertain shipyard and war workers.

New workers, including women, Caribbean blacks, and Hispanics,
flooded into Camden County to fill jobs in the labor-starved war industries.
African Americans from southern states formed the single largest group of
newcomers during the war. They swelled Camden City's African American population from 12,478 in 1940 to 17,434 by the end of the war, increasing the percentage of black residents from 10.6 to 14 percent of the
total Camden County urban population. Black war workers settled largely
in the Eighth Ward, where the total population increased from 7,297 to
8,423 between 1940 and 1950. Newcomers also settled in the Thirteenth
Ward, where the population rose from 15,311 to 16,344 during the war,
and in the Fourteenth Ward, which saw an increase from 9,094 to 10,781.
The greatest wartime urban population growth occurred in East Camden,
where many new workers were employed by the shipbuilding companies

Penn-Jersey, R.T.C., and Mathis Yacht. Population in the Eleventh Ward grew from 13,727 to 15,083 and in the Twelfth Ward from 11,506 to 16,733 during the decade.

Meanwhile, neighboring Pennsauken Township expanded from 17,745 to 22,767 residents, as many white workers relocated there during the war and the black influx into Camden City. Similarly, nearby rural Delaware Township doubled its population during World War II, from 5,811 to 10,358. Many of the 30,000 workers at the New York Shipbuilding Corporation of Camden and the 50,000 at the huge Philadelphia Navy Yard across the river began to seek housing in White and Black Horse Pike towns as well. Bellmawr, site of the government-subsidized Bellmawr Park and Crescent Park housing projects, grew from a sleepy horse farm community of 1,250 to a booming residential neighborhood of 5,213 suburban dwellers. The population of nearby Haddon Township increased from 9,708 to 12,379, Oaklyn from 3,869 to 4,449, and Audubon, with the government defense housing project of Audubon Park, from 8,906 to 9,531. Down the Black Horse Pike, war workers settled in Mount Ephraim, increasing the population of that historic farming community from 2,282 to 4,449, and Runnemede grew from 2,835 to 4,217 residents during the war.

POSTWAR OPTIMISM

Camden City emerged from World War II stronger than ever, as the war appeared to bring full economic recovery from the Great Depression. Urban riverfront industries expanded, created new jobs, and brought thousands of newcomers to spend money in the city. New Jersey and Pennsylvania established a joint Delaware River Port Authority in 1950, and New Jersey Governor Alfred Driscoll of Haddonfield predicted that it would be the "preface to the greatest expansion this area has ever known." Indeed, Camden City reached its greatest population during the war and immediate postwar decade, peaking at 125,000 urban residents by 1950. Together, the citizens of Camden and Gloucester Cities made up more than one-third of the county's total population of nearly 300,000.

Camden County residents continued to come to the riverfront city, as they had for generations, for entertainment, shopping, and banking. They attended movies at the Stanley, Towers, and Savar Theatres in center city and live shows at the Walt Whitman Theatre on Westfield Avenue. They shopped at Hurley's Department Store downtown and bought "original torpedo rolls, Italian sliced Bread, Happy Pal Bread, and Cornell 'Hi-Protein' Bread" from Mighty Good Baking Company at Fourth and Walnut in South Camden. "At the end of the war, and for a few years afterward, Camden was the center of everything," recalled Joseph M. Nardi Jr., the son of a South Camden Italian American shoemaker. Sadly, two decades later Nardi was Camden's mayor when the city experienced the riots of 1971.

Following World War II, Camden County's big industries converted to peacetime production. Campbell Soup Company prospered, becoming the world's leading producer of condensed soup (at its plant on Second and Market Streets) and canned pork and beans (at its Delaware Avenue and Cooper Street factory). MacAndrew and Forbes of South Camden made 90 percent of the world's licorice products. Kind and Knox of North Camden continued as the sole American maker of "bone gelatin" products. RCA moved into the mass production of televisions and developed electronic warfare systems for missiles as the postwar United States became locked in a cold war struggle with the Soviet Union. The Radio Condenser Company expanded its postwar workforce to provide condensers for "TV tuners" and to fill cold war defense contracts. The cold war led to the recovery of the New York Shipbuilding Corporation, which had suffered a postwar slowdown and extensive layoffs. In the late 1950s the South Camden shipyard secured contracts to build the *Kitty Hawk,* one of a new postwar class of attack aircraft carrier, and the *Savannah,* the world's first nuclear-powered cargo ship.

The enthusiastic eightieth anniversary celebration of the founding of the Camden Chamber of Commerce, held in the ballroom of the Walt Whitman Hotel in downtown Camden in 1953, epitomized the postwar optimism. The organizers gave distinguished public service awards to Harry W. Pierce, president of the New York Shipbuilding Corporation, Ralph W. E. Donges, justice of the New Jersey Superior Court, and Dr. Lewis L. Coriell, director of the Camden Municipal Hospital. That same year, Coriell founded the Coriell Institute for Medical Research in Camden, soon the world's largest repository of living human cells for research. William Zeckendorf, president of Webbe and Knapp Real Estate of New York City, gave a keynote address. Zeckendorf had just completed a multimillion-dollar deal to convert the defunct Central Airport in Pennsauken into "the largest shopping project in the nation."

THE POSTWAR CRISIS GROWS

In 1958, five years after its gala anniversary celebration, the Camden Chamber of Commerce honored Edward L. Teale, current president of the New York Shipbuilding Corporation, at the new Cherry Hill Inn in suburban Delaware Township rather than at the increasingly seedy Walt Whitman Hotel. Camden City's leading hotel showed signs of urban decay that symbolized, in many ways, the larger problems that lay beneath the surface of apparent postwar economic recovery.

Despite war-induced prosperity and industrial expansion, the urban center suffered deep-rooted problems that stemmed from its rapid, largely uncontrolled industrial growth during the late nineteenth and early twentieth centuries. Large factories, railroad lines, and commercial streets choked with shops and stores mixed with crowded working-class neighborhoods that had formed along narrow streets, and all were jammed against the river on less than ten square miles of land. Nearly every inch of Camden's urban residential and industrial real estate had been developed, and much of it was already decaying from years of neglect during the Depression and World War II. Meanwhile, industrial and residential waste fouled the city's water and air, corroding metal and eating away at bricks, mortar, and wood. The water supply was so rusty in East Camden that residents could not use it.

Although the city had acquired federal housing projects during war, returning soldiers found overcrowded older row houses, particularly in the working-class central and southern sections of the city to the west of Haddon and Mount Ephraim Avenues and extending to the riverfront. Public services seemed totally inadequate to deal with a larger, more ethnically diverse postwar population that included an increasing number of blacks and the first Hispanic migrants. Already juvenile delinquency and youth unrest plagued the city, some of it racially motivated. In the first years after the war, youth gangs smashed windows along Broadway and Kaighns Avenue and vandalized public and private properties. Shopkeepers recognized that the city was becoming a less and less desirable place to do business.

There were other signs of the city's declining role as the center of county life. In 1952, facing a $1.4 million annual deficit, the 114-year-old Philadelphia and Camden Ferry (founded in 1836 by John W. Mickle) closed. Those travelers who still chose the ferry after the dedication of the Delaware River Bridge in 1926 now no longer entered the city to cross to Philadelphia on the ferryboats *Haddonfield* and *Millville.* Work on a second bridge, linking South Philadelphia to Gloucester City, started in 1953, and the Walt Whitman Bridge opened in 1957. The new bridge bracketed the city with the older span located three miles upriver, renamed the Benjamin Franklin Bridge in 1955. Together, they rushed people past, rather than through, both urban business sections. The Hurley's store and the Stanley and Towers Theatres felt the impact and closed their doors between 1956 and 1958. Other center city merchants saw that the future lay in rural Delaware Township, which had undergone a real estate and business boom during the war and had been rezoned to attract industrial development. Even the *Camden Courier-Post,* which had operated in the city since 1875, left its overcrowded and unsafe plant, moving its presses to Delaware Township in 1956.

George E. Brunner's Postwar New Deal

Suburban leaders warmly supported the second Delaware River bridge because it would open Gloucester Township and the lower county to development. Yet the urban Democratic machine that opposed the bridge still exerted tremendous influence in county politics. George E. Brunner, Camden City's mayor from 1936 to 1958, led the county's urban political coalition and Democratic party organization. With its large population and well-financed party organization, the city continued to dominate elections and policies during the immediate postwar period. Brunner opposed policies that benefited the rising suburban communities, where the Republican party dominated. He decried expensive county road development and warned that the second span over the Delaware River would be "a jacket of steel" that would completely isolate Gloucester and Camden

Cities from the rest of the county. Brunner favored instead a massive urban public works project to build a tunnel under the river and city.

Brunner approached postwar problems with the same New Deal–type programs that had revived the city during the Depression. For instance, Brunner had secured the support of women voters in 1935 through a temporary political alliance with Mary Walsh Kobus. Now he appointed Marguerite C. Rudderow to the city's postwar food committee and Jane Stretch, editor and part owner of the *Courier-Post,* to a Citizen's Study Committee on "slum clearance and rehabilitation." Mostly, Brunner confronted a growing urban crisis, as he had the Depression, by seeking massive federal relief programs and public works for Camden City, similar to Roosevelt Plaza, which had been built in front of City Hall in 1936 with New Deal funds and labor. Brunner's postwar New Deal–inspired public works project was the creation of a center city parkade (parking garage and shopping mall) to be located near Roosevelt Plaza.

Brunner expected the parkade to revive downtown businesses by providing a thousand parking spaces. "It represents what Franklin Roosevelt called the joy of achievement in creative effort," Brunner announced. Brunner and New Jersey Governor Robert Meyner dedicated the parkade in 1955. The mayor proclaimed that it added a "new and brilliant chapter to the history of Camden." But Robert J. Kiesling, president of the Camden Trust Company, noted that the project had not really solved the parking problem that caused the "deterioration, which is now taking place in the life and business of the city." Kiesling urged the formation of a municipal parking authority in 1958 to organize the chaotic automobile situation in the city.

Mayor Brunner next appealed for aid to the administration of Harry S Truman, which announced an updated New Deal program, called the Fair Deal, and the GI Bill to assist returning veterans with housing and education. Under Federal Housing Authority (FHA) policies, the local government had to show that an area was blighted before it could receive federal aid. So the Brunner regime condemned entire neighborhoods and started bulldozing properties to demonstrate the existence of urban blight. Unfortunately, federal funds to rebuild these razed properties—many of them in the traditionally black neighborhoods of the Eighth Ward in South Camden—never arrived because applicants failed to meet FHA guidelines, leaving strips of empty lots. (Meanwhile, the FHA encouraged loans to suburban housebuyers.) Camden's African American leader, Dr. Ulysses S. Wiggins, the head of the Camden branch of the National Association for the Advancement of Colored People (NAACP) and recently appointed as the first black physician to the staff of Cooper Hospital, severely criticized the Brunner urban renewal project. Wiggins alleged that the administration practiced a form of segregation by razing ethnically mixed neighborhoods (black, Polish, Russian, Irish) and forcing blacks to cluster in planned federal housing projects.

ULYSSES S. WIGGINS FIGHTS BACK

Dr. Wiggins decided to run for city commission in 1951. He had the support of a rising black middle class, including Reverend David M. Harmon, named bishop of the Union African Methodist Church in 1951, Reverend Charles S. Lee of the Kaighns Avenue Baptist Church, and his wife Edith Lee, a director of the "Colored" YWCA on Kaighns Avenue. He received encouragement from black schoolteachers Rachel C. McNeill of Mount Vernon School and Walter L. Gordon, principal of the Charles Sumner School and treasurer of the Camden NAACP, and from YWCA physician Bascom S. Waugh. Behind the scenes, Camden's first black prosecutor, Robert Burk Johnson, the Worshipful Master of the Oriental Lodge, Free and Accepted Masons, provided the support of that influential black fraternal and Masonic order. In the end, Wiggins made a vigorous, but unsuccessful, attempt to win election as the first black to sit on the Camden City Commission. Some black leaders believed that planned urban renewal projects, which would destroy African American religious, fraternal, business, social, and political organizations and structures along Kaighn, Ferry and Central Avenues, were really attempts to undermine the black political power base in these South Camden neighborhoods, where support for Wiggins had been so strong.

Finally, North Camden and Cramer Hill residents, unhappy with rusty water, crumbling streets, and continued neglect, organized a movement in 1958 to recall Brunner. These largely Republican wards blamed the Democratic urban machine for deliberately ignoring their concerns. Although the recall failed, discontented city Republicans found a leader in local war hero and East Camden lawyer Alfred R. Pierce, the city school board's solicitor. Pierce formed Citizens to Save Our City, building a new political coalition "to do something to prevent [Camden] from becoming a dead city." Save Our City embraced the predominently black, Italian, Jewish, and Hispanic voters of North and East Camden, who had been ignored by Brunner over the years as his power base became increasingly isolated in the Fairview section of the city.

THE HISPANIC COMMUNITY

Pierce actively courted Hispanic voters for the first time in Camden history. Camden County's Hispanic heritage can be traced back to the early nineteenth century, when the Esther Nunes family arrived from a Spanish-speaking community in Florida and settled for a short time on the Camden Town waterfront. More immediate roots lay in the arrival in 1928 of the Cuban–Puerto Rican American Mario Rodriguez family to work in the cigar factory. Camden's Hispanic community experienced its first large influx of residents during World War II, when labor-starved local industries recruited women, blacks, Jews, and Caribbean laborers to fill wartime jobs or to work in South Jersey farm fields. Campbell Soup Company, in particular, hired Puerto Rican laborers.

After the war, many Puerto Ricans decided to stay in Camden, working for the DiPaolo Coat Factory and other Italian American–owned businesses. Farm workers, too, moved into the city for jobs. Some rented apartments along Stevens and Berkeley Streets, forming by 1947 the first identifiable Spanish-speaking neighborhood in Camden. Other Puerto Ricans, employed by the Campbell Soup Company, rented rooms in North Camden houses owned by Irish, English, or German families.

Camden County's Hispanic community continued to grow during the 1950s. The Diocese of Camden recognized the increasing importance of the Spanish-speaking residents, establishing Our Lady of Fatima parish in South Camden in 1953 to provide pastoral care. Nevertheless, the Brunner government ignored Hispanics. In 1958 the Save Our City candidate for city commission, Frank C. Italiano, an attorney whose family once worked with Puerto Ricans at the DiPaolo Coat Factory, urged Pierce to court the Hispanic vote. They met with Victor Montes, president of the Spanish Civic Club, Juan Rios, president of the Puerto Rican Association, and fifty other Spanish-speaking residents of the city. Cuban–Puerto Rican attorney Joseph Rodriguez provided liaison. The Hispanic representatives voiced their concerns over the lack of bilingual education and of Spanish-speaking police officers, teachers, and city officials.

SAVE OUR CITY

Hispanic support contributed to the 1959 election victory of the Pierce-Italiano ticket, which unseated the Brunner organization that had controlled city government for twenty-three years. The only Save Our City candidate who failed to win a seat on the five-member commission was Isadore Borstein, a city electrical supply company executive, but Pierce appointed him as city business administrator. Pierce quickly launched a charter reform movement, securing a change in the form of Camden City government in 1961 from the Progressive/New Deal commission system to a mayor and seven-member council organization, thereby broadening the voter base. City voters elected Pierce mayor and returned every one of Pierce's Save Our City coalition to city council.

The composition of the first city council reflected the ethnic diversity of Camden's urban neighborhoods as they existed in 1961. Elijah Perry, a jazz vocalist with the Lionel Hampton band and an accountant with a degree from the University of Pennsylvania's Wharton School of Business, became the first black elected to Camden City government and the first black chairman of the city's Democratic party organization. Pierce also appointed black civic leader J. Allen Nimmo as his director of civil defense and disaster control. Michael J. Piarulli and Andrew A. Corea represented the large Italian American constituency, Matthew R. Casper the Polish American section of Liberty Park, and Harry A. Kerr the city's still influential Jewish community. Elizabeth B. Hawk spoke for the rapidly fading Irish American urban community and Mario R. Rodriguez for the rising Hispanic interests.

Pierce saw the election of 1961 as a mandate to save the city from further disintegration by stimulating private investment in the development of a North Camden shopping and business center, an industrial park at Kaighn's Point in South Camden, and a "City within a City" project for the East Camden waterfront. He envisioned creating in downtown Camden

City an urban version of the new Cherry Hill Mall that opened in Delaware Township in 1961. Pierce's blueprint (which won the American Institute of Planners award in 1966 for the best urban renewal concept in America) called for shopping plazas, high-rise apartments, and a high-speed federal highway through the center of town. It also proposed an expanded cultural and educational center around the Rutgers University campus in North Camden.

There were some initial successes, particularly in North Camden, where the Pierce administration secured the Northgate high-rise apartments and the expansion of nearby Rutgers University's Camden Campus of Arts and Sciences and Law School. However, such progress uprooted older Irish, German, and English residents and more recent Hispanic families from North Camden.

In the end, Pierce's approach to urban renewal differed little from that of the discredited Brunner Democratic organization. Like the New Deal mayor, Pierce sought to level entire neighborhoods. To make way for downtown urban renewal and multilane highways, he also destroyed the elevated railroad trestles and bridges known as the Chinese Wall (for the massive earth-filled brownstone structures built between 1902 and 1908, which reminded observers of the Great Wall of China). Driven by the spirit of the John F. Kennedy New Frontier and Lyndon B. Johnson Great Society national programs, the Pierce administration's plans proved more grandiose even than Brunner's. Pierce had designs to renew North and East Camden, center city, Kaighns Avenue, Centerville, and Liberty Park, and he secured a federal highway through the city.

East Camden's residents, however, blocked the "City within a City" project with lawsuits to prevent the razing of blighted brick row houses, factories, and buildings in their neighborhoods. When private developer Jerry Wolman, owner of the Philadelphia Eagles football team, went bankrupt, the East Camden waterfront project died. Meanwhile, the center city demolition forced out the vibrant Greek American community from its Mickle Boulevard properties to make room for parking lots. The dispossessed community quickly relocated to Cherry Hill, where it built St. Thomas Greek Orthodox Church and Hellenic cultural and educational facilities.

The most devastating destruction of a traditional Camden residential and business neighborhood during the 1960s occurred in South Camden along Kaighns, Ferry, and Central Avenues and Kossuth Street. Between 1960 and 1968 the Centerville–Liberty Park urban renewal project removed more than a thousand families, or 8 percent, of the entire urban population. Although mostly African American families were affected, the destruction also displaced Polish, Russian, German, Lithuanian, and Jewish working-class families, shopkeepers, and small businesses. Those who could afford to leave went to the suburbs or urban fringes. Middle-class blacks relocated to nearby Whitman Park and Parkside or more distant East Camden and Pennsauken, where several historic black enclaves had existed for more than a century. This movement contributed, at least in part, to Jewish evacuation of Parkside and South Camden for suburban Delaware Township (Cherry Hill), Pennsauken, Merchantville, and White and Black Horse Pike towns. For a time, the Polish American community in Whitman Park resisted pressure to move, heeding the call of their revered parish priest, Monsignor Arthur B. Strenski, to stay in the city. Meanwhile, the Camden Housing Authority relocated poorer African American and Polish American families, unable to afford suburban property, to rental apartments in Parkside and other neighborhoods, accelerating the flight of middle-class whites and blacks from these urban communities. The Federal Housing Authority refused to lend mortgage money for poorer families, regarding most of Camden City as an area of unacceptably high risk.

Pride in Camden

Disillusionment with Pierce's urban renewal and relocation policies brought about the return of an old-style New Deal administration in 1969. Camden's Democratic party boss, Angelo J. Errichetti, a former city purchasing agent and director of public works, and his handpicked mayoral candidate, Joseph M. Nardi Jr., a former assistant Camden County prosecutor, led the Pride in Camden movement. Nardi promised to restore urban neighborhood pride and reverse the flight of white families and business from the city.

The 75 percent decline in manufacturing jobs—from 43,267 in 1950 to 13,500 by 1980—had contributed to the exodus. The situation became most urgent in 1967, when Camden City's second largest employer

(10,000) and tax base, New York Shipbuilding Corporation, plagued by poor management that was interested in relocating to the South and by mounting environmental problems, closed its doors. Almost at once, white middle-class people and businesses started to leave, accelerating the gradual movement that had begun shortly after World War II. Camden County's urban population declined, falling from 117,000 in 1960 to 102,551 in 1970. At the same time, the number of black and Hispanic residents seeking jobs with Campbell Soup Company and other city firms increased. Hispanics constituted more than 6 percent of the population in 1970 and reached well over 20 percent by 1980; the black proportion rose from more than 23 percent in 1960 to 39 percent by 1970.

Meanwhile, urban renewal failed to attract new business or stop the exodus of whites from the city. Jobs continued to disappear, and the lower-income residents who remained in the city slipped into poverty. Property values continued to fall every year after 1960. Camden was rapidly becoming one of the poorest, most racially polarized cities in the United States. The city housing authority admitted that 51.6 percent of Camden City housing was unfit for habitation, boarded up, in abysmally poor condition, or overcrowded.

Nevertheless, Nardi had reasons for optimism. He received the support of Hispanic leaders Joseph and Mario Rodriguez, African American councilman Elijah Perry and political newcomer Melvin R. Primas, Polish American city council president Daniel Ciechanowski, and the still-effective Irish and Italian urban Democratic party organizations. He appointed J. A. Nimmo as director of the City Health and Welfare Department, a new agency created at the national level by President Lyndon B. Johnson's Great Society program. Nardi selected Arnold Cream, an African American former heavyweight boxing champion (known as Jersey Joe Walcott), as the city's director of community relations.

Unfortunately for Nardi, nationwide social and political revolutions, including the Vietnam war protests and the feminist and Black Power movements, convulsed his administration from the beginning. Demands for full participation in Camden government came from "black nationalist freedom fighter" Charles A. "Poppy" Sharp, founder of the Black Believers of Knowledge (1967) and the Black People's Unity Movement (BPUM) and an unsuccessful candidate for a seat on city council in 1968 on the Peace and Freedom party ticket. Antiwar priests Samuel Appel and

Michael J. Doyle befriended the Black People's Unity Movement, and activist Hispanic leaders Hector Rodriguez and Angel Perez voiced the growing unrest in that community.

The moderate middle-class black, Hispanic, and white leadership seemed threatened by the radicals. Nardi relied on a tough ex-Marine police chief, Harold E. Melleby, to keep law and order. He used veteran schoolteacher Josiah C. Conwell, the black principal of Camden High School (who had once spanked Poppy Sharp in a Mount Vernon School class for "incorrigible boys"), to suppress student unrest and prevent sit-ins such as the one in May 1968 that shut down the local high school. To enforce peace in the school system, Camden hired imposing former Camden High School and professional black athletes William Smothers (later Camden High School's head basketball coach), Reggie Hammond, and Frank Stewart to secure the school. Nardi also expected veteran City Councilman Perry to calm the African American community in the city, appointing the U.S. Army veteran as director of the Department of Community Relations. Likewise, the Nardi administration relied on moderate Hispanic leaders, such as Camden County's first Hispanic attorney, Joseph Rodriguez, to keep the lid on younger Puerto Ricans, who chafed at the lack of city services and jobs for the fastest-growing ethnic group in the city.

RIOT OF 1971

Nardi inherited a revolution already simmering in the city. It stemmed, in part, from an August 1967 speech at the Camden Convention Center by H. Rap Brown, chairman of the Student Non-Violent Coordinating Committee and leading Black Power advocate. Brown prevented moderate Camden County NAACP and Congress of Racial Equality leaders from speaking and stirred the crowd of primarily young black activists to defend itself with guns against the "Hunkies" (white establishment) and "Uncle Tom's" (black moderates who served the white power establishment). After the inflammatory speech, blacks surged into the streets. Though kept in check by a massive display of police force, bands of restless youth broke windows along Broadway and Kaighns Avenue. More ominously, blacks destroyed white-owned corner grocery and variety stores in Central and South Camden.

It would be four years before Camden City burned in riots, but already shopkeepers along Haddon, Kaighns, and Mount Ephraim Avenues and Broadway reported constant vandalism. Many boarded up for good after 1967 and began the exodus to the suburbs. Meanwhile, older white residents in Parkside, who sought to live in harmony with middle-class black residents and formed a number of interracial religious and educational organizations, reported increasing destruction of property and growing neglect by city government in their once quiet and well-maintained neighborhood. Violence against white students at Camden High School in Parkside during a sit-in in May 1968 was the final straw for most remaining white families. Nearly a thousand black students demanded more black teachers, athletic coaches, and courses in black history and culture. The following October, 330 of the 700 white students enrolled in the deteriorating fifty-year-old Camden High School did not return to classes, many reportedly attending the county's newer Catholic high schools and schools in Cherry Hill, Collingswood, and Pennsauken.

The summer of 1969 saw periodic violence in Camden City. Civil disturbances rocked a twenty-block section of Camden surrounding the corner of Seventh Street and Newton Avenue, where, allegedly, white police officers had molested black girls. At the same time, snipers killed a white policeman and a black girl, and a black householder killed two white police officers. It took the arrest and fatal beating of Puerto Rican motorist Horacio Jimenez by Camden City police officers during the summer of 1971, though, to unleash the most destructive riots in Camden County history.

The violence started in late August 1971, when city police tried to break up a nonviolent, predominantly Hispanic crowd that had marched with their children to City Hall to protest the treatment of the Puerto Rican motorist and to demand suspension of the police officers. Trapped, the crowd panicked and, joined by more militant marchers, began to smash windows and loot stores along Federal Street, Broadway, and Mickle Boulevard. Black activist Sharp put on a black armband and led the BPUM into the streets. "We support the Puerto Rican community because we too have been victims of police brutality," he announced. Reportedly, black activists armed Puerto Ricans. Several days of rioting followed. Hispanic neighborhoods in North and Central Camden burned down, including El Centro, the Puerto Rican social services agency. Ironically,

Hispanic leaders blamed "young black people" for the arson and looting, and accused the city police of contributing to the arson and violence. Only the Hispanic youths Jose Molina and Manuel Nieves suffered serious gunshot wounds.

During the rioting, antiwar demonstrators broke in to the Camden Federal Building on Market Street on 23 August to raid the local draft board records as a protest against the seemingly never-ending war in Vietnam. Jesuit priests and Catholic draft resisters from Massachusetts and New York led the twenty-eight protestors. However, Camden residents played a critical role in the Camden 28 antiwar movement. Michael J. Giocondo, an unsuccessful city council candidate who was employed by the city drug abuse program, Lutheran minister Milo M. Billman, a member of the Camden Community Development Council, and Reverend Michael J. Doyle of Sacred Heart Church in South Camden participated in the break-in and protest. Doyle, particularly, opposed the use of federal money to fight an imperialistic war in Vietnam rather than the war on poverty at home in cities such as Camden. Long after the others had left, Doyle continued to fight for the poor and dispossessed in his South Camden parish. Meanwhile, antiwar protestors closed down the campus of Rutgers University in North Camden for a short time.

FINAL FLIGHT TO THE SUBURBS

The riots of 1971 marked a watershed for Camden County's urban industrial center, culminating a quarter century of economic and social decline. The final migration of whites and businesses from the city began. At the same time, blacks, Hispanics, and Asian Americans (mostly Vietnamese driven from Saigon when the Americans pulled out in 1975) remained in the city. By 1980, nonwhites composed 75 percent of Camden City's population. The Jewish community left first, followed closely by Irish and Italian Americans. Hispanics moved into abandoned Irish and Italian neighborhoods, churches, and stores. A small Polish American community remained in South Camden around St. Joseph's parish, but St. Joseph's High School, founded by Monsignor Strenski in 1951, closed, and other Polish American organizations disappeared from the city, only to be revived in the suburbs. Several white Euro-American neighborhoods remained in East

Camden as well, although these too began to fade during the 1970s. Businesses followed. The closing of Lit Brothers in 1975 started the final exodus, until not a single department store or large grocery or shop remained in downtown Camden.

For a time, the traditional urban political leadership resisted change. Democratic city boss Errichetti, a tough former Camden High School football star, became mayor in 1973 and tried to put the city of his Italian ancestors back together. He formed the familiar New Deal–type Democratic coalition of blacks (Melvin "Randy" Primas Jr. and Golden Sunkett Sr.), female (Helen McHugh), Italian (Joseph DiRenzo), Polish (Daniel Ciechanowski), and Hispanic (Felix Montes) council members. Errichetti showed signs of turning the city around, securing a transportation terminal, urban renewal funds, waterfront development, and promise of a veterans' hospital. But indictment and imprisonment for bribery and corruption shot down his rising star in 1981. His fall also meant, in many ways, the end of the city's political domination of Camden County. Never again would the city be the center of county politics.

However, Errichetti's political coalition continued to run Camden City through Primas, elected the first black mayor in 1981. Primas came from an old Camden family that had resided in East and Central Camden for generations. His uncle, Theodore L. Primas, was the first black Camden deputy chief of police. Randy Primas envisioned leading the city to recovery. He placed in a positive light the years of urban renewal that had torn down hundreds of buildings, claiming that it opened up the city to new development. "We are a city that is not land poor," he insisted. He hoped to develop the waterfront and a "Gateway North" access to the waterfront. However, Primas inherited a $5 million budget deficit, the product of fiscal mismanagement and a declining tax base, and he was forced to increase taxes, further hindering recovery. The State of New Jersey began to monitor the city's budget process, a pattern that recurred for the next twenty years, until the state took over city finances in 2000.

Primas left in 1990 to work for New Jersey Governor James Florio's administration, and the city's Democratic machine selected African American councilman Aaron Thompson to fill out the term. Elected mayor in 1990, Thompson tried to revive the city, but the lifelong Centerville resident was overwhelmed by the problems. The city machine dumped Thompson in 1993 in favor of school board president Arnold W. Webster, who promised "Hope, Change, and Responsibility." He continued the Cooper Plaza historic district, central business district, and waterfront developments begun earlier, but he struggled for power with the Hispanic community, the Delaware River Port Authority, and the county government. Eventually, opposition from the Hispanic community, led by city council president Milton Milan, along with Webster's indictment for misuse of school board funds, ended his career. Meanwhile, Milan capped a remarkable rise from the streets of North Camden to become the first Hispanic mayor in Camden County in 1998. Like his predecessors, Milan promised to improve life for city residents, demolish drug-infested buildings, clean up refuse, and build new housing. In hopes of solving the money problem, Milan assumed direct control over the city's finances.

Milan confronted a diverse and changing urban population. His own Hispanic community, which now composed 40 percent of the city, fragmented into feuding Puerto Rican political groups while Dominicans, Nicaraguans, and other Spanish-speaking peoples arrived in increasing numbers. Dominicans operated at least a hundred corner grocery stores (bodegas) in the city. The Vietnamese population continued to grow, and Cambodians, Koreans, and other Asian Americans added to the ethnic mix—and ultimately to problems in governing such a diverse set of neighborhoods. Moreover, like Errichetti and Webster, Milan was saddled with an indictment in 2000, and convicted for corruption. By this time, though, the future of the county seemed to lie not in the city that once served as the center of its life, politics, and economy but in the dramatic growth of its last suburbs—Cherry Hill, Gloucester, and Voorhees Townships.

9

"There Is No Dearth of Open Land in the County"

Postwar Vacant Land

At the end of World War II, Camden County's riverfront cities and urban fringe communities contained little vacant land. Yet, more than half of the entire county remained undeveloped, primarily rural Delaware, Voorhees, and Gloucester Townships. In 1957 farmland and vacant lots still dominated 60 percent of Delaware Township (renamed Cherry Hill in 1962). "There is no dearth of open land in the County for purposes of development and most of the vacant lands are suitable for development," observed county planner John D. Tomaselli. Some postwar commercial and residential enterprises had taken root in these townships and "spread out from this core along the highways toward the South-eastern end of the County," Tomaselli added, but "they fade away due to lack of urbanization."

Delaware and Voorhees Townships, on Camden County's easternmost border with Burlington County, and Gloucester Township, along the central border with Gloucester County, were dotted with horse and cattle farms, fruit orchards, and villages that had changed little over the past century. Here, unlike other areas, the railroad had made slight impact on development. A Camden and Atlantic branch line served Delaware Township for a few years, and the main line touched a corner of Voorhees Township, but neither stimulated suburban growth. The Philadelphia and Reading's Atlantic City main line and its Gloucester branch line, which passed through parts of Gloucester Township, had led to the establishment of only a few isolated suburban neighborhoods. Clusters of single-family dwellings lay along narrow country roads, some paved and straightened as recently as the decade before World War II. There were few stores, businesses, or industries to provide a tax base to support schools and public utilities and services. The lumber, glassmaking, marl, and dairy industries that once dominated these townships had faded long ago, and the Lucas paint works, the only large industry in the county's last developed suburbs, lay in the borough of Gibbsboro, which separated from Voorhees Township in 1924.

Over the next fifty years, however, this last open space became the county's most populous, ethnically diverse, and affluent section. Between 1950 and the end of the century, Delaware/Cherry Hill Township grew from 10,000 people to more than 70,000, Gloucester Township from 8,000 to 54,000, and Voorhees from 1,800 to 25,000. Major businesses and industries moved into the region, building commercial and industrial parks. Shopping malls and strip shopping centers dotted the residential neighborhoods. The value of taxable properties here far surpassed that of the rest of the county. Cherry Hill ranked first, Gloucester Township second, and Voorhees fourth (behind sprawling industrialized Pennsauken Township). By the end of the twentieth century, these last suburbs had become the economic and political centers of an emerging Camden County middle-class metropolitan region. At the same time, the increasingly impoverished Camden City, the county's former center, steadily declined. Its population fell from 125,000 in 1950 to less than 87,000 by the 1990s, as businesses and the white middle class left for good.

DELAWARE/CHERRY HILL TOWNSHIP

The development of these last suburbs reflected, in many ways, Camden County's entire history. The emergence of Delaware/Cherry Hill Township as the county's leading political and economic section by the 1970s best exemplifies this historical process. Delaware Township separated from

Waterford Township and was incorporated in 1844, just a month before the state legislature created Camden County itself. The original township boundaries extended from the Delaware River southeast to present-day Evesham Road, which once led from the Clementon glassworks to the Burlington County line, and from Cooper Creek to the south branch of Pennsauken Creek. A few years later Delaware Township annexed Petty's Island, in the Delaware River just off the entrance to Cooper's Creek. Later, in 1859, the island and northern part of the township became part of Stockton Township.

In 1844 Delaware Township encompassed some of the best farmland, tidal creek pastures, and timbered forests in the newly formed Camden County. Ancestors and kin of the first tidewater planter elite families owned most of the farms, orchards, and saw and gristmills, and they provided the leadership to create the new township. Samuel T. Coles, Joseph W. Lippincott, and Joseph A. Burrough sat on the first township committee. Josiah Ellis served as judge of elections, and Joseph H. Ellis as township surveyor. William E. Matlack and Job Coles oversaw the highways, including the King's Highway, which ran from Haddonfield through the township to Moorestown (Burlington County), and Cooper's Landing Road (the Marlton Pike [Route 70]), running from the Cooper's Ferry landing eastward through the township to Marlton in Burlington County. George Haines was overseer of the poor, and Joseph Ellis and Jonathan Fetters served as pound keepers for stray animals. In 1844 Benjamin W. Cooper, Joseph Stafford, and Joseph A. Burrough sat on the school committee to manage the one-room schoolhouse located at the crossroads of the two main highways in Delaware Township. Dr. Richard M. Cooper set up practice as a physician, and Joseph Kay Jr. represented the township on the Camden County Board of Chosen Freeholders and in the New Jersey State Assembly. These men and their families dominated Delaware Township's and Camden County's social, political, and economic life.

ELLISBURG

The Simeon Ellis family founded the first hamlet in the community at the end of the seventeenth century. A county road surveyor, Ellis knew that the Board of Justices and Freeholders planned to extend the Salem Road to Burlington, crossing the head of Cooper's Creek, and build a highway from Pyne Poynt to the fast land at the head of the south branch of Pennsauken Creek. Ellis therefore bought four hundred acres of prime woodland where the proposed routes would cross, and near a large Lenape village. The Kay, Matlack, Burrough, and Cooper families also purchased large tracts of land in the vicinity, cleared pastures, and built brick and frame plantation houses and saw and gristmills. Ellis's crossroads property became the center of the Ellisburg community. Cattle dealers, farmers, and timber merchants brought their products to the Ellisburg market. Stables, a blacksmith shop, tavern, inn, and tiny schoolhouse grew up around the neighborhood. When these local planter elite formed Delaware Township in 1844, Ellisburg naturally served as the seat of township government, which met in the schoolhouse or inn.

Elsewhere in Delaware Township, clusters of houses formed around sawmills, gristmills, taverns, or churches in a pattern characteristic of the development of rural nineteenth-century Camden County. Although none of these places achieved the importance of Ellisburg, several contributed to early township history. North of Ellisburg, near the King's Highway as it approached the Burlington County border, the Rudderow family and other former Quakers organized a meeting in 1703 and eventually built St. Mary's Protestant Episcopal Church (circa 1751) on the plantation lands originally owned by pioneer settler Samuel Coles. Several houses, a sawmill, fulling mill, and inn (located on Crooked Lane) clustered near the church and a burying ground that was incorporated in 1858 as the nonsectarian Colestown Cemetery. Colestown remained little more than the church and burying ground until after the Civil War, when the discovery of mineral-rich sulfur waters in a nearby millpond led to creation of a small resort community around the Fountain Hotel.

Southeast of Ellisburg, local planter William Bates operated the Blazing Rag Tavern, reputedly a favorite hangout during the Revolutionary War variously for British and patriot troops and later a watering spot for less temperate Haddonfield residents, who crossed Cooper's Creek to carouse in Batesville. As available Haddonfield property disappeared, newcomers settled along both sides of the creek, where Bates had laid out lots. By the mid-nineteenth century, Batesville boasted an inn, blacksmith shop, wheelwright shop, general store, and several large frame residences along the road from Haddonfield to Longacoming (Berlin), where it met the Milford Road (Kresson Road). This dirt highway led to Matthias Simmerman's

Milford Glass Works, founded in 1838, but by 1844 called Lippincott, Wisham and Company, manufacturers of hollow glassware.

Scattered plantations dominated nineteenth-century Delaware Township. Wealthy farmers christened their home places with names that later became prominent in twentieth-century Cherry Hill schools, roads, housing developments, and subdivisions. In the nineteenth century Abraham Browning owned Cherry Hill Farm, namesake for the township, while Benjamin Cooper built Locustwood Farm. Joseph O. Cuthbert and then Jacob Lippincott ran Deer Park Farm, founded originally in the eighteenth century by Samuel C. Davis as a fenced hunting preserve. Brookfield Farm was the Nicholson property, and Cooperfield Farm the Cooper and Kaighn holdings. Samuel M. Heulings owned Murrell Farm and Joseph Hinchman the Pleasant Valley Farm. Aquilla Hillman operated Locust Hill Farm, Joseph H. Coles the New Orchard Farm, Hannah D. and William T. Lippincott the Thorndale Farm, and the Burrough family the Cedar Grove and Woodland Farms. Edward Winslow Coffin, the son of glass baron and railroad entrepreneur William Coffin, owned Hickory Hill Farm at Coffin's Corner (near Ashland) on the southwestern boundary of Delaware Township.

THE PHILADELPHIA, MARLTON AND MEDFORD RAILROAD

Elwood Evans, owner of the three-hundred-acre Locust Grove Farm, envied the location of Coffin's Hickory Hill Farm in western Delaware Township, near the Camden and Atlantic railroad tracks. Evans lived in the remote eastern portion of the township and felt isolated from Coffin's bustling business community in the western part of the county. Evans had a difficult time bringing his prize Jersey cattle, milk, grain, and timber to Camden City and Philadephia markets along the often muddy and impassable Marlton Turnpike. Coffin's father had helped to secure the Camden and Atlantic Railroad stop in Haddonfield in 1853. This line turned south on the other side of Cooper's Creek, bringing passengers and goods to Longacoming, to the glassworks in the lower county, and, by 1854, to the planned resort town of Atlantic City on the Jersey shore. The possibility of building an expensive railroad line through the wilderness of Delaware Township appeared remote, especially because conservative farmers opposed the passage of the dirty, noisy machines across their meadows. In the late 1870s, however, the Camden and Atlantic desired a rail connection to the Pennsylvania Railroad's Amboy Division station in Medford, Burlington County. Evans's long-cherished wish finally coincided with the Camden and Atlantic's need to develop a branch line.

Evans discussed with Camden and Atlantic executive John Lucas the construction of a line from the railroad's stop in Haddonfield across Delaware Township to Burlington County. Lucas owned the Gibbsboro White Lead, Zinc and Color Works, located a few miles below Evans's farm, and would benefit from any railroad expansion in the neighborhood. Lucas and Evans thus helped to organize the Philadelphia, Marlton and Medford Railroad Company. As incorporators of the new company, they included Camden and Atlantic directors and real estate entrepreneurs Enoch A. Doughty, George T. DaCosta, and Charles D. Freeman, along with Edmund E. Read, a Camden City banker and Lucas business partner. Meanwhile, Evans mobilized Delaware Township farmers to support the railroad. Connected by marriage to the Cooper, Lippincott, Haines, Matlack, and other Camden and Burlington County planter elites, Evans interested these local farmers in the railroad project, particularly Benjamin W. Cooper, the largest landowner. Evans and Lucas promised to run the railroad near their farms, with stations located conveniently for shipping agricultural products to Haddonfield, Camden, and across the Delaware River to Philadelphia. After some problems financing the line, Evans used his personal fortune to ready the Philadelphia, Marlton and Medford Railroad for business in 1881. As promised, the railroad boasted five stations between Haddonfield and Marlton for the Delaware Township farmers: Freeman Station on the Haddonfield-Berlin Road, Orchard Station on the Milford (Kresson) Road, Springdale Station on White Horse Road, Evans's own Locust Grove Station at his farm, and Cropwell Station on the Marlton Pike, where it crossed the south branch of Pennsauken Creek into Burlington County.

THE FIRST BUILDING BOOM

The Philadelphia, Marlton and Medford Railroad carried mostly local passengers and farm products between Haddonfield, Marlton, and Medford until the end of World War I, when improvements to the Marlton Pike and other township roadways and bridges allowed easier automobile, bus, and truck travel. South Jersey historian Alfred Heston, writing in the

1920s, found Delaware Township "entirely lacking in railroad facilities" (although the Pennsylvania Railroad operated a passenger service until 1927 and did not close the line officially until 1931). Heston reported that the inauguration of a bus service on the Marlton Pike promised that the "opening up for suburban development cannot be long delayed." Dedication of the Camden-Philadelphia bridge and boulevard in 1926, which rushed automobile traffic directly to the Marlton Pike (Route 70) and the Kaighns Avenue extension (Route 38) in Delaware Township, increased interest in the creation of a commuter suburb. Indeed, real estate speculator J. Robley Tucker and suburban real estate entrepreneurs Earl R. Lippincott, Henry Howard Chew, Horace Roberts (of the Barlow [Real Estate] Development Company), and Patrick McPhelin bought large tracts of Delaware Township land, laid out lots and streets, and put in curb stones and cement sidewalks.

Lippincott, Chew, and other entrepreneurs developed Haddonfield Estates, Erlton (named for Earl R. Lippincott), Colwick (Coles family), Barlow, and East Merchantville neighborhoods of single-family dwellings and enjoyed brisk sales of their building lots. The children of newcomers filled existing Delaware Township schools. The Still School, in the black enclave of Matchtown (Homesteadville) on the township's northern border with Pennsauken, became so overcrowded that students were relocated to a portable building at the Hinchman School. The township built the Wesley R. Stafford School on the Haddonfield-Berlin Road in 1925 to serve the new Haddon Towne and Brookmeade housing developments. In 1927 the township built the J. Huelings Coles school for the Colwick neighborhood, and the following year the Sharp family donated an acre of land for construction of the Joseph D. Sharp School for the Old Orchard residential development on Marlkress Road.

The Great Depression hit Delaware Township particularly hard because much of the growth (as on the stock market) had been based on speculation, loans, and long-term mortgages; when one part collapsed, the entire structure fell apart. Unemployed homeowners failed to meet mortgage payments and lost their homes. Few newcomers bought property in the township. Many projects remained little more than concrete sidewalks wandering through weed-choked building lots. During the 1930s, Delaware Township's population grew by only 1 percent, from 5,734 in 1930 to 5,811 in 1940. The township went bankrupt, paid its salaries and taxes in scrip, and surrendered government to the state Municipal Finance Commission. The state's takeover provided some improvements, particularly the construction of local roads (Springdale, Evesham, Mill, and Hampton Roads), but even these apparent benefits had their cost. The widening of the Marlton Pike as State Route 40 (later Route 70) and the construction of the Ellisburg traffic circle in the early 1930s leveled the historic schoolhouse, store, and tavern.

GARDEN STATE RACE TRACK

World War II brought recovery and expansion to Delaware Township. By the end of the 1940s, the population had doubled, from 5,811 at the beginning of the decade to 10,358 by the end. Township Committeemen John L. Vossen, the director of real estate, and Harry L. Cranmer, the director of revenue and finance and commander of the township defense council, reorganized finances and promoted development. Their efforts released Delaware Township from state control by 1942. Vossen foreclosed on hundreds of acres of undeveloped, tax delinquent land that had been bought up during the speculative boom of the 1920s and left vacant during the Depression. The township sold the property during the 1940s to the workers who crowded into the booming wartime industrial centers of Camden, Philadelphia, and Gloucester City and then decided to move their families to the fresh air and open spaces in the suburbs during and immediately after the war.

Meanwhile, New Jersey State Senator Bruce Allen Wallace (a resident of Colwick and a member of the Delaware River Bridge Commission) contributed to the effort to lift state restrictions against gambling and horse racing. The state had banned horse racing in 1850, when Delaware Township residents feared that a syndicate of Philadelphia, Camden City, and Cape May gamblers planned to build a sporting club and racetrack at Bloomfield Cottage Farm (near the present-day junction of Routes 38 and 70 on Browning Road). Removal of the ban allowed automobile dealer, banker, and racetrack entrepreneur Eugene V. Mori of Vineland to build the Garden State Race Track on land foreclosed by the township committee. Receiving special exemptions to use rationed materials and gasoline during the war, Mori rushed the racetrack to completion and opened for business in June 1942.

The Garden State Race Track provided a tax base and brought thousands of prospective suburban dwellers to the township each race day. Although the greatest suburban expansion would not come until the 1960s, the building boom was at last revived, much of it stimulated by Mori's land speculation and development of inns, hotels, shopping centers, and private dwellings. By 1949 Camden City Jewish business leaders A. J. Rovner and Kolman Goldstein had moved to the township, and the growing Jewish community opened its community center on Route 70 in 1956. William Stark, founder of the Beth Jacob congregation (which later combined with Beth Israel in 1976), recalled that at first there were "only a few scattered Jewish families in the vicinity, and I never dreamed that one day we would have a real Jewish community here." But in 1988, when Beth Jacob congregation dedicated a new synagogue in Cherry Hill, Rabbi Lester Hering observed that "we are now in a flourishing vibrant Jewish community that will ensure the continuity of our Jewish Congregation."

The 1950s proved to be a golden age for Delaware Township development. Expansion occurred so rapidly, with population tripling to 31,522 by 1960, that a Camden County grand jury investigation in 1956 led Judge A. J. Cafiero to charge that "impropriety" between developers and local government had contributed to "abnormal growth." The township used the state zoning revision law of 1952, which gave suburbs license to write their own land use laws, to rezone major highways through the township for commercial development. Mori built the Cherry Hill Inn in 1955 and signed leases with Strawbridge and Clothier, J. J. Newberry, and Food Fair in 1957 for a proposed indoor shopping center to be located on Mori's property along Haddonfield Road and Route 38, near his racetrack. The Latin Casino dinner theater, Garden State Drive-In Theater, Camden County Music Fair, Hawaiian Cottage restaurant, Kenney's Suburban Steak House, and Cinelli's Country House restaurant opened near the two major highways through Cherry Hill, Route 38 and Route 70. Construction of a shopping center started at the Ellisburg Circle in 1953, and the Kingston Shopping Center opened in 1955 on King's Highway and Chapel Avenue. Camden City businesses moved many of their facilities to business parks in Delaware Township in the 1950s, including RCA, Samuel Langston Company, Hussman Refrigeration, and Holt Rug Company.

Most important, the Devon Development Company, along with the Carl T. Mitnick, Cinkowski, Samuel C. DeCou, and other Camden City real estate entrepreneurs and developers built several high-rise apartments and hundreds of single-family residences throughout the township, including the Old Orchard and Cherry Hill Estates developments in 1958. The majority of newcomers were Irish and Italian American urban Catholics. Bishop Bartholomew J. Eustace of the Camden Diocese dedicated Queen of Heaven parish in Erlton in 1955, Holy Rosary in Ashland in 1958, and, three years later, St. Mary's in Deer Park, St. Pius X in Brookmead, and St. Peter Celestine in Kingston Estates. After the devastating fire that destroyed Camden Catholic High School on Broadway in Camden City on Easter night in 1960, the diocese decided to rebuild the high school in Delaware Township on a plot of land purchased along Route 38 and Cuthbert Boulevard.

THE CHERRY HILL MALL

The dedication of the Cherry Hill Mall on 16 October 1961 by New Jersey Governor Robert Meyner and Delaware Township Mayor Christian Weber symbolized the birth of Cherry Hill Township. Mori and township planners had laid the groundwork for the shopping center during the mid-1950s. But it took the brilliant architectural design for an enclosed mall by Victor David Gruen, who had fled from Nazi-occupied Austria in 1938, and financing and planning by the Rouse Community Research and Development Corporation to create the first modern shopping mall in the eastern United States.

The Cherry Hill Mall had a profound impact on the township, prompting an immediate name change in 1962. The mall created an absolute frenzy for development of similar malls and strip shopping malls, such as the Erlton, Barclay, Kingston, and Woodcrest shopping centers. The Cherry Hill Industrial Park opened on Springdale Road, located near the New Jersey Turnpike, which had been constructed through the township in 1952. "At least five more regional shopping centers can be reasonably justified," Camden County planner John Tomaselli reported in 1963.

Housing developments remained the backbone of this burgeoning suburban community on the outskirts of Camden City. Building lots for single-family homes sold briskly in the East Gate, Barclay Farms, Croft Farm, Woodcrest, Locustwood, and Fox Hollow developments between 1960 and 1963, while Candlewyk, Cherry Downs, Springdale, and

Willowdale attracted buyers between 1963 and 1965. Township officials reported in 1963 that Cherry Hill contained more than ten thousand single-family dwellings, six high-rise apartment buildings, and twenty-seven industrial complexes. Leaders of the remaining Jewish communities of Parkside and East Camden gathered at the Cherry Hill Inn to vote 79–19 to build Congregation Beth El in the suburban township. Likewise, the Greek American community, dispossessed by urban renewal in the city, settled in Cherry Hill and opened St. Thomas Greek Orthodox Church in 1967. To meet the tremendous population increase, Cherry Hill built the John Brainerd, Horace Mann, and A. Russell Knight schools between 1962 and 1965, along with Cherry Hill East High School on Kresson Road opposite Fox Hollow. Completion of the Port Authority Transit Corporation (PATCO) high-speed rail line through the township in 1969 and the opening of the Ashland and Woodcrest stations in 1980 further accelerated growth in Cherry Hill Township.

THE *MOUNT LAUREL* DECISIONS

After World War II, the attractions of rural life rather than the decline of Camden City brought buyers to Delaware Township. Although the city showed signs of postwar social and economic decay, there was no immediate abandonment of Camden City or mass exodus to the suburbs. In the 1950s Camden City remained an ethnically diverse, busy, and seemingly prosperous urban center. Most of the 117,000 residents agreed with reform-minded Mayor Alfred Pierce that Camden could be saved. Property values continued to rise until 1959 and remained relatively stable throughout the 1960s. But panic selling began during the student unrest and black power and antiwar movements that tore the city apart during the late 1960s and early 1970s, culminating in the riots of 1971. White urban middle-class workers and businesses abandoned the city for Cherry Hill and other immediate suburbs, following their Irish, Italian, and eastern European neighbors who had chosen earlier to settle in the quiet rural retreats.

Instead of escaping urban problems, however, these new residents of Cherry Hill confronted issues during the 1970s and 1980s that were brought about, in part, by the conditions that they had tried to avoid in the first place. A series of court cases between 1971 and 1986, known collectively as the *Mount Laurel* decisions, brought the urban housing crisis and problems of poverty to Cherry Hill. The issue had started back in Camden City in 1970, when crusading civil rights attorney Peter O'Connor of the Camden Regional Legal Services sued the city to stop the destruction of poor neighborhoods, claiming that such "urban renewal" meant "Negro removal." Meanwhile, a group of black families in the nearby Burlington County suburb of Mount Laurel were denied access to affordable housing in that rapidly growing middle-class rural community. The Camden Regional Legal Services, fresh from its urban battles, came to Mount Laurel to represent the rural black community, filing the case in May 1971 as *Southern Burlington County NAACP et al. v. Township of Mount Laurel.*

While the New Jersey Superior Court was hearing the case, O'Connor visited Cherry Hill, next door to Mount Laurel, where the same type of rezoning for upper-middle-class, single-family dwellings that had prompted the Mount Laurel case was going on. O'Connor hoped to persuade the Cherry Hill planning board to provide low-cost housing for minority residents voluntarily, before it too faced a lawsuit. After the court found in 1975 that Mount Laurel must provide low-cost housing, O'Connor again visited Cherry Hill, urging the township to set aside 5 percent of all new construction for affordable housing. Challenges in 1983 and 1986 upheld the first Mount Laurel decision, but in 1986 the federal Fair Housing Act transferred power to enforce a percentage of low-cost housing upon suburban communities from the more aggressive New Jersey courts to a federal bureaucracy known as the Council on Affordable Housing.

All along, Cherry Hill had allowed construction of new developments, mostly single-family, upscale houses. Officials insisted that the 6 percent of new construction that resulted in apartments for low-income families complied fully with the Mount Laurel edicts. The Fair Housing Act, however, required 20 percent. Moreover, the township purchased the only tract of land available for such apartments as open space in 1985, drawing suspicion that Cherry Hill sought to prevent urban minorities from entering the suburban refuge. "That was the last straw," affordable housing crusader O'Connor observed. "They actually spent millions of taxpayer dollars to get around building apartments for the poor. It was racial discrimination, pure and simple." Cherry Hill Mayor Susan Bass Levin shot back that it was a question of saving the last available open space in a township that for years had been overdeveloped and now faced massive sewage, drinking water, and traffic problems. Connection to the Camden County Municipal Utilities Authority (CCMUA) in 1987 helped with sewage treatment, but the state Department of Environmental Protection announced the following year that Cherry Hill was part of a critical water area threatened by salt contamination.

Meanwhile, the New Jersey Council on Affordable Housing placed a moratorium on new home construction in 1987, until Cherry Hill complied with federal housing guidelines to set aside one thousand low- and moderate-income housing units in undeveloped tracts in Short Hills, Sergi Farms, and Holly Ravine. Two years later the Delaware Valley Regional Planning Commission suggested that building should not stop, because Cherry Hill was the Delaware Valley's "newest growth corridor," offering more than 30 percent of countywide job opportunities. The regional commission defined the corridor as the three-mile radius around the intersection of the Evesham and White Horse/Springdale Roads, and particularly through Cherry Hill's southern neighbor, Voorhees Township.

Voorhees Township

Voorhees Township replicated Delaware Township's postwar suburban experience, though at a later date. If the opening of the Cherry Hill Mall in 1961 can be regarded as the turning point in Delaware Township's suburbanization, the dedication of the Echelon Mall in 1970 launched Voorhees Township into its period of greatest suburban growth. Like its northern neighbor, Voorhees was once part of Waterford Township, and many of the same tidewater Quaker families who settled Delaware Township, most notably the Matlacks, planted future Voorhees Township. However, the area was even more remote from the main avenues of travel and commerce. The township's only hamlet of note, Milford (renamed Kresson after the Kress family of farmers and glassblowers), featured a small glass factory and weaving mill for rag carpets and blankets, but its location in the northeastern corner along the Burlington County border left it miles from any other settlement.

The Haddonfield-Longacoming (Berlin) Road was the only major thoroughfare crossing the entire portion of heavy woods and open fields. Along the road, the Matlack family built a sawmill and several residences, and John Collins erected a brick house at Glendale. This hamlet obtained some importance in the mid-nineteenth century, when Ephraim Tomlinson, a wealthy farmer, mill owner, and banker, opened a store and in 1855 built a Methodist Episcopal church there. Soon strawberry farmer Josiah C. Engle added a second store to the growing Glendale neighborhood.

Two miles from Glendale, on the White Horse Road, a tavern greeted travelers traversing the lower county to Longacoming or going west from Burlington County toward the Delaware River through Gloucester Township. The White Horse Tavern (near present-day Stratford) served as a political and social center for the neighborhood during the first half of the nineteenth century. Local planter elites who favored the creation of Camden County in 1844 and the establishment of a county seat in Longacoming met at the tavern. The stagecoach from Camden to the Atlantic shore and from Burlington to Woodbury stopped regularly there, and vacationers from Philadelphia stayed in summer cottages along nearby lakes. However, construction of the Camden and Atlantic Railroad in 1853 took stagecoach business away from the tavern and diminished its place in county affairs.

GIBBSBORO

As the importance of the tavern stop at White Horse declined, that of the village of Gibbsboro, two miles away, increased. The Gibbsboro White Lead, Zinc and Color Works expanded production and built more factories and residences for skilled craftsmen around Edward Gibbs's former millpond. Philadelphia paint manufacturer and merchant John Lucas, recently arrived from England, established the color works at Gibbsboro in 1852 because the iron- and lime-free spring water nearby made possible the production of uniquely colored paints. Moreover, as a director of the Camden and Atlantic Railroad Company in 1853, he knew that the line would run near his proposed factory. Innovative products, careful management, and effective advertising made the Gibbsboro paint works a national business success. Lucas sold large building lots at low cost to his employees and built St. John's in the Wilderness Protestant Episcopal Church (founded in large part by his wife, Harriet Anne Brown-Lucas of Philadelphia). By 1880 Gibbsboro boasted 255 residents, two stores, the church, and the paint works, but no direct railroad connection to ship the ever-expanding line of Lucas paints and varnishes. Lucas thus persuaded his fellow railroad directors to build a one-mile-long spur in 1887 from the Lucaston railroad station to his Gibbsboro paint works.

With the decline of the glass manufacturing industry in Camden County, the Lucas paint works remained the only major industry in rural southeastern Camden County at the close of the nineteenth century. Lucas grew tired of paying taxes to support the less prosperous farming parts of the township and so lent his support to the attempt to separate Gibbsboro and the surrounding area from Waterford Township, an effort led by his business partner Peter Voorhees, a Camden attorney and relative of the acting governor of New Jersey, Foster M. Voorhees. The state legislature incorporated Voorhees Township in 1899, named after the locally popular Republican governor, whose family held interests in Camden and Burlington County banking, railroad, real estate, and marl fertilizer businesses.

In 1900 a tight-knit community of nearly one thousand English and German American craftsmen and Italian, African, and Irish American laborers and farmers made up Voorhees Township's population. Seventy-five percent had been born in New Jersey or Pennsylvania. Sixty-two owned their own farms, a hundred worked as laborers on those farms, and more than a hundred English and German Americans (including female can labelers) ran the Lucas enterprises. Irish American females labored as house servants for the Lucas family and company managers and foremen. Meantime, more newcomers arrived in Gibbsboro, attracted by the expanding Lucas paint and varnish works, research laboratories, and railroad connection. The population in the surrounding rural areas of the township remained the same, however. By 1924 the Lucas Company confronted the same issue that founder John Lucas had faced in 1899. To avoid paying taxes to support the rest of the undeveloped township, Gibbsboro incorporated as a borough in 1924, breaking away from Voorhees Township.

The wild real estate speculation and building boom that swelled neighboring Delaware Township during the 1920s also had an impact on rural Voorhees. The township experienced an 8 percent increase in population during the decade, despite the loss of Gibbsboro's population. Like Delaware Township, Voorhees suffered through the Depression with almost no growth. After World War II, Voorhees rebounded along with its neighbor to the north, although its growth remained much slower and more modest.

The population of Voorhees Township increased from a little more than one thousand by the end of the war to around two thousand by 1960. Nevertheless, signs of future expansion during the 1960s could be seen as new businesses moved into the township, including the Camden Lime, Tri-Borough Sand and Stone, Lafferty Asphalt, Abbott's Dairies, and Moyer-Mitchell Poultry companies.

ECHELON PLANNED UNIT DEVELOPMENT

The introduction of the PATCO high-speed rail line from Camden to nearby Lindenwold in 1969, with a stop at Ashland station, and construction of the Echelon Mall the next year on the site of an old airfield, catapulted Voorhees to the center of county life. Township population increased dramatically, growing from 6,201 in 1970 to 12,919 in 1980, 24,500 in 1990, and nearly 30,000 by the end of the century. Assessed property value of $1.4 billion was the fourth highest in the county by 1998, trailing only the larger municipalities of Cherry Hill, Gloucester Township, and Pennsauken.

The Rouse Corporation, the same firm that planned and built the Cherry Hill Mall in 1961, conceived and constructed the 82-acre Echelon Mall in 1970. The shopping mall itself, however, was only the first step in Rouse's 425-acre Echelon Planned Unit Development (PUD), a type of metropolitan community already operating in Columbia, Maryland, and other sections of the country. The PUD integrated clusters of industrial, corporate, residential, shopping, and open space units into a self-contained metropolitan neighborhood. Camden County would eventually locate its county library there. The development comprised in "one lively area," Rouse advertised, "the full range of business, retail, office and institutional services that are usually scattered throughout a suburban region." Satellite PUDs surrounded Echelon's metropolitan center, growing in the last decade of the century along Route 73 and the Evesham, White Horse, Haddonfield-Berlin, Gibbsboro-Marlton, and Kresson Roads.

The PUD adjusted to changing conceptions of suburban housing, prompted in part by the *Mount Laurel* decisions. It provided low-cost, multi-family "garden" apartment rental units, middle-class condominiums, rental flats above shopping centers (in the Main Street development), and upscale single-family dwellings in the same planned residential development. This housing philosophy stimulated "a housing boom unmatched in Camden County's history," according to the *Courier-Post,* along with the relocation of a widely diverse population to Voorhees Township. Asian and Latino Americans from Camden City, Philadelphia, Pennsauken, and Cherry Hill joined earlier waves of Italian, Irish, Polish, Russian, and other Euro-Americans in the PUDs of Voorhees. One-fifth of the newcomers settling in the township between 1980 and the end of the century came from the Philippine Islands, China (Taiwan), India, and the Dominican Republic. In 1998, 13 percent of the schoolchildren in Voorhees Township had been born in Central, East, or Pacific Asia. One class at Osage School brought together students born in Hong Kong, Taiwan, Turkey, Korea, India, Lebanon, and Russia.

GLOUCESTER TOWNSHIP

Gloucester Township's development between World War II and the end of the century mirrored that of Voorhees and Delaware Townships. Like those townships to its east, Gloucester developed much later than other municipalities and can be considered one of the last suburbs. Although there were some signs of suburbanization along the railroad during the late nineteenth century, the lack of a major roadway through the township until the completion of the Black Horse Pike in 1931 hindered the development of automobile-commuter neighborhoods.

The sprawling township lying along central Camden County's western boundary with Gloucester County grew dramatically during the last decades of the twentieth century. Gloucester Township's population increased from 7,952 residents in 1950 to 53,797 in 1990. By 1998 the value of the township's assessed property was second only to Cherry Hill and just ahead of Voorhees. Moreover, Gloucester Township replicated the experience of its neighbors in attracting an ethnically diverse population, showing a dramatic increase in Asian Indian, Chinese, Filipino, Latino, Hispanic, and other non-European peoples, who joined the Italian, British, Polish, Russian, and German Americans who had settled there after World War II. Indeed, by 1990 Gloucester Township contained 41.3 percent of Camden County's Filipino population.

But here the similarities to Cherry Hill and Voorhees ended. Gloucester Township lacked the geographic, social, and economic identity achieved by Cherry Hill and Voorhees, with their malls, business parks, and definable clusters of residential communities. Gloucester even lacked a separate post office address. Camden County residents sometimes confused Gloucester Township with Gloucester County, Gloucester Town Township, or, later, Gloucester City. To make matters more confusing, the 523-acre Camden County Health Services Center, Hospital and Farm at Lakeland were part of Gloucester Township but stood across Timber Creek in Gloucester County. Likewise, Gloucester Township's Camden County neighborhoods of Blackwood and Grenloch had mirror images in Blackwood Terrace and Grenloch Terrace directly across the creek in Gloucester County.

Moreover, Gloucester Township contained an unusual number of "lost" cemeteries or dead towns, many of which had been little more than clusters of mill or factory workers' houses. These included Upton, a colonial settlement established in the 1680s along Timber Creek near Blackwood that had disappeared by 1700, Good Intent, Mechanicsville (now Blenheim), and Watsonville or Brownstown. Other places in Gloucester Township had disputed origins. Tradition made freed slave Solomon Davis the founder in 1850 of the black enclave of Davistown and Solomon Wesley United Methodist Church, the only African American church in Gloucester Township. But local scholarship suggests that Lindley Davis, the freed female slave of the Daniel Bates family, established Davistown as a haven for freed slaves. Furthermore, constant cannibalization of the original Gloucester Township lands, established as a constable wick in 1694–95, added to the destruction of Gloucester Township's identity as a separate municipality.

Nevertheless, Gloucester Township remained one of the most historic areas in Camden County. It boasted some of the oldest colonial neighborhoods, including the Timber Creek community of Blackwoodtown. The settlement took its name from John Blackwood, a Scottish-Irish Presbyterian farmer and miller who bought a tract of land along the headwaters of Timber Creek in 1741 from Upton landowner George Ward. A few years later Blackwood purchased Charles Read's fulling, saw, and gristmills, and his brother Samuel established a public house on the winding trail that came down from Haddon's Town and crossed the creek. The

Blackwoods built a Presbyterian church (circa 1750), making the community a center of the county's opposition to British economic and political control. Consequently, the area became active in the resistance to British rule during the 1760s and 1770s. After the American Revolution, Blackwoodtown grew as a crossroads and tidal creek commercial center. Uriah Norcross established a daily stagecoach line from Camden to Blackwood to Longacoming, and his father-in-law, Edward Middleton, ran a large public house, tavern, and inn.

In the early nineteenth century Philadelphia manufacturer Garrett Newkirk established the Good Intent textile mill in Blackwoodtown. The small factory town featured the Temperance Hotel, a boarding school, and a collection of stores and houses. After the Civil War, Blackwoodtown's Good Intent mills produced woolen goods and horse blankets. In 1855, Camden City and Gloucester Township entrepreneurs and farmers incorporated the Camden and Blackwoodtown Turnpike Company to build and maintain a good toll road connecting Haddon Avenue in the city to the tidal creek factory town. The turnpike company failed to maintain a safe road, however, making inadequate repairs to washed-out parts of the turnpike and to bridges that crossed the many tributaries of the Timber Creek system. Poor access to remote Gloucester Township discouraged the type of late-nineteenth-century suburban growth that was apparent just to the east along the heavily traveled White Horse Turnpike toll road, the Camden and Atlantic Railroad (1853), and the Philadelphia and Atlantic City Railway (1877).

The construction in 1873–75 of the narrow gauge Camden, Gloucester and Mount Ephraim Railway from the Kaighn's Point Ferry in Camden to David S. Brown's Gloucester City textile mills and the farming village of Mount Ephraim promised to boost Gloucester Township's suburban development. Indeed, the company announced in 1876 that it planned to extend the line from Mount Ephraim to Blackwood and up the King's Highway to Haddonfield. A ground-breaking ceremony was held for the rail line, and subscriptions were raised to build the extension. But Brown, the project's warmest backer, died in 1877, and plans to connect Blackwood to the Camden, Gloucester and Mount Ephraim Railroad ended.

After the Philadelphia and Reading system took over the bankrupt Philadelphia and Atlantic City Railway in 1883, it negotiated to buy the

Gloucester "Peanut Line" branch to Mount Ephraim and convert it to standard gauge track in 1885. It looked as though the new company might complete the long-planned Blackwood extension. Still, nothing happened for four years, until Frank Bateman of the Spring Mills factory that produced Iron Age farm equipment in a manufacturing village just below Blackwood organized the Camden County Railroad to run a line from Mount Ephraim to Spring Mills (renamed Grenloch). The Reading Railroad, anxious to block any attempt by the rival Pennsylvania Railroad system to move into the area, backed the project, and the railroad reached Blackwood and Grenloch by 1891. Certainly, the new railroad had an impact on settling new suburban developments along its line and encouraged expansion of the summer cottage resort business on Blackwood Lake. But Blackwood, and most of Gloucester Township, never experienced a suburban boom similar to that seen among the towns along the railroad main lines to the east.

Camden County purchased the Camden and Blackwoodtown Turnpike in 1903, removed the tolls, and encouraged developers to survey building lots along the road. Once again, this highway suffered by comparison with the major arteries through the county to the north and east. The county's poor maintenance of the road to Blackwood (the name now given to the railroad stop) further retarded suburban house building in the rural Timber Creek region. Blackwood resident E. Frank Pine, a Gloucester Township freeholder, Camden County sheriff, and New Jersey state legislator, led a Black Horse Pike movement. Between 1915 and 1923 he made the Gloucester Township roadway equal to the nearby White Horse Pike, which had contributed to development of booming early-twentieth-century suburban communities. At first, he received support from the Greater Camden Movement, but opposition appeared from rival White Horse Pike and Berlin Township entrepreneur Dr. Frank O. Stem.

Stem, county physician and arguably the most powerful local political figure in Camden County during the 1920s, made certain that the Black Horse Pike project moved slowly. Pine and the Black Horse Pike Boosters Association lobbied the county and state governments for years to get a paved Black Horse Pike through Gloucester Township and an extension to the Atlantic City seashore that would boost local business. Obstacles continued, and the Black Horse Pike was not completed until

1931. The trials of the road help to explain why Gloucester Township lagged behind other rural regions of Camden County during the suburban building boom of the 1920s.

Located at the head of navigation on the north branch of Timber Creek, about a mile west of Blackwoodtown, Chew's Landing was the only other definable early community in what is today Gloucester Township, and it may be considered to have played an even more important role in the township's history than Blackwoodtown. "It is a place of considerable business in lumber and cord wood, and contains 2 stores, 2 taverns, 2 grist mills, and between 30 and 40 dwellings, 1 Episcopal and 1 Methodist church," New Jersey chronicler Thomas F. Gordon observed in 1834. The community took shape around 1699, when Richard Chew and John Roe bought land on the outskirts of Upton. Chew's son Jeremiah built a wharf landing for timber flats, a tavern, and a store, making the place at once a colonial commercial center. Farmers and mill owners from the lower county around Longacoming used Chew's (and other Timber Creek landings) to ship goods downstream to the Delaware River, Camden, and Philadelphia markets. Chew's Landing boasted Presbyterian, Baptist, and Methodist churches and, like neighboring Blackwoodtown, was a hotbed of revolutionary unrest. Jeremiah's son Aaron became a local Revolutionary War hero for his resistance to British rule.

The Brewer family established a shipyard at Chew's Landing in the early nineteenth century, where lighters, flats, barges, small craft, and several large schooners of up to three hundred tons were constructed. The Brewers launched these larger schooners into the still deep headwaters of the tidal creek and floated them downstream to the Delaware River for installation of masts and rigging in Philadelphia or Camden shipyards. The Brewer family became political as well as economic leaders in mid-nineteenth-century Camden County. Edmund Brewer, son of the boatyard founder, served on the Camden County Board of Chosen Freeholders (1849–52) and as county sheriff (1856–59), while his son George became a freeholder (1851–59) and Camden County clerk (1861–66). Chew's Landing achieved such prominence in county affairs that it received consideration as the location for the county seat.

Depletion of timber supplies and the silting of Timber Creek killed the Brewer shipbuilding industry. More important, the opening of the Camden and Atlantic Railroad in 1853 meant that goods formerly brought to the landing from the Longacoming region now moved by rail to the Camden waterfront. As Chew's Landing faded in significance, Gloucester Township once again became a backwater in the rapidly suburbanizing late-nineteenth-century county, making its revival and expansion during the post–World War II era all the more remarkable.

During the building and real estate speculation boom of the 1920s, the Clementon Estates Corporation laid out "Clementona: Summit of South Jersey, Gloucester Township." Developers advertised Clementona as "the highest ground in South Jersey, being 210 feet above sea level, and each lot is planted with bearing fruit trees or grape vines." Depression burst the Clementona bubble, but by 1940 Gloucester Township's population had reached six thousand and continued to grow steadily throughout the war as urban war workers sought commuter housing in Audubon and Bellmawr. School construction reflected the growth, with new schools built in Blackwood, Blenheim, Glendora, Erial, and Grenloch.

The Black Horse Pike commercial zone expanded and, after the war, became a commuter-choked artery filled with gas stations, restaurants, shops, and motion picture theaters. Shore traffic in the summer and the growth of Bellmawr, Runnemede, Blackwood, and other neighboring communities stimulated business. On either side of its main artery, however, Gloucester Township remained rural farmland. Suburban development took off in the 1960s, with the population climbing to 26,511 by 1970 and doubling to 53,797 twenty years later, a growth matched only by Cherry Hill. The Federal Housing Authority financed 1,700 townhouses, and private developers built the Brittany Woods, Revere Run, and La Cascata neighborhoods. By the end of the twentieth century, Gloucester Township's intense, but often erratic, development had become a case study in suburban sprawl.

10

"A Breath-taking View of the Philadelphia Skyline"

The Camden Metropolitan Region

Camden County provides an ideal historical model with which to study the evolution of an American metropolitan community. It has undergone each of the stages of urbanization used by the Federal Census Bureau and the "new urban" historians to define an American metropolis. Camden County contains one central city that for much of the twentieth century had a population of more than 100,000 people. Rings of suburban development radiated out from the central city, including an inner ring of older suburbs, a middle buffer zone of railroad towns, and an outer ring of newer sprawling suburban neighborhoods generated by improved highways. Historically, these zones integrated into one mutually interdependent metropolitan county.

Originally, an ethnically homogeneous, white middle-class rural tidewater society controlled county life. Over time, the county's only sizable manufacturing town along the Delaware River grew into a large urban industrial center that dominated political, cultural, and economic life. As the riverfront city expanded during the nineteenth century, it spread along turnpikes and rail lines into the nearby rural countryside, forming early suburbs. All roads and rails led to Camden City and the waterfront ferries that connected the county to Philadelphia across the river. City, suburb, and rural hamlet remained closely linked to and dependent upon the urban center for business, government, and cultural development.

So long as the city grew, the county prospered. But intractable problems with Camden City's location and its poorly planned urban development—combined with a century of mismanagement, political corruption, and unrestrained industrial and residential expansion—began to reveal urban decay. Signs of slowdown and decline appeared during the Great Depression and World War II. The war brought more heavy industry, pollution, crime, and nonwhite unskilled labor to the already overcrowded waterfront city.

DESTROYING THE METROPOLIS

White urban middle-class veterans returning from World War II found a housing shortage in the city. Provided with funds to buy new houses under the GI Bill, they started a gradual exodus from Camden City. There was no conscious decision to abandon the city, only a desire to relocate to the fresh air, open space, and improved quality of life provided by the still rural neighboring regions. But the effect of their choice was that the city stopped growing in the 1950s, peaking at 125,000 residents. For the first time since the founding of the county in 1844, Camden City's population declined. As primarily white middle-class residents left the city, blacks and Hispanics (and later Asian Americans) moved in, increasing their percentages among the declining total population. In 1950 whites made up more than 85 percent of Camden City's residents. Forty years later, people of color composed the same percentage of the county's inner-city population. During these decades too, older manufacturing industries closed or left because of the changing nature of the economy, lack of space to expand, a shortage of skilled labor, and increasing environmental regulations. Most of the businesses headed for the nearby suburbs, taking jobs and tax revenues with them.

As the city grew poorer, the suburbs became richer. The widening economic and ethnic inequity between city and suburbs created for the first time in Camden County history a distinct separation between urban and rural sections. As the gap widened, Camden City ceased to be the dominant force in a metropolitan region. Suburban residents no longer came to shop or visit the city. Those who continued to work in the county government or remaining industries in the city rushed back home to the suburbs in the evening. Those who used the city's hospitals or attended Rutgers University's Camden commuter campus spent as little time in the city as possible. As the racial imbalance, poverty, violent crime, and drug trade increased, fear of the city escalated, and suburbs began to build informal (and sometimes legal) walls against the city. The suburbs hesitated to develop low-income housing, probably to keep the poor, mostly nonwhite urban residents from moving into their communities. By the end of the century, Camden had become, as urban scholar David Rusk insisted, "a city without a suburb."

Regional Development

Nevertheless, Camden City and Camden County are inextricably connected. The county seat still provided, as always, the gateway to southern New Jersey and a passageway to Philadelphia. All roads and a high-speed rail line came to Camden City, even if only to cross the bridges. An active port that employed suburban residents connected the city to the county. Most important, what happened in Camden City deeply affected the inner ring of older suburbs, most directly Gloucester City, Pennsauken, Collingswood, Oaklyn, Woodlynne, and Audubon. By the last decades of the twentieth century, these nearby suburbs were suffering from increased poverty and crime and the loss of businesses and white middle-class residents, replicating the process that had started in Camden City after World War II. The decline of these neighborhoods eroded the buffer zone between the city and the newer suburbs in the county's outer ring, where the preliminary signs of suburban sprawl could be detected. The newer suburbs experienced overcrowding, traffic congestion, pollution, and crimes of increasing intensity. Clearly, the suburban county could not escape its metropolitan and urban origins. If the city fell ill, it infected the rest of the county, spreading problems from the inner suburbs to the outer ring of distant neighborhoods.

County civic and business leaders had long recognized the interconnection between city and suburban development. City planner Charles W. Leavitt tried to develop a "sensible regional plan" for the county during the 1920s. However, these early plans were based on continued growth and perpetual annexation of new neighborhoods as they developed new roads and bridges and undertook constant building. After World War II, county leaders witnessed increased suburban growth but a decline in the urban environment. As early as 1961 (coinciding with the opening of the Cherry Hill Mall), executives from Camden County's largest employers organized a new Greater Camden Movement to rehabilitate Camden City and its surrounding municipalities. Original members included Campbell Soup, RCA, New York Shipbuilding, Esterbrook Pen, Samuel M. Langston, and the *Courier-Post* newspaper companies. RCA, Esterbrook Pen, and Langston corporate chiefs, with offices in Camden and new facilities in Cherry Hill, and the *Courier-Post* Company, which had moved from Camden City to Delaware Township, were intimately aware of the connection between city and county. They hoped to use this nonprofit organization to rebuild the county's metropolitan economy.

During the 1960s, federal and state governments created new agencies to help metropolitan regions nationwide address inner-city poverty, control water and air pollution, remove solid waste, and confront other pressing social and economic needs. At the local level, Camden County created a planning board under chairman John A. Healey and planning director John D. Tomaselli to study land use, water resources, population trends, and the economic base. However, early attempts to develop a master plan for "the Camden Urban Region" suffered from fundamental flaws. County planners admitted in 1963 that their land use plan failed to take into account the impact on future county development of a planned Delaware River Port Authority (DRPA) rapid transit line between Camden and Lindenwold or of the proposed Atlantic City Expressway from Blackwood to the Jersey shore. Nothing so deeply affected settlement patterns and economic development or more clearly defined the metropolitan character of the county over the next forty years than these two transportation and communication systems. The failure to consider the future impact of these vital growth corridors revealed that from the beginning the county responded to rather than coordinated planning with the Delaware River Port Authority and other regional agencies.

CAMDEN COUNTY MUNICIPAL UTILITIES AUTHORITY (CCMUA)

The county's first major post–World War II regional planning initiative occurred in the early 1960s in response to growing problems with chemicals and sewage fouling the county's drinking water, streams, and tidal creeks. Cooper River had become so deadly that it was closed permanently to boating, fishing, swimming, and other water activity. Each new housing development in the suburbs destroyed trees that had stopped soil erosion and runoff into nearly every local water supply. Once beautiful Crystal Lake became choked in 1966 with debris from builders of the Van Sciver tract in Haddon Township. In 1962 the Delaware River Basin Commission organized to plan the cleanup of the Delaware River and subsidiary waterways. In 1972 the Federal Water Pollution Control Act earmarked $1 billion in federal grants for upgrading local sewage systems, and Camden County used a federal grant under this act to develop a countywide sewage system.

The county had created a sewage authority in 1967, but suburban municipalities refused to join; only Camden City accepted the authority hookups. Consequently, in 1972, the Camden County Board of Chosen Freeholders created the Camden County Municipal Utilities Authority (CCMUA) to take advantage of federal grants for clean water and environmental recovery, and it hired county planning board director Tomaselli as executive director. Tomaselli confronted constant crisis. The New Jersey Department of Environmental Protection banned any CCMUA development until the authority had prepared a regional plan for the populated inner urban zone and another for the distant rural suburbs of Winslow, Waterford, and Berlin Townships. Moreover, constant accusations of mismanagement, political influence peddling, and corruption plagued CCMUA. Tomaselli resigned in 1976 amid implications of fraud and graft in the county organization.

The main obstacles came from intensely local attitudes. The concept of home rule was deeply ingrained in the history of Camden County's boroughs. Most had incorporated after breaking away from a larger township so that they could take care of their own affairs. These municipalities refused to join the CCMUA. The mayors of Bellmawr and Somerdale led opposition to county control of their sewage plants because they would have to pay exorbitant rates while Camden City received lower rates and higher prices for land on which to place sewer lines.

In 1976 twenty-three suburban Camden County towns defied a state superior court order to connect with the CCMUA system and hired lawyers and consulting engineers to negotiate with CCMUA. The first sewer pipes were finally laid in 1984, extended to Cherry Hill, Pennsauken, and Cooper River by 1987, Timber Creek in 1991, and Waterford, Chesilhurst, and Winslow by 1996. The cost of the project constantly escalated, from $56 million in 1972 to $300 million in 1976 and more than $700 million by the mid-1980s. When the final hookup of the ninety-mile-long underground sewer system occurred in 1996, the Camden County Board of Chosen Freeholders estimated that its project was worth $1 billion to any private firm that might take over operations. Despite the exorbitant cost, high sewer rates, and years of political patronage, the CCMUA markedly improved the county environment, contributing particularly to the restoration of Pennsauken and Newton Creeks and the Cooper River.

CROSS ACCEPTANCE PROCESS (CAP)

The same fierce localism that had delayed regional sewage treatment appeared throughout Camden County in response to state initiatives to develop county planning mechanisms, particularly the so-called Cross Acceptance Plan of the State Development and Redevelopment Plan of 1986. This scheme called for the county to coordinate planning with each municipality for resources, housing, land use, and transportation and for each county to coordinate with the State Planning Board. In the process, municipalities could express their particularly local needs and characteristics, and the county and state would acquiesce to those that did not conflict with larger regional development. School funding and other state aid depended upon municipal acceptance of the New Jersey State Development and Redevelopment Plan. In 1989 thirty-two out of thirty-five

Camden County municipalities offered their responses to CAP, ranging from enthusiastic acceptance by Camden City, which desperately needed outside help, to outright opposition from suburbs under assault along the White Horse Pike. Other townships, such as rapidly developing Winslow, expressed lukewarm acceptance. Haddonfield, which had developed an elaborate local master plan that fit its own unique situation, showed indifference to the countywide initiative.

HADDONFIELD'S MASTER PLAN

The first effort to develop a suburban plan to control urban growth, regulate land use, and define the relationship to other municipalities occurred in Haddonfield before World War II. The Great Depression revealed that the apparently wealthy suburban borough of Haddonfield suffered from the same problems that plagued poorer neighborhoods of the big city next door. There was a perception of overcrowding, unemployment, unkempt streets, inadequate public utilities, and abandoned, boarded-up storefronts along King's Highway. Haddonfield Borough government introduced zoning codes during the 1930s designed to control future growth. At that time, Haddonfield decided to re-create its past as a quiet colonial market and residential town.

World War II delayed these efforts, but in 1959 Haddonfield introduced a master plan (revised in the 1970s) that outlined development of a colonial-theme shopping center along King's Highway and residential clusters on either side of the main road. Owners had to apply to the borough historic commission for permission to make any changes to buildings, stores, and private residences or undertake new construction. The borough would grant permission to remodel or build structures only to individuals who abided strictly by the code on building height and size, color of paint, architectural style, and use of open space. Violators faced penalties and stiff fines.

Haddonfield Borough explained that the purpose of the zoning ordinances was to "prevent the over crowding of land or buildings; [and] avoid undue concentration of population." Using its master plan and zoning powers, Haddonfield built a model suburban enclave based on the re-creation of its colonial heritage, even though only the Indian King Tavern and a few original colonial residences remained. Surrounded by troubled urban neighborhoods to the west and suburban sprawl on the east, and crossed by the high-speed commuter line, Haddonfield nevertheless managed to isolate itself from regional troubles. The value of property there continued to increase, and the borough became one of the most affluent and desirable residential neighborhoods in the county. In the 1980s, however, the county expected Haddonfield to adopt the Cross Acceptance Plan and show how the borough would interact with the rest of the region. Haddonfield's response was curt and succinct. The "Borough is concerned that the State Plan will interfere with traditional *home rule*" and the "unique" master plan that had saved Haddonfield from decay and sprawl.

SUBURBAN OPPOSITION TO CAP

Most of its older White Horse Pike borough neighbors shared Haddonfield's disdain for CAP. Long a buffer zone between the inner city and the outer reaches of the suburban county, these municipalities were under assault from both sides and wanted nothing to do with either. There is "no visual indication as to where one town ends, and another begins," worried Norman T. Brecht, Audubon Borough's director of public works and parks and public property. Greedy land developers had filled every inch of the area, destroying farms, fields, and woods. He thought that the county "should replace the plows on the county seal with dollar signs." Brecht demanded a moratorium on building and refused to cooperate with CAP, calling county planning and development "a disgrace." The borough public works director branded CAP "a diabolical plan to this generation and future generations to come."

Magnolia Borough leaders agreed. Left to determine its own development, Magnolia had escaped both the "ghetto-like areas" of the inner city and the sprawl of the outer ring of suburban townships. "We are a pretty typical suburban town concerned with taxes, education, services and keeping and attracting businesses. We do not have much land to develop or redevelop so we are mainly concerned with keeping up what we have." Hi-Nella (founded in 1929), a tiny White Horse Pike municipality of 1,250 residents, 126 single-family dwellings, and two large low-income apartment housing complexes, blamed earlier cooperation plans for creating "a blighting condition on the rest of the community." In the 1970s Hi-Nella had cooperated with the county to develop a low-cost housing complex that had caused nothing but hardship for the rest of the borough. "When this complex is late with its tax payment, the rest of the taxpayers face several hundred dollar increases."

A CONCEPT PLAN FOR THE LAST SUBURBS

The newest suburban communities of Cherry Hill, Voorhees, Gloucester, Waterford, and Winslow Townships, along the outer edges of the heavily developed parts of the county, wanted to maintain home rule as well. However, they realized that CAP could be used to contain urban sprawl and assist in solving an emerging sewage, transportation, and housing crisis. These last suburbs approached CAP with great caution. Cherry Hill planners suggested that "it would be impractical to provide an infrastructure analysis" until the state and county granted funds and technical support for further study of local and regional issues. Voorhees Township Planner Virginia C. Lamb wanted to accept CAP but doubted that either county or state had the resources to implement the plan. "State and county agencies are currently so minimally staffed that they are unable to fulfill their own requirements much less be available to local municipalities," she observed.

Winslow Township took a slightly different approach. More isolated than Cherry Hill and Voorhees, and much later in suffering from suburban sprawl, the township early developed its own comprehensive planning organization, with a township planning board, economic development council, environmental commission, and housing and school planning agencies. The township met regional challenges along the way. "Winslow Township has exceeded its fair share as far as affordable housing, including rental assisted units, low/moderate income units, housing for senior citizens and existing [federal] housing," Winslow planners explained. The township also maintained the "highest ideals" of the regional planners in developing the 692-acre Wilton's Corner tract, which combined commercial, environmental, public use, and mixed (income) residential areas. The township cooperated fully with the state Pinelands Commission, the U.S. Fish and Wildlife Service, and federal scenic rivers and endangered species laws in pursuing developments that protected the environmentally sensitive wetlands and pinelands that covered much of its area.

When the county asked for the township's response to CAP in 1989, however, Winslow confronted a "new suburban sprawl" that defied local solutions. The placement of a park-n-ride stop at Sicklerville on the Atlantic City Expressway, the construction of a stop at the Berlin/Atco station on the New Jersey Transit train line to Atlantic City, and the improvement of the Berlin–Cross Keys and other local roads had created a mass migration to the township. Winslow's population had grown from a modest 11,000 residents in 1970 to well over 30,000 by 1990. Township schools were overcrowded, roads congested, sewage treatment troubled, and planning for open space and wetland preservation disorganized. Winslow planners admitted that no one sat on the township environmental commission until 1987, when the new mayor, Norman Tomasello, appointed five men and women to hold the first meeting. Clearly, Winslow needed CAP.

CAMDEN REDISCOVERS ITS WATERFRONT

At the other end of the county, Gloucester and Camden Cities wanted CAP even more than rural Winslow Township. In many ways, both riverfront cities were dying industrial relics, wracked by poverty, pollution, and poor planning. And remarkably, both chose as their plan for recovery the use of CAP to bring them back to the river where it all began more than 350 years earlier. Gloucester and Camden Cities (and to a lesser extent Pennsauken Township to the north) envisaged re-creating their historical waterfront heritage as the way to stimulate a rebirth of the urban center and a revival of metropolitan Camden. The construction of appealing riverfront facilities would bring suburban visitors to spend money, boost revenue, attract investment in the impoverished area, and create larger economic recovery in the neighborhoods. As Camden City Mayor Melvin R. Primas explained in "City of Camden: Cross-Acceptance Report" (1989), waterfront property for development remained plentiful.

DRPA, the Camden County Board of Chosen Freeholders, Rutgers University, the Cooper's Ferry Development Association, and various other private corporations and "empowerment zone" organizations (funded under federal government grants during the 1990s) seized the opportunity to develop Camden City's abundant waterfront land. In 1983 RCA, Campbell Soup, and the American Cities Corporation (a subsidiary of the Rouse Company that had developed the Cherry Hill and Echelon Malls, among other Delaware Valley architectural innovations) called for creation of a public-private organization to develop Camden's seventy-five-acre waterfront district. They envisaged a project similar to Baltimore's Inner Harbor. Re-creating the Camden waterfront as the economic, entertainment, and cultural center it had been for so much of the county's history promised to bring money to the city that could be used, ideally, to rebuild surrounding residential neighborhoods and provide jobs to inner-city residents. DRPA's executive director, Paul Drayton, announced that his agency intended to make Camden "a playground for adults and children."

Beginning with development of the Wiggins Waterfront Park in 1981, through ground-breaking ceremonies in 2000 for a minor league baseball stadium on the Camden waterfront, planners pressed ahead with the vision of re-creating Camden County at its riverfront birthplace. Ferry service between Camden and Philadelphia, a cornerstone of Camden County's history, was reinstituted after a forty-year absence with the introduction of the *Delawhale* in 1992. The state funded the Thomas H. Kean New Jersey State Aquarium, and the public-private Cooper's Ferry Development Association (created in 1983) promoted the Camden Children's Garden. Private corporations constructed the Entertainment Center, and the county secured the battleship *New Jersey* from the U.S. Navy for installation nearby as a floating museum. Plans for an aerial tramway from Camden to Penn's Landing in Philadelphia, a minor league baseball stadium, and the conversion of old waterfront factories into townhouses followed. The state cleaned up the long decaying Admiral Wilson Boulevard gateway to Camden County, in part to make a pleasant impression on summer 2000 visitors to the Republican National Political Convention in Philadelphia.

Skeptics of the waterfront approach to recovery suggested that it had little to do with improving the life of impoverished inner-city residents. Yet Camden City already possessed the models for such recovery in neighborhoods such as Fairview, extolled by "new urban" planners as a "smart growth" approach to rebuilding metropolitan America. Conceived originally for shipyard workers during World War I, Fairview was designed on the model of an English garden community by architect Electus Litchfield, who created circles of attractive row houses radiating out from a central community plaza, where residents could visit or shop within walking distance of their homes. Each house had an attractive yard and a personality that was individual yet unified into a single compact neighborhood. This creative use of urban space, the new urbanists contended, provided an "antidote to suburban sprawl."

GLOUCESTER CITY'S PLAN

Gloucester City, like its neighbor upriver, chose the waterfront path, bringing the county back to its birthplace along the banks of the Delaware River. Gloucester City's waterfront projects at the end of the millennium occurred near the reputed spot of the first European settlement in the county at Fort Nassau in the 1620s. Though just as old as Haddonfield, and in some ways more historic, Gloucester City approached CAP much differently. Unlike the residential borough of Haddonfield at the head of Cooper's Creek, Gloucester City had not preserved its colonial heritage during its development in the mid-nineteenth-century as a riverfront mill town. While Haddonfield had held on to its historic tavern, Gloucester City had lost its equally historic Hugg's Tavern to demolition in order to build a county playground and swimming pool. What Gloucester City had to offer was the remains of a once prosperous waterfront industrial complex, with rows of three-story brick residences for skilled workers at the Washington Textile Mills and old brick "smoke stack type industry" factories along the river.

Gloucester City's plan called for refurbishing the Washington Mills row houses as modern apartments and developing the riverfront factory section for a public boat landing, hotels, fishing pier, marina, and perhaps malls or townhouses with "a breath-taking view of the Philadelphia skyline." Planners started to convert a former U.S. immigration building into a waterfront restaurant. However, the overall redevelopment plan required massive help to clean up years of pollution from thorium at the site of the old Welsbach Gas Mantle factory and mercury and lead poisoning from the grounds around former iron foundry, paper mill, shipbuilding, and other sites. Consequently, Gloucester City welcomed CAP, which offered to use money from stable municipalities to assist recovery in impoverished urban centers. "The State of New Jersey must spearhead the cleanup of this area in order to replenish the lost tax base and employment opportunities that Gloucester City has lost over the past six years," explained Gloucester

City Mayor Robert S. Bevan. If this vision could be accomplished, perhaps once again Camden County could become an attractive and prosperous riverfront metropolis.

REINVENTING CAMDEN COUNTY

As Camden County entered the new millennium, it sought to reinvent itself by returning to its historical origins on the Delaware River. Long the center of government, business, and entertainment for the county, the waterfront area had suffered crippling economic and social decay in the second half of the twentieth century. Decline of the urban riverfront region deeply affected the social and economic future of the surrounding urban neighborhoods and the sprawling suburban developments beyond. But with the decay of the inner city and urban suburbs, more rural suburban communities turned their backs on Camden City and the waterfront from which they had arisen. The once truly metropolitan Camden County community of the first half of the twentieth century disintegrated.

Gradually, county businesses and public officials determined that, in order to protect the county from future social and economic troubles, they needed to rebuild the city, and particularly the urban waterfront. Shortly before her death in 1994, Camden County's first African American female freeholder, Aletha Wright, director of Camden City's human services, predicted that Camden City would one day be reborn on the waterfront. The county's economic strength had derived originally from the riverfront's role as a ferry and railroad terminal and a resort and entertainment center that brought thousands of visitors from Philadelphia and suburban southern New Jersey to spend their money in Camden City. If Camden County could re-create the city as this center, the entire county would benefit. Thus in recent years a combination of public and private corporations and agencies has reinvented the county's past glory.

An entertainment center, aquarium, children's garden, baseball park, and battleship museum have attempted to reimagine the prosperous nineteenth-century Camden City world of pleasure gardens, amusement parks, racetracks, billiard and bowling halls, baseball fields, waterfront bathing and fishing resorts, and even a tiny children's garden railroad. In the summer of 1834, William Cooper's Garden at Cooper's Point Ferry became one of the most popular amusement and resort centers in Camden City's history. It installed a "Circular Pleasure Railway," where happy children could pedal their way round and round a tiny oval track while their parents drank beer at the waterfront picnic grounds nearby. Exactly 166 years later, a tiny railroad was introduced to the Camden Children's Garden to bring children and their parents to the Camden waterfront once more.

The plans to rebuild the Camden City waterfront addressed only one aspect of Camden County's future as it entered the twenty-first century. The urbanized fringes of Pennsauken, Haddon Township, and Collingswood continued to suffer gradual decay in neighborhoods and abandonment of businesses. The booming suburbs of Cherry Hill, Voorhees, and Gloucester Townships approached the end of available open space and land to build upon. As population increased dramatically, the regional sewer system, water supply, roads, and public services barely kept pace. Moreover, the water table threatened to drop to a dangerous level and become tainted with the salt water that moved farther up the river with each period of drought in the Delaware Valley. In the more distant suburbs of the once wild lower county townships of Winslow and Waterford, developers of housing, shopping, and industrial centers coexisted uneasily with the fragile pineland and wetland environments.

Furthermore, the rebuilding of Camden City no longer had as much relevance to the health of the county's political economy as in the past. Political leadership and economic power now resided in Cherry Hill, Gloucester, Voorhees, and Winslow Townships and in other suburban municipalities. Camden City, once the center of county business and government, was plagued by political corruption, intractable poverty, and crime. The city to which the county looked for rebirth could not manage its own financial affairs and constantly faced a state takeover. Camden City continued as the seat of county government. But without substantial improvement in the urban environment, how long could the county support this arrangement?

Nor did the reconstruction of the Delaware riverfront in 2000 have much to do with the changing nature of Camden County's incredibly diverse ethnic population. Hispanics became the largest ethnic group in Camden City by the end of the century, followed closely by the much older African American community. At the same time, Russian, Caribbean, Latino, and Asian Americans came to the Philadelphia–Camden County metropolitan waterfront region in search of jobs. But as urban factories closed and businesses moved to the suburbs, urban conditions deteriorated into poverty. Those who could moved to the urban suburbs or outer suburban peripheries beyond. Asian Indian Americans ran gas stations and small businesses throughout the county. Filipino Americans became a vibrant new middle class in some suburbs. Korean and Chinese Americans opened restaurants, shops, and stores in many suburban communities. Others tried to survive in the hostile urban environment. Dominican, Colombian, Honduran, Mexican, Korean, Vietnamese, Cambodian, Asian Indian, and Chinese Americans operated dozens of stores and small businesses and worked in the service industries or as unskilled labor in Camden City.

Current population trends promise to lead to the development of a truly multicultural society in Camden County in the twenty-first century. Some population studies predict that by the middle of the next century Hispanic and Asian Americans will outnumber Americans of European ancestry. Whether or not this trend continues, the constantly changing ethnicity of Camden County's society places great demands on local and county governments to provide schools, social services, employment, and opportunities so that a multicultural society and economy can adjust to and prosper in an American metropolitan community.

FURTHER READINGS

BIBLIOGRAPHIES

For more extensive bibliographic notes on primary archival material, newspapers, and secondary literature about Camden County, see Dennis G. Raible, *Down a Country Lane* (Camden: Camden County Historical Society, 1999), and Jeffery M. Dorwart and Philip English Mackey, *Camden County, New Jersey, 1616–1976: A Narrative History* (Camden: Camden County Cultural and Heritage Commission, 1976). See also Jean D. Creszenzi, *List of Directories on Microfilm in the City & County Directories Collections of the Camden County Historical Society and the Gloucester County Historical Society* (Camden: Paul Robeson Library, Rutgers University-Camden Campus, 1993).

ARCHIVES FOR FURTHER RESEARCH

Those who wish to pursue research in the original manuscript sources should begin in regional archives, including the Camden County Historical Society in Camden, the Gloucester County Historical Society in Woodbury, and the Historical Society of Pennsylvania in Philadelphia, among others. In addition, the Urban Archives at Temple University in Philadelphia, the rare book room in the Paul Robeson Library at Rutgers University in Camden, and the Frank H. Stewart Collection in the Savitz Learning

Center library at Rowan University in Glassboro hold manuscript material about Camden County's history. Specialists need to examine the rare books and manuscript collections at Alexander Library, Rutgers University Libraries, in New Brunswick, New Jersey, the New Jersey State Archives and Library in Trenton, and county records in the clerk's offices at the Gloucester County Courthouse in Woodbury and the Camden County Courthouse in Camden.

HISTORIES OF CAMDEN COUNTY AND CITY

The standard introductions to the county's history remain: George R. Prowell, *The History of Camden County, New Jersey* (1886; rpt. Camden: Camden County Historical Society and Camden County Cultural and Heritage Commission, 1974); A. Charles Corotis and James M. O'Neill, *Camden County Centennial, 1844–1944* (Camden: Huntzinger, 1944); Paul F. Cranston, *Camden County, 1681–1931* (Camden: Camden Chamber of Commerce, 1931); and Alfred M. Heston, *South Jersey: A History, 1664–1924*, 5 vols. (New York and Chicago: Lewis Historical Publishing, 1924–26).

Charles S. Boyer, longtime president of the Camden County Historical Society, published a number of valuable studies on specific aspects of the county's history, including: *History of the Press in Camden County, New Jersey* (Camden: Sinnickson Chew, 1921); *The Civil and Political History of Camden County and Camden City* (Camden: privately printed, 1922); *Old Inns and Taverns in West Jersey* (rpt. Camden: Camden County Historical Society, 1962); *Old Mills of Camden County* (Camden: Camden County Historical Society, 1962); *Old Ferries: Camden, New Jersey* (Camden: privately printed, 1921); and *Rambles Through Old Highways and Byways of West Jersey*, ed. John D. F. Morgan (Camden: Camden County Historical Society, 1967). The Camden County Historical Society continues to publish scholarly articles in the tradition of Charles S. Boyer in its *Camden County Historical Society Bulletin;* see, for example, a publication by the society's president, David C. Munn, *The Legacy of the Cooper Family*, Bulletin 42 (Camden: Camden County Historical Society, 1995).

The county histories listed above devote much space to the history of Camden City. However, the city is treated in more detail by Charles S. Boyer in *The Span of a Century: A Chronological History of the City of Camden* (Camden: Centennial Anniversary Committee, 1928) and by Howard M. Cooper in *Historical Sketch of Camden, N.J.* (Camden: Horace B. Ketler,

1909). In recent years, dozens of studies related to the rebuilding of the decaying city have appeared, including City of Camden Division of Planning, *City of Camden, Camden County, New Jersey, Comprehensive Plan 1977–1992: Technical Summary Report* (Philadelphia: Wallace, McHarg, Roberts and Todd, Urban and Ecological Planners, 1992). However, the best sources for Camden City's history remain the Camden City directories and the Camden City and County sections of the *Philadelphia Bulletin Almanac*.

HISTORIES OF OLD GLOUCESTER COUNTY

Official records concerning the origins of Gloucester County can be found in Frank H. Stewart, ed., *The Organization and Minutes of the Gloucester County Court, 1686–87* (Woodbury: Gloucester County Historical Society, 1930), and *Gloucester County under the Proprietors* (Woodbury: The *Constitution*, 1941). Early Gloucester County society and economy can be reconstructed from New Jersey Archives, first series, *Calendar of New Jersey Wills: Documents Relating to the Colonial History of the State of New Jersey* (Paterson: Press Printing and Publishing, 1901), *Documents Relating to the Colonial History of the State of New Jersey, 1631–1687* (Newark: Daily Journal, 1880), and *New York Colonial Records, Documents Relating to the History of the Dutch and Swedish Settlements on the Delaware River* (Albany: Argus, 1877).

For an introduction to the Lenape, see Dorothy Cross, *The Archaeology of New Jersey*, 2 vols. (Trenton: New Jersey State Museum, 1941, 1956), and Clinton A. Weslager, *The Delaware Indians: A History* (New Brunswick: Rutgers University Press, 1972). For the Swedish cultural heritage, see Carol E. Hoffecker, et al., eds., *New Sweden in America* (Newark: University of Delaware, 1995), and Clinton A. Weslager, *New Sweden on the Delaware, 1638–1655* (Wilmington: Middle Atlantic Press, 1988). Fort Nassau, the first European settlement in what became Camden County, is treated in Clinton A. Weslager, *Dutch Explorers, Traders and Settlers in the Delaware Valley, 1609–1664* (Philadelphia: University of Pennsylvania Press, 1965). The Anglo-American Quaker tradition in the founding of the county is captured in John Clement, *Sketches of the First Emigrant Settlers, Newton Township, Old Gloucester County, West New Jersey* (Camden: Sinnickson Chew, 1877), and Isaac Mickle, *Reminiscences of Old Gloucester or Incidents in the History of the Counties of Gloucester, Atlantic and Camden, New Jersey* (1845; rpt. Woodbury: Gloucester County Historical Society, 1968).

REVOLUTIONARY WAR ERA

Insight into eighteenth-century Gloucester County can be found in New Jersey Archives, first series, *Documents Relating to the Colonial and Revolutionary History of the State of New Jersey: Extracts from American Newspapers, 1740–1780* (Paterson, Trenton, and Somerville: *Press, Call,* John L. Murphy, and *Unionist Gazette,* publishers, 1895–1923), and Frank H. Stewart, ed., *Notes on Old Gloucester County, New Jersey,* 3 vols. (Camden and Woodbury: New Jersey Society of Pennsylvania, 1917, and The *Constitution,* 1934, 1937). See also Job Whitall, *The Diary of Job Whitall, Gloucester County, New Jersey, 1775–1779, 1795,* ed. Florence DeHuff Friel (Woodbury: Gloucester County Historical Society, 1992), Samuel Mickle, *The Diaries of Samuel Mickle, Woodbury, Gloucester County, New Jersey, 1792–1829,* 2 vols., ed. Ruthe Baker (Woodbury: Gloucester County Historical Society, 1991), and Johann Conrad Dohla, *A Hessian Diary of the American Revolution,* trans. and ed. Bruce E. Burgoyne (Norman and London: University of Oklahoma Press, 1990). These firsthand accounts are invaluable for an understanding of life and war in late-eighteenth-century Gloucester County. Robert W. Harper, *Old Gloucester County and the American Revolution, 1763–1778, Including Atlantic, Burlington, Cape May, Cumberland and Salem Counties* (Woodbury: Gloucester County Cultural and Heritage Commission, 1986), is useful, although Samuel Stelle Smith, *Fight for the Delaware, 1777* (Monmouth Beach: Philip Freneau Press, 1970), is more accurate.

NINETEENTH-CENTURY CAMDEN

The single most important source for early-nineteenth-century county history and the creation of Camden County is Isaac Mickle, *A Gentleman of Much Promise: The Diary of Isaac Mickle, 1837–1845,* 2 vols., ed. Philip English Mackey (Philadelphia: University of Pennsylvania Press, 1977). Also, the *Woodbury Constitution and Farmer's Weekly Advertiser, 1835–52* (microfilm; Camden: Robeson Library, Rutgers University) provides the Whig perspective on the founding of Camden County. The politics of race in nineteenth-century Camden can be traced in the *Camden Democrat* (microfilm; Camden: Robeson Library, Rutgers University). Frank H. Stewart, *Notes on Old Gloucester County, New Jersey,* 3 vols. (Woodbury and Camden: New Jersey Society of Pennsylvania, 1917, and The *Constitution,* 1934, 1937), is an essential source for the county's history from 1800 to 1860.

The impact of the railroad is traced by George W. Cook, *Atlantic City Railroad, the Royal Route to the Sea: A History of the Reading's Seashore Railroad, 1877–1933* (Oaklyn: West Jersey Chapter, National Railway Historical Society, 1980).

SUBURBAN CAMDEN

Nearly every Camden County municipality published its own history for the New Jersey Tercentenary celebration (1964), for the American Bicentennial (1976), or for anniversaries of borough or township founding. Although most were brief narratives with little historical analysis, Louisa W. Llewellyn's *First Settlement on the Delaware River: A History of Gloucester City, New Jersey* (Gloucester City: Gloucester City American Revolution Bicentennial Committee, 1976) provided a detailed, analytical history of that municipality for the Bicentennial celebration. By far the most comprehensive and valuable suburban histories are William W. Leap, *The History of Runnemede, New Jersey, 1626–1976* (Runnemede: Borough of Runnemede, 1981), and Jack Raible's history of Haddon Township, *Down a Country Lane* (Camden: Camden County Historical Society, 1999). Also useful are Carol Benenson, *Merchantville, New Jersey: The Development and Marketing of a Victorian Commuter Suburb* (Camden: Camden County Historical Society, 1989), Robert J. Hunter, ed., *An Historical Guide Through Haddon Heights* (Haddon Heights: Borough of Haddon Heights, 1992), Barrington Historical Society, *History of Barrington, New Jersey* (Barrington: Historical Society, 1992), and Jack H. Fichter, *A History of Pennsauken Township* (Pennsauken: Pennsauken Historical Society, 1966).

Most recent literature about Camden County's suburbs deals with the concept of suburban sprawl. The best introductions are: David Rusk, "Camden's Future Depends on Suburbs: The Summit on the Future of South Jersey," *Courier-Post,* 21 November 1999; David, Rusk, *Cities Without Suburbs* (Baltimore: Johns Hopkins University Press for the Woodrow Wilson Center Press, 1995); David Rusk, *Inside Game Outside Game: Winning Strategies for Saving Urban America* (Washington, D.C.: Brookings Institution Press, 1999); and David L. Kirp, John P. Dwyer, and Larry A. Rosenthal, *Our Town: Race, Housing, and the Soul of Suburbia* (New Brunswick: Rutgers University Press, 1995). Robert Fishman, *Bourgeois Utopias: The Rise and Fall of Suburbia* (New York: Basic Books, 1987), Peter O. Wacker, *Land and People: A Cultural Geography of Preindustrial New Jersey, Origins and Settlement Patterns* (New Brunswick: Rutgers University Press,

1975), and Warren R. Hofstra, *A Separate Place: The Formation of Clarke County, Virginia* (Madison, Wis.: Madison House, 1999), are model studies of the historical roots of county suburbs. The basic introduction to the new urbanism is Andres Duany, Elizabeth Plater-Zyberk, and Jeff Speck, *Suburban Nation: The Rise of Sprawl and the Decline of the American Dream* (New York: North Point Press, 2000). Also helpful is Daniel A. Cirucci, "Sprawl Hitting Home: Halcyon Buffer Now Being Threatened in Cherry Hill," *Courier-Post,* 15 February 2000.

The Fairview model of "garden city" planning is discussed in: Electus D. Litchfield, "Yorkship Village," *American Review of Reviews* (December 1919): 599–602; Michael H. Lang, *Designing Utopia* (New York: Black Rose, 1999); and Kevin Riordan, "A Model Community: Fairview," *Courier-Post,* 29 April 1999. Haddonfield's plan is discussed in Douglas B. Rauschenberger and Katherine Mansfield Tassini, *Lost Haddonfield* (Haddonfield: Historical Society of Haddonfield, 1989). Early county planning efforts are revealed in *Report on the Preliminary Land Use Plan of the Camden Urban Region, October 1963* (Camden: Camden County Planning Board, 1963), and Camden County Planning Board, *Camden County Growth Coordinating Process: Responses of Municipalities and County to the New Jersey State Planning Commission's Preliminary Development and Redevelopment Process: Final Report February 28, 1990* (Camden: Camden County Board of Chosen Freeholders, Department of Policy, Planning, and Development, 1990).

CAMDEN ETHNIC STUDIES

There are few published histories about Camden County's multicultural society. The county's African American experience is documented by Spencer R. Crew, "Black Life in Secondary Cities: A Comparative Analysis of the Black Communities of Camden and Elizabeth, New Jersey, 1860–1920" (Ph.D. diss., Rutgers University, 1979). The County's Hispanic culture is treated in Richard G. Malloy, "Taino Transformations: Place, Pride and Power among Puerto Rican Leaders in Camden, N.J." (Ph.D. diss., Temple University, 1998). Joseph John Kelley, *The Irish in Camden County* (Camden: Camden County Historical Society, 1984), is a brief introduction to the Irish American community. Irish, German, Polish, and Hispanic American Catholics in Camden County are described briefly in Charles J. Giglio, *Building God's Kingdom: A History of the Diocese of Camden* (South Orange: Seton Hall University Press, 1987). There is little written about the Jewish experience in Camden County, although the Camden County Historical Society contains the files and historical pamphlets of the Tri-County Jewish Historical Collection. Also useful is Charles F. Westoff, *Population and Social Characteristics of the Jewish Community of the Camden Area, 1964* (Cherry Hill: The [Jewish] Federation, 1965).

INDEX

ABOUT THE AUTHOR

Jeffery M. Dorwart is a professor of history and former chair of the history department at Rutgers University, Camden, where he has taught since 1971. He has written *The Pigtail War: American Involvement in the Sino-Japanese War of 1894–95* (1975), *Camden County, New Jersey, 1616–1976: A Narrative History* (with Philip English Mackey) (1976), *The Office of Naval Intelligence: America's First Intelligence Agency, 1865–1918* (1979), *Conflict of Duty: The U.S. Navy's Intelligence Dilemma, 1919–1945* (1983), *Cape May County, New Jersey: The Making of an American Resort Community* (1992), *Eberstadt and Forrestal: A National Security Partnership, 1909–1949* (1992), *Fort Mifflin of Philadelphia* (1998), and *The Philadelphia Navy Yard, 1775–1996* (2000).